THE IMPURITY SYSTEMS OF QUMRAN AND THE RABBIS

SOCIETY OF BIBLICAL LITERATURE

DISSERTATION SERIES

Number 143

THE IMPURITY SYSTEMS OF QUMRAN AND THE RABBIS
Biblical Foundations

by
Hannah K. Harrington

Hannah K. Harrington

THE IMPURITY SYSTEMS OF QUMRAN AND THE RABBIS

Biblical Foundations

Scholars Press
Atlanta, Georgia

THE IMPURITY SYSTEMS OF QUMRAN AND THE RABBIS
Biblical Foundations

Hannah K. Harrington

Ph.D., 1992
University of California

Advisors:
Daniel Boyarin
William Brinner
David Daube
Jacob Milgrom

Library of Congress Cataloging in Publication Data
Harrington, Hannah K., 1958–
The impurity systems of Qumran and the rabbis: biblical foundations/ Hannah K. Harrington.
p. cm. — (Dissertation series; no. 143)
Originally presented as the author's thesis (Ph.D.)—University of California, 1992.
Includes bibliographical references.
ISBN 1–55540–844–3 (cloth). — ISBN 1–55540–845–1 (pbk.)
1. Purity, Ritual—Judaism. 2. Dead Sea scrolls—Criticism, interpretation, etc. 3. Rabbinical literature—History and criticism. 4. Purity, Ritual—Biblical teaching. 5. Bible. O.T. Leviticus—Criticism, interpretation, etc. I. Title. II. Series: Dissertation series (Society of Biblical Literature); no. 143.
BM702.H37
296.7—dc20 93–12316
CIP

This dissertation is dedicated to
my loving husband,
Bill Harrington

TABLE OF CONTENTS

PART ONE
The Impurity System of the Qumran Sectaries

PART TWO
The Impurity System of the Rabbis

LIST OF ILLUSTRATIONS

SIGLA FOR ILLUSTRATIONS

ʾAb	ʾAb Ṭumʾâ
ʾAbî ʾAbôt	ʾAbî ʾAbôt Ṭumʾâ
abo	item is located above the impurity bearer
b	bathe
br	break
bre	breathe
c	carry without direct contact
e	earthenware
eve	evening
F	food
f	fast
H	hands
i	intercourse
L	liquids
li	lies on
Mad	maddāp
o	overhang
P	person
Qod	qodōšîm
RV	rinsable vessels
s	sit on
sacr	sacrifice
sh	shave

shi	shift
sp	spit
spr	sprinkle
t	touch, direct contact
Tĕr	tĕrûmâ
w	wash
7	7-day impurity
//	a double line indicates that the persons/objects are still in contact

Note: Contamination is by direct contact only, unless otherwise indicated.

Sigla for Illustrations Prepared by D. P. Wright Different Than Those Indicated Above

a	denotes the "father contacting the "offspring" in the described manner
b	denotes the "offspring" contacting the "father in the described manner
B	bed
e	eating
F	purification by fire
L	launder
l	lie on
r	ride on
S	saddle
T	thing
u	located under
wp	water of purgation
x	indefinite length of impurity
1	1-day impurity
[ ]	a deduction from the text
	a shaded line indicates a deduced branch

Sigla for Illustrations Prepared by J. Milgrom Different Than Those Indicated Above

sp	sprinkle

ACKNOWLEDGEMENTS

This work would not have been possible without the instruction and support of certain, special people. My thanks goes especially to Professor Jacob Milgrom who first interested me in the subject of Jewish purity laws and practices in his graduate seminar on Leviticus. Following this course I worked independently with him and benefited from access to his written work as well as private consultations. Prof. Milgrom has been an exceptional example of biblical scholarship because of 1) his rare insight into the Hebrew text and 2) his thorough treatment of each verse based on a wealth of knowledge of ancient near eastern and rabbinic texts.

I also want to give thanks to Professor Daniel Boyarin for his guidance in helping me to structure this dissertation. Prof. Boyarin's constructive criticism has helped me to shape many arguments presented in the chapters below. Additionally, he has brought to bear on this effort expert knowledge and intuition of rabbinic literature that has questioned and improved my work in many places.

Other professors to whom I am especially indebted include: Prof. David Daube (University of California, Berkeley, Boalt Hall), for reading and commenting on this manuscript; Prof. Herb

Basser (Queen's College) for instruction in several difficult rabbinic texts; Prof. Robert Alter (University of California, Berkeley) for insight into biblical literary techniques, especially in his graduate seminar on Judges; Prof. Wilhelm Wuellner (Graduate Theological Union) for his time and consultation on New Testament scholarship relevant to this work.

I am also deeply grateful for the invaluable support of my friends, especially Dr. Priscilla Benham and Dr. Rebecca Patten of Patten College where I have worked as an instructor while pursuing this degree. I appreciate their unfailing confidence in me and efforts to push me ahead to greater achievements. Also, I thank Dr. Bebe Patten for her counsel and Dr. Gary Moncher for his encouragement and good humor.

Finally, the endurance of my mother, Constance Karajian, and my husband, Bill Harrington, have been remarkable. This work would have been impossible without their patience, kindness, and support. Much love and appreciation goes to both of them.

NOTE ON EDITIONS

Citations from Sifre Numbers are from the H. S. Horowitz edition. Line numbers are cited first followed by the page number from the Horowitz edition in brackets.

Translations of passages from the Mishna, Babylonian Talmud, and Palestinian Talmud are taken from the following sources unless otherwise indicated:

Bible	*The New Oxford Annotated Bible with the Apocrypha*. Revised Standard Version. Oxford: Oxford University Press, Inc., 1972.
Mishna	Neusner, J. *The Mishnah*. New Haven: Yale University Press, 1989.
Tosefta	Neusner, J. *The Tosefta*. 6 vols. New York: Ktav, 1981.
Babylonian Talmud	*The Babylonian Talmud*, ed. I. Epstein. 35 vols. London: Soncino Press, 1948.
Palestinian Talmud	Neusner, J. *The Talmud of the Land of Israel*. 35 vols. Chicago: The University of Chicago Press, 1989.

In this dissertation words taken from the Hebrew Bible and rabbinic literature are transliterated by the system established by the Society of Biblical Literature. Terms copied from the Dead Sea Scrolls are printed in unvocalized, Hebrew characters, as they appear in the Scrolls.

INTRODUCTION

The purpose of this dissertation is to analyze data from the sectarian community at Qumran and Rabbinic sources on the subject of ritual impurity.[1] This work is not merely an effort to chart the data into an easy reference tool, although that is provided throughout. Rather, I wish to uncover the motives of the sectarians and the Rabbis in developing their impurity systems in the manner in which they do. Where do they get their ideas from? from Scripture? from logic? from experience? To state the results at the outset, it is my conclusion that much of what appears to be innovation in contrast to biblical principles is actually a valid, astute reading of Scripture itself. Thus, this effort is based largely on a careful reading of Leviticus and Numbers. The sectarians and the Rabbis themselves were careful exegetes who had a sacred regard for the divinely appointed

---

1 I use the term, "sectarian," to refer to the Jewish community living near the Dead Sea at the turn of the era in recognition of the fact that these Jews have physically and theologically removed themselves from the large body of Jews residing in Judea and living out their lives in relationship to the existing cult at Jerusalem.

Torah. Their concepts of impurity grow out of Scriptural roots rather than out of a different stock.

Before proceeding any further, I will offer a working definition of ritual purity: a state of cleanness required for lay participation in the cult effected by physical purification rituals such as ablutions.

SCHOLARSHIP ON JEWISH PURITY ISSUES

The following is a survey of the work that has been done in this field and is presented in order to properly situate my own approach and to provide justification for it. Scholars from various disciplines have become increasingly interested in the Jewish concept of impurity and have contributed to the present state of the inquiry. The area studies of these scholars include: rabbinics, Bible, early Christian literature, and cultural anthropology.

The majority of the work, to date, has been the concern of rabbinic scholars. Beginning in the early half of this century, A. Büchler in two separate works, *Der galiläische ʿAm ha-ʾAreṣ* and *Studies in Sin and Atonement in the Rabbinic Literature of the First Century,* seeks to limit the concern for ritual ("levitical") purity in the Bible and in rabbinic literature. In the first work Büchler claims that ritual purity is necessary only for eating tĕrûmâ according to the Rabbis, thus, the whole matter is relegated to a priestly concern. Even eating secular food in purity is a reference only to the ḥullin which the priests eat as opposed to the tĕrûmâ.[2]

In the second work Büchler discusses, among other things, moral and ritual impurity in the biblical view. He stresses the fact that the former was the overwhelming concern not the latter and that various ritual purifications accompanied repentance. Thus, ritual impurity is viewed as merely symbolic of sin and had very little intrinsic effect on the cult. Büchler points out that according

2 A. Büchler, *Der Galiläische ʿAm ha-ʾAreṣ des zweiten Jahrhunderts,* 86, 161.

to the prophets sin defiles, figuratively speaking, the sanctuary. However, the prophet would allow the sinner to come to the Temple. Leviticus 16, in Büchler's view, discusses rules for expiation of moral impurity only; the term ṭumʾōt does not refer here to any real defilement of the sanctuary by those who are merely ritually impure.[3]

I disagree with Büchler's effort to downplay the role of ritual impurity in both the Bible and rabbinic literature. As will be clearer in the ensuing chapters, ritual purity was required to a certain degree by Leviticus for all Israel. Priests, indeed, had to maintain an even higher purity standard. The Rabbis interpret the levitical purity laws with great care and acumen. Not only the priests among them but even some of the laity ate ordinary food in ritual purity (See Appendix A).

G. Alon argues against Büchler's theory and suggests that Büchler's concession that some of the later Sages (after Temple times) followed stringent purity codes is untenable. In addition to the lack of the Temple and the sacrifices which gave meaning to the purity system, Alon says that "it is also far-fetched to suggest that the Sages of Usha promulgated many essential new Halakhot, that affected every Israelite and were a severe burden upon those who wished to observe them, without relying on earlier tradition."[4]

Alon's view is that there are restrictionist and expansionist elements with regard to purity throughout rabbinic literature.[5] On the one hand, there is a tendency to extend holiness to all Jews, thus requiring laity to observe strict purity laws which some might argue were only intended for the priests. On the other hand, there is a tendency among the Rabbis to adapt the laws of Scripture in a practical manner to everyday life, not increasing burdens on the average person unnecessarily. Alon grants that these two tendencies are supportable by Scripture since

---

3 A. Büchler, *Studies in Sin and Atonement in the Rabbinic Literature of the First Century*, 267.

4 G. Alon, *Jews, Judaism and the Classical World*, 214.

5 Ibid., 233.

sometimes the purity laws are addressed to the priests (Lev. 21:4; 22:4-8) and sometimes to all Israel (Lev. 11:2; 12:4; 15:2, 31; Num. 19:20).

Alon agrees with Büchler that the halakha as encoded by Maimonides restricts impurity to the realm of the cult, i.e., priests, Temple and consecrated food. However, he claims Büchler uses this later halakha to interpret food passages in Tannaitic literature as references to the priests. Alon uses literature of the second Temple period, e.g., the Gospels, Philo, and Josephus, to prove that these references are, in fact, to ordinary food in many cases. Despite the lenient halakha as understood in later talmudic times, there are both restrictionist and expansionist tendencies throughout rabbinic literature.

I agree with Alon that at the turn of the era there was a strong expansionist tendency among Jews with regard to purity matters. I note that if he had had access to the Temple Scroll from Cave 11 at Qumran, he would have found even further support for his thesis. The sectarians demanded a high standard of purity for all residents of ordinary cities and an even higher status for the residents of the Temple City (see Chapter 1). I think the argument can be strengthened further with more in depth recourse to Scripture.

Philo and Josephus are helpful in revealing the attitudes of at least some first century Jews, but they stand outside the rabbinic academies. The texts of the latter reveal that both the expansionist and restrictionist tendencies of the Sages are often directly derived from Scripture. In order to understand the origins of the expansionist tendency, I think it is important to analyze the biblical basis for those who advocated such a stringent lifestyle. Also, on what biblical basis does the lenient tendency stand? Alon has created an awareness of these two attitudes in biblical and rabbinic literature. I wish to explain how these attitudes are developed and supported in sectarian and rabbinic literature with the former preferring an expansionist and the latter preferring a more limited interpretation of the biblical laws of purity.

J. Milgrom, while agreeing with Alon that both lenient and stringent attitudes toward impurity are rooted in Scripture, takes issue with him regarding the source of these differences. Milgrom suggests that the dichotomy is not due to the difference in pollution of priests vs. laity but in the presence of two different priestly sources: the Priestly Code (P), most of Leviticus and parts of Exodus and Numbers, and the Holiness Code (H), primarily Leviticus 17-27 but evident in editorial comments throughout the Pentateuch. P limits the sacred sphere to the Tabernacle while H extends the sacred realm to the whole land requiring all who reside in it to maintain a certain degree of sanctity.[6]

As I noted above, the study of the sectarian literature from Qumran reveals an early Jewish community with an avid interest in the biblical laws of purity. Many of the laws of the sect reveal that expansionist attitudes not only existed but that they were similar to many found throughout rabbinic literature. Y. Yadin has translated a document from Cave 11, the Temple Scroll (11QT).[7] He provides a verse-by-verse commentary as well as a large section devoted to the purity laws. He compares sectarian with rabbinic traditions in an effort to prove the early existence of many rabbinic notions. Thus Yadin provides a source for the rabbinic laws of impurity which clearly pre-dates the first century. (He dates 11QT in the mid-second century B.C.E.) Yadin also compares sectarian ideas with relevant Scripture passages to reveal the emphases of the sect. I include below a survey of Qumran scholarship on purity so here I will refer only to Yadin.

For Yadin the "halakha" is that of Maimonides.[8] He does not treat rabbinic literature critically, but merely makes comparisons of select data with passages from 11QT to which they are similar providing an early reference for many rabbinic traditions. Yadin is not interested in establishing the rabbinic system or uncovering its origins but merely selects random

---

6 J. Milgrom, "The Qumran Cult: Its Exegetical Principles" in *Archaeology and History*, ed. L. H. Schiffman, 166-67.

7 Y. Yadin, *Megillat ha-Miqdaš;* English ed. *The Temple Scroll*, 3 vols.

8 Yadin, I, 277, 325.

traditions which he proves to be early because of their existence at Qumran.

The first scholar to give the subject of ritual purity in Judaism monographic treatment is Jacob Neusner. In his work, *The Idea of Purity in Ancient Judaism,* Neusner surveys the subject throughout ancient and classical Jewish writings from the Bible through the Talmuds. Also, Neusner's translations of rabbinic literature, several of which are the first translations of the text into English, have attracted a broader range of scholars to the study of rabbinic texts.

In a more critical manner Neusner analyzes the Order of Tohorot in a 22-volume series dedicated to translation, commentary, and discussion of literary and historical problems. It is this series to which I refer repeatedly in the chapters below. Neusner argues that unless the subject is treated thoroughly as a system of ideas, it cannot be understood at all.[9] To this I heartily agree.

Neusner attempts to distinguish a sequence in the logic of the Mishna by establishing the outgrowth of one idea from another. He begins with the premise that concepts can only evolve if the proper conceptual groundwork is already in place. Thus, if the Sages attribute to an early Sage an idea that depends on the existence of other concepts which had not yet been introduced, the attribution is to be discounted.[10] Using this method, Neusner has produced a three-volume work entitled, *Rabbinic Traditions of the Pharisees Before 70 A.D.*

While I appreciate Neusner's effort to present the rabbinic laws of impurity as a system and to analyze all of the relevant traditions critically before making generalizations about the system, I find Neusner's conclusions untenable at times because he fails to recognize the systemic nature of the Torah's impurity laws. It is my belief that the Rabbis derive their information from the Torah by reading its purity laws as a system. The Rabbis construct this system by filling in the gaps of the text, where it is

---

9 J. Neusner, *A History of the Mishnaic Law of Purities*, XXII, 12-13.

10 J. Neusner, *The Evidence of the Mishnah.*

silent or ambiguous, in a way consistent with its internal principles. The validity of the Rabbis' gap fills may not be obvious to a superficial reader, but the Rabbis were not superficial readers. They were reading a sacred text, one which was plumbed for its maximum yield as to instructions on how gaps should be filled. The Rabbis do not see themselves as creators of a new religion but as continuators of a long tradition.

In his effort to distinguish it from biblical religion, Neusner misrepresents rabbinic Judaism at times as a separate religion for Jews without a cult having little or no linkage to the Priestly Code of the Bible.[11] In Neusner's picture it stands even in opposition to the biblical tradition because it is interested in creating holiness outside of the Temple. Thus it operates on a different agenda than Scripture entirely. Another aspect of this rabbinic agenda is an emphasis on man's power in the interdynamics of purity and impurity, an innovation which, according to Neusner, stands in contrast to Scripture's premises.[12] Again, I think this distinction is contrived, as I discuss in the chapters below.

There are numerous concepts in the purity data of the rabbinic sources which Neusner regards as innovations, and he dates their origins at various periods of history, e.g., pre-first century, Yavneh, Usha. These apparent innovations include such concepts as **ṭĕbûl yôm**, **midrās**, human intention, and degrees of impurity. I will argue below that many of these concepts are not instituted by the Rabbis because of some outgrowth of logic or due to the destruction of the Temple but rather they are rooted, to varying degrees, in Scripture. The Rabbis are exegetes not inventors.

Neusner claims that because various groups read Scripture differently proves that their results did not originate in exegesis of the text:

> The chief evidence that the systems do not necessarily originate in Scriptural exegesis, of course, is the simple fact that other groups

---

11 J. Neusner, *The Idea of Purity in Ancient Judaism*, 53; *Purities*, XXII, 2, 37, 52, 298-99.

12 Neusner, *Purities*, XXII, 186.

> reading the same Scriptures hardly reach the same conclusions as to the appropriate point of emphasis and structure for their societal and conceptual systems.[13]

I disagree with this notion of exegesis. Just because different groups reached different conclusions when studying Scripture does not imply that they were not exegeting the text. Scripture, because of its gaps and at times ambivalence, is often variously interpreted even within a single group. The Sages of the Talmud and Midrash provide numerous examples of different and even contradictory interpretations of Scripture. To provide a modern example, many of the scholars discussed in this introduction are studying the same Scripture and seeking to interpret it correctly, however, they often reach very different conclusions.

D. Boyarin explains that it is the Torah itself which is dialogical and ambiguous:

> It is the incompleteness in the Torah's explanation of itself which provides the space within which these antithetical readings can be created. However, the material for filling the gaps is not a subjective creation of the reader but rather a strong production of the intertext.[14]

Thus, the Rabbis recognize a gap in the text and then begin to fill it, not with pure invention, but with information gleaned from other passages of Scripture. These interpretations often differ from Sage to Sage because, although all are based on Scripture, the Torah itself is at times ambivalent and thus is capable of supporting multiple interpretations. Boyarin comments elsewhere, "The Text of the Torah is gapped and dialogical, and into the gaps the reader slips...."[15] For groups such as the Rabbis and the yaḥad at Qumran, differences notwithstanding, Scripture was the foundation upon which decisions had to be based, the axis upon which the world turned.

---

13 Ibid., 52.

14 D. Boyarin, *Intertextuality and the Reading of Midrash*, 48.

15 Ibid., 14.

Gaps in the Torah could only be filled by reference to other texts of Scripture.

Another of Neusner's claims which I have difficulty accepting concerns the relationship of the Sifra to the Mishna. Neusner says that the Mishna represents a system which rests wholly on logic.[16] Unlike the Pentateuch, which depends on the divine revelation at Sinai for credentials, the Mishna appeals to no authority, e.g., it does not claim to originate in divine revelation. After the closure of the Mishna, others claimed that its traditions were transmitted from generation to generation starting with Moses. Neusner states that the destruction of 70 C.E. gave rise to the philosophy of the Mishna, and he describes its central agenda as follows:

> The Mishnah's system therefore focused upon the holiness of the life of Israel, the people, a holiness that had formerly centered on the Temple. The logically consequent question was, what is the meaning of sanctity, and how shall Israel attain, or give evidence of, sanctification.[17]

Thus, the Mishna consciously ignores the vacuum created by the destruction of the Temple by claiming that all Israel is holy; the Temple is not necessary for Israel's sanctification:

> That sanctification, as a matter of fact, from the viewpoint of the system now endured and transcended the physical destruction of the building and the cessation of sacrifices. For Israel the people was holy, enduring as the medium and the instrument of God's sanctification.[18]

Neusner explains that although the Mishna itself does not derive its principles from Scripture, the Sifra, written in the period from 200-400 C.E. does claim Scriptural basis for the Mishna's traditions. The editor of the Sifra is looking for ways in which to link Mishna's philosophy, which has separated from a

---

16 J. Neusner, *Sifra: An Analytical Translation*, 46.

17 Ibid., 39.

18 Ibid., 40.

stock independent of Scripture, to the Torah and thus supply it with sacred authority. Thus, many passages are quoted verbatim from Mishna-Tosefta and substantiated by recourse to Scripture.

The Sifra makes an express effort to prove that logic alone is not a valid criterion for law; Scripture is. Thus, the Sifra demonstrates in many cases that logic can produce improper conclusions and hence is not to be trusted as a pillar on which to base law.[19]

I cannot agree that the simplest understanding of the work of the editors of the Sifra was to provide a Scriptural basis for Mishna-Tosefta. First, as Neusner himself points out, one-third of the Sifra is unknown to Mishna-Tosefta.[20] Neusner explains that this material was simply not of interest to the authors of Mishna-Tosefta. My question is: why include it in the Sifra if the sole agenda of the document is to substantiate the Mishna? Secondly, what could have given rise to the Mishna's system of holy things and purities if not the laws of Leviticus and Numbers? Neusner admits that the Sifra has a special interest in the purification rites which is not evident in the Mishna.[21] Why discuss these? It seems more logical to me that the Sifra is exegeting the text and that the Mishna is merely interested in the results of the exegesis: the practical guideline for daily living in a world in which the cult would be renewed. I simply do not find the outside impetus which informed the Rabbis of the Mishna how sanctification should be effected. I do find direction for this inquiry in the laws of the Priestly Code.

R. P. Booth has evaluated Neusner's work on purities in his book, *Jesus and the Laws of Purity: Tradition History and Legal History in Mark 7*. Booth is concerned primarily with the authenticity of the Pharisaic allegation against Jesus' disciples for not washing hands before eating. After his work on the tradition

---

19 Ibid., 46-47.

20 Ibid., 31.

21 Ibid.

history of this idea, Booth concludes that the saying in Mk. 7:5 is authentic.[22]

Of interest here is Booth's evaluation of Neusner. Booth is skeptical of Neusner's reliance on the Mishna's attributions of sayings to the generations of named Rabbis. He questions the link of Rabbis to specific generations. He feels that these generations have been delineated by H. Danby, H. L. Strack, and the Soncino Rabbinical Index based on the content of the Rabbis' dicta - precisely the criterion Neusner uses to determine if the particular Sage belongs to a certain generation. Thus, he finds the attestations artificial and the argument circular.[23]

Booth also points to the critique of A. J. Saldarini who suspects the Mishna's reliability for attributions since it is, in his opinion, the most edited document in rabbinic literature. Any consistency to be noted in it may be due to editorial harmonization.[24]

Booth, while admiring Neusner's efforts to track the logic of the Mishna, suggests that custom and experience are responsible for a large part of the development of the purity laws.[25] The institution of laws represents a final stage after the impression of certain ideas on the social consciousness. Customary ways are often determinants in court proceedings. Also, judges must often provide fair, practical decisions based on custom rather than logic. Indeed, many cases were no doubt settled by the people and not brought to the Sages at all.

However, Booth does place large importance on the interpretation of Scripture as the source for much of rabbinic law:

---

22 R. P. Booth, *Jesus and the Laws of Purity: Tradition History and Legal History in Mark 7*, 217.

23 H. Danby, *The Mishnah*, 799-800; H. L. Strack and G. Stemberger, *Einleitung in Talmud und Midrasch*, 65-103; *The Babylonian Talmud*, ed. I. Epstein, index, 621-730; Booth, 141.

24 A. J. Saldarini, "'Form Criticism' of Rabbinic Literature," *JBL* 96 (1977) 264; Booth, 141.

25 Booth, 146-47.

> It was the interpretation of the relevant Scripture rather than logic which was the theoretical discipline followed by the Sanhedrin and the Sages.[26]

I agree with Booth, who argues against Neusner, that certain rabbinic principles are inherent in the Priestly Code and hence should not be relegated to the invention of post-70 C.E. Rabbis. Rules concerning what is susceptible to impurity and how that impurity is transmitted are in large part determined by the laws of Leviticus and Numbers. Booth refers in particular to the susceptibility of a vessel and its contents to the impurity of a carcass but the insusceptibility of a spring of cistern (Lev. 11:32-36). He uses Leviticus 15 to illustrate sequences of transmissibility: the zāb defiles the saddle which in turn defiles anyone touching it. I will explore these and other such Torah-derived purity principles below.

As to Booth's insistence that custom is a large determinant for the Rabbis' purity laws, he is no doubt correct. However, the problem of proving that custom is the source for particular laws is out of the scope of this dissertation. Proving the Scriptural basis for much of the system *is* the goal of this study. It is easy to relegate anything for which one cannot find a source to the category of custom. What is needed is a thorough examination of what can be demonstrated to be biblical.

E. P. Sanders, who has done considerable work on the Jewish background of Jesus and Paul, takes issue with Neusner's emphasis that the early Sages wanted to extend sanctity to the laity and that they ate ordinary food in a state of ritual purity. In contrast to Neusner, and Alon before him, Sanders says that the "Houses applied 'purity' only to the priests' food."[27] Sanders says, against Neusner, that cleanness was not extended from the cult to the profane world by the Pharisees. Rather, certain purity laws are in effect for the laity already in some Leviticus passages (cf. 11:2; 15:2, 31).[28] However, I think Sanders misunderstood

---

26 Ibid., 147.

27 E. P. Sanders, *Jewish Law from Jesus to the Mishnah*, 174.

28 Ibid., 165.

Alon because the latter does recognize this duality in Scripture and suggests that it is the reason for the same duality in rabbinic literature.[29]

Sanders does not think the Sages extended priestly laws but that Leviticus 11 is understood just as it should be, a requirement on the laity.[30] However, Sanders then offers an even more difficult proposition than Alon by stating that the Pharisees extended biblical laws of "corpse impurity and then tried to avoid contracting it from their new sources as a kind of gesture towards living like priests."[31] It seems more reasonable to me (and I attempt to prove it below) to assume that the Rabbis are developing Scripture rather than that they are inventing new sources of impurity.

Sanders points to the impracticality of observing purity laws in the way Neusner and Alon suggest and so concludes that they were inoperable.[32] This is an argument based on a modern perspective. For the early Sages the Torah was sacred and, when the law was unambiguous, practicality was not a consideration. Biblical penalties for failure to observe the laws were the main concern.

Sanders supports Neusner's efforts to define strata in the Mishna and considers his dating of sayings by their attributions to various Sages a reliable technique (although Neusner himself has since become skeptical of his earlier claim).[33] He points out that the most common attribution is to Rabbi Judah, the redactor of the Mishna, not Hillel or Aqiba, eminent Sages of the first and early second centuries, respectively.

The biggest problem I have with Sanders' work is that his understanding of Leviticus is not thorough and, hence, provides a shaky base on which to build the rest of his argument. Two points stand out. One, the laws form a system. Even though all parts of

---

29 Alon, 232.

30 Sanders, 166.

31 Ibid.

32 Ibid., 174-175.

33 Ibid., 168; Neusner, *Reading and Believing*; idem. *Purities*, XVIII, 161.

the system are not explicitly defined, some elements can be proven implicitly from the given data. Sanders only treats as biblical the exact data stated. He makes few inferences from that data. For example, since Scripture does not explicitly require the menstruant to immerse, he assumes that she did not bathe after her impurity until first century times.[34] He does not recognize the hierarchy of impurities in the Priestly Code and the implications of that hierarchy, for surely, if the person who touches the menstruant's bed must bathe (Lev. 15:21), the menstruant herself must bathe. This is a logical understanding of the text.

Secondly, Sanders makes no reference to the Sifra, the rabbinic commentary on Leviticus. Since the Mishna rarely explains how it derives its laws from Scripture, the Sifra is a necessary tool in uncovering the way in which the Rabbis read Leviticus. Sanders focuses more on the Pharisaic debate and overlooks the way in which the Rabbis derive their views from Scripture.

Nevertheless, Sanders has provided a thorough critique of the works of Alon and Neusner on the Pharisees and on purities. In addition, he gives a valuable survey of archaeological findings on miqvāʾôt in Israel as well as a good comparison of Hellenistic traditions regarding food impurity.

Most recently, another New Testament scholar, Marla Selvidge, has examined Jewish ritual purity in the first century on the basis of Scripture as well as rabbinic literature. Like Booth on handwashing and Sanders on foods, Selvidge concentrates on one aspect of the purity code, in her case, menstruation. In her book, *Woman, Cult and Miracle Recital*, Selvidge compares Jewish and Greek attitudes toward women. However, like Sanders, she makes untenable conclusions because she does not have a thorough, systemic understanding of Leviticus. For starters, two-thirds of her quotes from the Hebrew Bible are incorrect.[35]

---

34 Sanders, 143.

35 Selvidge, *Woman, Cult and Miracle Recital*: ʾîš is equated with woman, 49; niddâ is represented as kiddâ or biddâ, 56.

Selvidge's main thesis, based on Leviticus 15, is that women are repressed in Judaism because of their biological difference.[36] They cannot participate fully in the cult, certainly not while menstruating and never as officiants. They are only a liability to men since they can contaminate them, although the reverse is not true: men cannot contaminate women. Although men are made unclean by flows from their genitals, they are not repressed nearly as much as women. Baby girls contaminate the mother twice as much as baby boys. The menstruant herself is contagious but the impure man described in Lev. 15:1-5 only effects objects. Women are never told to launder their clothes after contact with impurity; only the contamination of men is of any concern. Women were secluded at least 80 days a year if pregnant and up to 91 days a year if not. Perhaps the ultimate indignity is the use of the term, **niddâ**, menstruant, as a metaphor for sin throughout the Hebrew Bible.

By contrast, Selvidge regards Greek attitudes toward women in the Hellenistic period liberal and unprejudiced.[37] Women are allowed in the cult even as priestesses, temple workers, and oracle mediums. Menstruation was a cleansing not a defiling process.

These arguments are based on a superficial reading of Leviticus 15 and a selective use of Greek material. Although not an expert, my feeling toward the Greek attitude toward women is that although women are allowed to be mediums in the mystery cults, the State religion appears even more repressive than that of Israel. The vestal virgins are allowed no sexual intercourse for the almost 40 years of their service. Israel places no value on denying a woman fulfillment of the normal desire for sex and family (cf. Jephthah's daughter is mourned for her death as a virgin, Jud. 11:38-40).

Other examples from Greek literature do not concur with Selvidge's presentation of the liberated woman. While the status of women may improve in the Hellenistic world as compared to

---

36 Ibid., 57.

37 Ibid., 78-79.

that of the early Greeks, (e.g., Homer and Hesiod), antifeminism continues. E. Cantarella, who has examined the role and status of women in both ancient and classical Greece with numerous examples from both legal and mythical literature, concludes: "To speak of recognition of the 'female' role and of women's power, however mediated and occult, in Greek history is altogether unfounded. The function of women in Greece was exclusively that of reproducing citizens, if they were free, and servile labor, if they were slaves."[38]

The Greek attitude toward women was often violently misogynistic. S. de Beauvoir has demonstrated that the Aristotelian attitude regards woman as not only inferior to man but as constituting an aberration or anomaly.[39] Lines from the classical dramatists support this idea:[40]

> [From Euripides:] Would that mortals otherwise could get their babes, that womankind were not, so no curse had lighted upon man.
>
> [From Aristophanes:] I don't believe there's a single fault he has not accused us [women] of; calling us double dealers, false, faithless, tippling, mischief-making gossipers, a rotten set, a misery to men.
>
> [From Menander:] Though many the wild beasts on land and sea, the beastliest one of all is woman
>
> [From Menander:] For a woman is a necessary evil.

Accepted practice in Athens reflects this type of thinking. Women were not to go out in public; only those of the lower classes went shopping. In Athens, women were restricted to quarters in their homes (*gunaekeion*).[41] One Greek attorney

---

38 E. Cantarella, *Pandora's Daughters*, 177; cf. also *Reflections of Women in Antiquity*, ed. H. P. Foley.

39 S. de Beauvoir, *The Second Sex (Le Deuxieme Sexe)*, 27-28.

40 Euripides, *Medea*, ll. 573-575; Aristophanes, *The Thesmophoriazsae*, LCL, 165; Menander, LCL, 481.

41 Aristophanes, *The Thesmophoriazusae*, l. 414; W. K. Lacey, *The Family in Classical Greece*, 159, 175; T. Friedman, "The Shifting Role of Women, From the Bible to Talmud," *Jud* 36 (1987) 479-87; cf. also J. R.

declares, "A woman who goes out of the house ought to be at a stage of life at which those who meet her do not ask whose wife but whose mother she is." Athenian men did not eat with their wives especially in front of guests. Women were considered inferior to men in every way.[42] It is a man's reputation not his physical body which he is afraid a woman will soil. A man's name can be dragged to the ground by the promiscuous conduct of an ill-controlled wife.

Controverting Selvidge's position further, there are statements concerning the ill effects of menstruation. Aristotle said that a menstruant dims the mirror in front of her. Hesiod suggests that a man not bathe in the water in which a woman has washed. According to the Cyrene cathartic law (about 300 B.C.E.), parturients contaminate all who are in the house for three days.[43]

By contrast, the Israelite woman, although a definite danger to the cult during menstruation, is never denigrated because of her biological difference. She commands the utmost respect. Proverbs 31 extols the virtuous woman. Abraham listens to Sarah (Gen. 16:2; 21:10-14). Deborah leads the Israelite army in a holy war as well as functions as judge (Jud. 4:4). Huldah, the prophetess, is consulted by the king even when the prophet Jeremiah was probably available (2 Chr. 34:22). Esther valiantly saves the Jewish nation from destruction (Est. 9:12). Naomi buys and sells land (Ru. 4:9). The daughters of Zelophehad inherit land (Num. 36:2).

Even in cultic matters women do participate when pure. Hannah prays and sacrifices at the sanctuary (1 Sam. 1:24-26). Every woman after childbirth comes to the Temple to offer a sacrifice (Lev. 12:6). Her exclusion from the sanctuary (Lev. 12:4) implies that normally she is allowed to participate in public worship there. Mary is not secluded after the first week of childbirth but comes to the Temple area with Joseph for the

---

Wegner, "Tragelaphos Revisited: the Anomaly of Woman in the Mishnah," *Jud* 37 (1988) 160-72.

42 Plato, *Republic*, 455cd, 431c.

43 R. Parker, *Miasma*, 78, 102-3, 336.

circumcision of Jesus (Lk. 2:27). The same passage mentions Anna, a widow, who, according to the text, never left the Temple area (Lk. 2:37).

It is not the interest of this dissertation to defend Jewish attitudes of purity as superior to Greek attitudes, but rather it is to show the value of a thorough understanding of Leviticus 11-15 before any scholar ventures to make conclusions about Jewish purity in any era. If Selvidge had read Leviticus 15 in Hebrew systemically, she would not only have avoided several linguistic mistakes but would have become aware immediately that many of her conclusions are unfounded. Below are a few suggested corrections.

A parturient must offer an offering, but not, as Selvidge states, for sin. What sin is committed in bearing a child? A better translation is "purification offering."[44]

Selvidge points out that a man who has a seminal discharge is only unclean until evening; a menstruant is banished for seven days.[45] This is not as discriminating as Selvidge presents: the menstruant continues to exude blood during her week of uncleanness. The man is no longer producing uncleanness; if he does have a flow of longer duration, he is unclean for the whole time he is in this condition and does not undergo a week of purification until after he is healed (Lev. 15:13). Selvidge points out that the woman is put at the top of the list of contagious items in Lev. 15:19-30, whereas the impure man's list begins with impure objects. Rather, the man's list begins with the statement of his own categorical impurity (15:2).

Furthermore, Selvidge says the woman who contacts impurity does not need to bathe or launder.

> When comparing the laws concerning who must take a bath or wash his clothes because of coming in contact with someone or something contagious, it appears that the woman is omitted.

---

44 Selvidge, 54; J. Milgrom, *Leviticus*, I, 759.

45 Selvidge, 53.

> Leviticus specifically speaks of washing clothes in masculine terms.[46]

This is contradicted explicitly by Leviticus 15:18 which stipulates that the woman must bathe after sexual intercourse. Laundering too appears to be necessary, and a whole verse is devoted to explaining it in detail (Lev. 15:17).[47] If this is the case for a light, one-day impurity, *a fortiori*, for a more lengthy impurity. To say that a woman does not contract impurity from an impure man is controverted by the text's repeated reference to **kol**, "all": all whom the man with an abnormal discharge, who has not washed his hands, touches are made impure (Lev. 15:11, 21-22).[48] To say that laundering appears only with the male pronominal suffix and hence women were not required to launder is a misunderstanding of Hebrew syntax. The male term is often inclusive of the female, e.g., the term **mĕṣōrāʿ** does not refer only to males affected with scale disease, cf. Lev. 13:45 with 13:29, 38. Chapter 15 too provides an example in the masculine phrase, **wĕhazzāb ʾet-zôbô**, which is followed by **lazzākar wĕlannĕqēbâ**, rendered: "... and for anyone who has a flow, male or female...." (Lev. 15:33, translation mine). Here the writer is clearly using the term **zāb** generically (Lev. 15:33).

It is an unfair evaluation of Leviticus to state that the woman was only given occupations of childbearer, sex object, cook, and necromancer.[49] Leviticus is warning against possible incursions of impurity in Israel, both ritual and non-ritual. The book is not interested in listing valid occupations for men and women.

With regard to non-Levitical biblical passages on impurity, Selvidge misunderstands both the the purity required at Sinai (Ex. 19:10, 14-15) and David's plea of sexual abstinence in order to partake of the bread of presence (1 Sam. 21:5). In the latter episode Selvidge claims that for the biblical writer keeping away

46 Ibid., 55.

47 D. P. Wright, *The Disposal of Impurity*, 196.

48 Selvidge, 54.

49 Ibid., 49.

from women was more consequential than murder.[50] Selvidge does not seem to recognize that in order for God to accompany them on their mission David and his men must be ritually pure, and that all military expeditions in Scripture were considered holy wars requiring purity observance as outlined in Dt. 23. However, in both the David and Sinai stories impurity does not come from the woman's body but from the man's. It is the flow of semen which contaminates. At Sinai, the concern is not to segregate women but to be free of any impurity, including that resulting from sexual intercourse. Thus, all persons were exhorted to bathe and launder their clothes.

A final irritation with Selvidge's evaluation of Jewish attitudes toward women is the anachronism involved. In the ancient world, most cultures held strong taboos regarding the sequestering of a woman during menstruation as well as a strong exploitation of women.[51] Israel stands in stark contrast to her neighbors because while retaining the menstrual taboo, she guarantees rights for women unheard of in neighboring cultures. One such example concerns the woman suspected of adultery. Contrary to the suspected woman in Mesopotamia who is thrown alive into the river to drown even if there was only a suspicion of guilt, the Israelitess suspected of adultery but not apprehended is only judged by supernatural intervention.[52] She is, in fact, protected from the wrath of the shamed husband, because judgment is removed from his jurisdiction. It is up to God to vindicate or punish the woman according to a prescribed, harmless ritual. Thus a pagan, ritual ordeal has been remodeled in Israel and rendered harmless to guarantee certain rights for women.[53]

---

50 Ibid., 57.

51 Milgrom, *Leviticus*, I, 763-65.

52 Cf. Hammurabi, no. 132: the suspected adulteress is supposed to throw herself into the river to preserve the honor of her husband, J. B. Pritchard, *Ancient Near Eastern Texts Relating to the Old Testament*, 171; cf. also Ur-Nammu, ll. 281-90, Pritchard, 524; The Middle Assyrian Laws, no. 17, Pritchard, 181.

53 J. Milgrom, *The JPS Torah Commentary: Numbers*, 350-54.

The segregation of women at the Temple comes in the Hellenistic not in the biblical era. The superstitious fear of menstruants is not in the rabbinic halakha but in stories reflecting the attitude of the population at large. This is not a biblical taboo but a universal one. I agree with T. Friedman that it is not in the biblical but the Hellenistic era in which elements of repression toward women appear in Judaism.[54]

To conclude my argument with Selvidge, it is the Levitical basis of her thesis which is not sound since it is neither systemic nor understood in the context of the ancient world. By contrast, I wish to provide a solid basis for understanding the rabbinic concept of purity by recourse to a systemic interpretation of Leviticus.

The work of S. Cohen, grounded in a strong understanding of rabbinic texts, provides a stark contrast to that of Selvidge. However, he inadvertently errs when explaining the immersion requirement for menstruants. In his article, "Menstruants and the Sacred in Judaism and Christianity," Cohen claims that menstruants were not required to bathe according to the Torah and even questions that this was the intention of the Mishna:[55]

> The Mishna assumes that both a zābâ and a parturient must immerse in water in order to be purified (m. Nidda 10:8) but unless I am mistaken the Mishna nowhere states explicitly that a menstruant must also immerse.

Cohen does acknowledge the fact that both the Babylonian and Palestinian Talmuds take for granted that the menstruant must immerse after her impurity. Nevertheless, according to Cohen, this lack of immersion in the early period did not restrict the menstruant with regard to the cult. Cohen cites m. Nid. 10:7 as proof that the menstruant can separate ḥallâ for the priests, but he has misunderstood the referent of the passage.[56] The Mishna

---

54 Friedman, 479.

55 S. Cohen, "Menstruants and the Sacred in Christianity" in *Women's History and Ancient History*, ed. S. B. Pomeroy, 275, 277.

56 Ibid., 284.

is referring not to the menstruant but to the parturient in her second stage of impurity in which she has immersed and is merely counting days to be considered completely pure (cf. Bekh. 27a).

In Chapter 6 below I discuss in detail the contamination power of the menstruant according to the Mishna. It is inconceivable that the Sages would allow a person who contaminates as a Scriptural source of impurity to participate in worship at the sanctuary. This will be clear after careful examination of the Mishna and the Sifra which demonstrate the Rabbis' understanding of Scripture.

Selvidge and Sanders do not see the presence of a system in the impurity laws of the Priestly Code. Cohen does not see it even in the rabbinic system where it is more clearly evident. What is needed then is an in-depth look at 1) the impurity laws of Scripture and their implications and 2) the rabbinic reading of those laws.

There is another discipline which has informed the study of Jewish purity issues, i.e., cultural anthropology. Scholars in this field help to define ritual impurity, to explain which taboos are universal, and to posit reasons for them. Cultural anthropologists say that we can understand a particular society better by examining their rules concerning the body because the latter is, in effect, a symbol of society itself. These scholars have elevated the study of rituals even over myth.[57]

J. Frazer attributed the existence of impurity to the fear of the unknown or fear of demons.[58] However, many things are unknown but only certain items are continually considered impure cross-culturally (e.g., menstrual blood, semen, scale disease, death). Although they may not be interpreted in the same way, these items seem to be feared universally.[59]

---

57 M. Douglas, *Purity and Danger*, 16; E. Leach and D. A. Aycock, *Structuralist Interpretations of Biblical Myth*, 17.

58 J. Frazer, *The Golden Bough*, III, 150-55, 186-88; VIII, 36-37; R. Smith, *The Religion of the Semites*, 447.

59 Milgrom, *Leviticus*, I, 820-21, 949-52, 1001.

M. Douglas attempts to define impurity. She states that uncleanness is "matter out of place."[60] Dirt in the garden is the same substance as dirt in the house, but in the garden it is not considered impure. This is because it is in its rightful place. It is considered socially acceptable in the garden, but in the house it is unacceptable.

S. Meigs has refined the definition of Douglas as follows:

> Impurity is 1) substances perceived as decaying, carriers of such substances and symbols of them; 2) in those contexts in which the substances, their carriers, or symbols are threatening to gain access to the body; 3) where that access is not desired.[61]

Thus, impurity is not just identified with items which are socially displaced, but rather the term refers to substances symbolic of decay which threaten the body.

J. Milgrom notes that Meigs' conclusions concur with those of A. Culpepper who analyzed Zoroastrian practices. Culpepper states, "All sickness and body excretions were understood to participate in death-impurity."[62] R. Parker, too, comes to a similar conclusion with regard to the Greek attitude towards impurity.[63]

Thus, impurity has a life-threatening component even if it is only symbolic. Some sort of threatening access to the body is assumed, whether it be death itself, a symbol of it, or a process involving loss of life forces.

Working from Douglas' definition of impurity as matter out of place, crossed boundaries, and forbidden mixtures, New Testament scholars have made neat models of first century Palestine's value systems.[64] Notwithstanding the contributions

---

60 Douglas, *Purity and Danger*, 2, 35.

61 S. Meigs, "A Papuan Perspective on Pollution," *Man* 13 (1978) 313.

62 A. Culpepper, "Zoroastrian Menstrual Taboos" in *Women and Religion*, ed. J. Plaskow, 205; J. W. Burton, "Some Nuer Notions of Purity and Danger," *Anthropos* 69 (1974) 530.

63 Parker, 32-73.

64 Cf., for example, the work of B. Malina, *The New Testament World: Insights from Cultural Anthropology*.

of these scholars, some of their basic assumptions are untenable. One, there is too much reliance on Douglas' work which is replete with false inferences from the biblical text.[65] For example, she assumes that live animals can be unclean if they are of the forbidden categories. This mistake is important for it hurts Douglas' thesis that uncleanness inheres in certain types of persons and animals.

Also, Douglas emphasizes that impurity results from boundary crossing.[66] She states that the way a society formulates rules about the body illustrates how it thinks about the larger social body. She points to the example of Israel's rules concerning impure flows explaining that these are impure due to the fact that they cross the boundaries of the body. However, not all excretions from the body are labelled impure. Saliva (except that of the zāb), sweat, excrement, and tears are not considered impure by the priestly writers, yet all of these cross body boundaries. These inaccuracies often go unnoticed, but they are crucial for drawing a correct map of Jewish purity.

Another overly emphasized connection is that between purity and "wholeness." J. Soler, following Douglas, states that to be pure is to be whole.[67] This is not the case for the Priestly Code, at least, for which there is no castigation of the handicapped, who are allowed to enjoy all aspects of Israelite worship except to officiate as priests.[68]

Also, contrary to the view of some scholars, there is no biblical justification to label "abnormal" bodily functions such as

---

65 Milgrom, *Leviticus*, I, 721.

66 Douglas, *Purity and Danger*, 115.

67 J. Soler, "The Dietary Prohibitions of the Hebrews," *New York Review of Books* (June 14, 1979) 24-30.

68 Although the sectarians at Qumran apply this restriction to the laity as well (11QT 45:12-14; 1QM 7:4-5; 1QSa 2:3-11). Malina adds to this category of impurity, resulting from abnormal, not "whole," conditions, those who have had "contact with a cadaver," 137. I do not see how burial rites make a person less "whole."

menstruation and seminal emission.[69] This seems to me to be a cultural anthropologist's imposition on the text.

E. Leach has rightly criticized Frazer and Douglas for their application of cross-cultural comparisons to the Bible. Leach says, "My own view is that the observations of the 'travelers and ethnologists of modern times' cannot help us at all."[70] Douglas' study of the Nuer and Lele tribes in Central Africa is interesting, in Leach's opinion, but cannot be conclusive when supporting an argument about Leviticus. The situations, both economically and historically, are too disparate.

I agree with Leach and point out that in the work of these cultural-anthropologists there is little if any attention given to the terminology of the Jewish sources themselves. Hence, items assumed by modern or other societies to be impure sometimes affect their assertions about the ancient Israelites. It is impossible not to make such mistakes when one has not examined the language of the sources carefully.

Two cases in point are the following. J. Neyrey assumes that nakedness and excrement are impure in Judaism.[71] However, nowhere in the Priestly Code or in the Mishna are these items classified impure. If one considers Genesis, Chapters 1-2, as the paradigm for the pure state, based on Yahweh's concept of the ideal state of man, then one must note that it is only after their sin that Adam and Eve are clothed. Although nakedness is certainly not enjoined for public life it is never labelled *impure* and never figures in the ritual purity system of the Priestly Code. Excrement is not impure in the priestly or rabbinic systems.

In the work of W. Countryman one finds another serious weakness. Operating under the premise that the ancients did not distinguish between ritual and ethical purity, Countryman equates the impurities of Lev. 11-15 with those of Lev. 18. This

---

69 Malina, 137; Douglas, *Purity and Danger*, 41-57; Neusner, *Purities*, XXII, 95; W. Countryman, *Dirt, Greed, and Sex*, 26.

70 Leach and Aycock, 20-21.

71 J. Neyrey, "The Idea of Purity in Mark's Gospel," *Semeia* 35 (1968) 101, 103.

leads him to the conclusion that since the Church annulled the Jewish purity system, certain sexual laws which he considers linked to that system, e.g., the homosexuality or incest prohibitions, are likewise neutralized.[72] Countryman ignores the character of the impurities of Lev. 11-15 which are purifiable and often due to uncontrollable circumstances of every day life as opposed to those of Lev. 18 (tô^cebot = abominations) which cannot be purified but must be eradicated by the death of the offender.

Thus, what is needed is a comprehensive approach in which cultural anthropology is not ignored but neither is it imposed on the sources. Rather, the sources and their interpretations by the society which held them to be sacred texts are carefully analyzed to yield specific notions of impurity of that society. Thus, for an accurate understanding of the sectarian and rabbinic concept of impurity one must understand the system of the biblical priests, not just in principle but in detail, as well as the Tannaitic interpretation of that system.

In light of the above survey of scholarship on Jewish purity issues it is clear that anyone who wishes to make claims about the rabbinic concept of purity must understand the system of purity in the Priestly Code thoroughly. Thus, the aid of biblical scholars must be enlisted. Until recently commentators on Leviticus and Numbers have not treated the purity laws systemically. Most of these scholars offer valuable philological, cross-cultural, or comparative linguistical exegesis of the phenomena in Leviticus 11-15, but none reconstruct the laws as a workable system.[73] J. Milgrom, in his many articles on impurity, and most recently his commentaries on Leviticus (Anchor Bible, 1991) and Numbers (Jewish Publication Society, 1990) has combined his excellent knowledge of the Ancient Near East with a wealth of exegesis from classical and medieval rabbinic scholars and has presented a plausible understanding of the priestly system of purities.

---

72 Countryman, 109-23.

73 M. M. Kalisch, *Leviticus*; B. Baentsch, *Exodus, Leviticus und Numeri*; K. Elliger, *Leviticus*; D. Z. Hoffmann, *Leviticus*; B. A. Levine, *Leviticus*; G. P. Wenham, *The Book of Leviticus*; A. Dillmann and V. Rysell, *Die Bücher Exodus und Leviticus*.

Milgrom's reading of Scripture employs a technique literary critics would call "gap-filling."[74] Scripture, because of its gaps and ambiguities, demands that the reader infer from the data presented the unwritten data, the rest of the picture. For example, although we know the mĕṣōrāʿ, the person affected by scale disease, is a very potent impurity bearer from Scripture's isolation and purification rules of ṣāraʿat (Lev. 13-14; Num. 5:2), the Torah tells us nothing about the ability of the mĕṣōrāʿ to contaminate other persons and objects. Milgrom fills this gap in accordance with principles identified within the text itself. In this case, the house affected by the same disease is said to contaminate by means of its overhang (Lev. 14:36, 46). Thus, it is logical, and early rabbinic exegetes concur, that the mĕṣōrāʿ too contaminates in this manner.

Boyarin, who has recognized the necessity for and common practice of gap-filling in rabbinic midrash in order to make sense of the text, makes this statement:

> It is not exploitation of the text; it is exploitation of the gaps in the text, which are there, as it were, precisely to be exploited.[75]

Filling in where the text is silent based on data explicitly given elsewhere in the text is the responsibility of the reader. These inferences are then tested against the backdrop of larger principles inherent in the text.

D. P. Wright has contributed to and continued the work which Milgrom began. In his book, *The Disposal of Impurity*, Wright compares biblical with Hittite and Mesopotamian modes of purification. He constructs convenient "trees," diagrams of the dynamics of impurity, i.e., what contaminates what, to what extent, and requiring what purification. He helpfully distinguishes between explicit and implicit data from the text and explains the basis for the latter. Several of his "trees" are

---

74 A. Berlin, *Poetics and Interpretation of Biblical Narrative*, 137; M. Sternberg, *The Poetics of Biblical Narrative*; cf. R. Alter, *The Art of Biblical Narrative*, on ambiguity, 67.

75 Boyarin, *Intertextuality*, 45.

reprinted in this dissertation for easy comparison with rabbinic models.

THE BIBLICAL AND RABBINIC IMPURITY SYSTEMS

Below is a general overview of the biblical and rabbinic systems of impurity setting forth the basic elements of Leviticus 11-15 and their rabbinic interpretation. The concept of purity at Qumran will be treated separately in Part One below. Until recently the scholarship on the sectarians' concept of impurity has been meager. However, with the recent emergence of many new documents it is possible to recreate, at least in sketch, the impurity system of the sectarians.

The Biblical System

The Torah clearly states (Lev. 15:31) that it is God's residence in Israel which makes it necessary for all Israelites to maintain a certain standard of purity. Only God is truly holy. J. Milgrom has said that holiness is "the extension of his nature; it is the agency of his will."[76] If certain things are called holy (e.g., land, priest), it is only because Yahweh has designated them such. Milgrom describes holiness as follows:

> That which man is not, nor can ever fully be, but that which man is commanded to emulate and approximate, is what the Bible calls qādôš, "holy."[77]]

Milgrom offers a system which clarifies the technical use of the following terms in the Priestly Code (which represents the nucleus of the purity material in the Torah): qādôš, holy; ṭāhôr, pure; ḥōl, common; and ṭamēʿ impure. The diagram below illustrates the dynamic between these four states:

---

76 Milgrom, I, 718-36.
77 Ibid., 731.

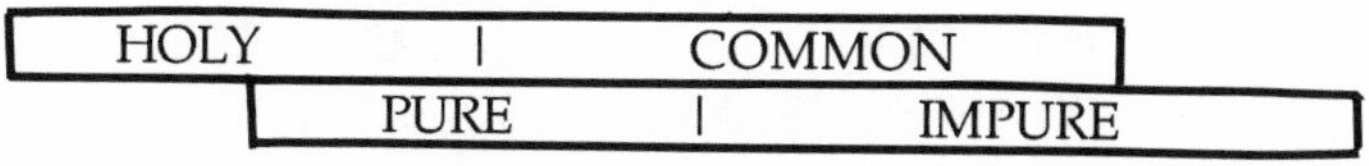

Holy can never become impure, and impure may never become holy. Rather, both try to influence what is pure or common. The latter are non-active categories: common is the absence of the holy and pure is the absence of impurity.

According to the Priestly Code, a pure person who comes into contact with what is holy is normally not adversely affected.[78] The exception to this is the pure layperson who enters holy areas or comes into contact with most holy offerings (minḥâ, ʾāšam, and ḥaṭṭaʾt), after they have been sacrificed, or with sacred furniture. Under these circumstances, the person becomes an encroacher who has trespassed on sancta and deserves death.[79] Like an impure person who has come into contact with holiness, he or she incurs the death penalty.[80] P does state that *objects* which come into contact with sancta become holy (Ex. 29:37; 30:26-29; Lev. 6:11, 20).

Impurity stands for the forces of death; holiness stands for the forces of life. God, who alone is truly holy, is the source of life and purity. Death provides no possibility of contact with God.[81]

Those who officiate at the sanctuary must maintain holiness since they are the "housekeepers" of the divine residence. They handle sancta, mediate the cult, and share God's food (Lev. 21:6). However, according to the Priestly Code, they cannot transmit holiness. The hierarchy can be illustrated in terms of space and persons by concentric circles as in Milgrom's diagrams represented below as Figure 1.[82]

---

78 This view stands in direct contrast to Ezekiel's according to which all sancta are contagious (even priestly garments, Eze. 44:19; 46:20) to persons who touch them and therefore lethal. Laity are not allowed to enter the inner court (Eze. 46:3) or to slaughter their own sacrifices (Eze. 44:11; 46:24).

79 Milgrom, *Leviticus*, I, 443-44; cf. Lev. 6:11.

80 Milgrom, *Leviticus*, I, 978.

81 For the symbolic equation of impurity and death, purity and life, cf. Milgrom, *Leviticus*, I, 1002.

82 Ibid., 718-36.

FIG. 1 THE HIERARCHY OF IMPURITY WITH REGARD TO PERSONS, ANIMALS AND SPACE

(copied from J. Milgrom, *Leviticus*, I, 722, 725)

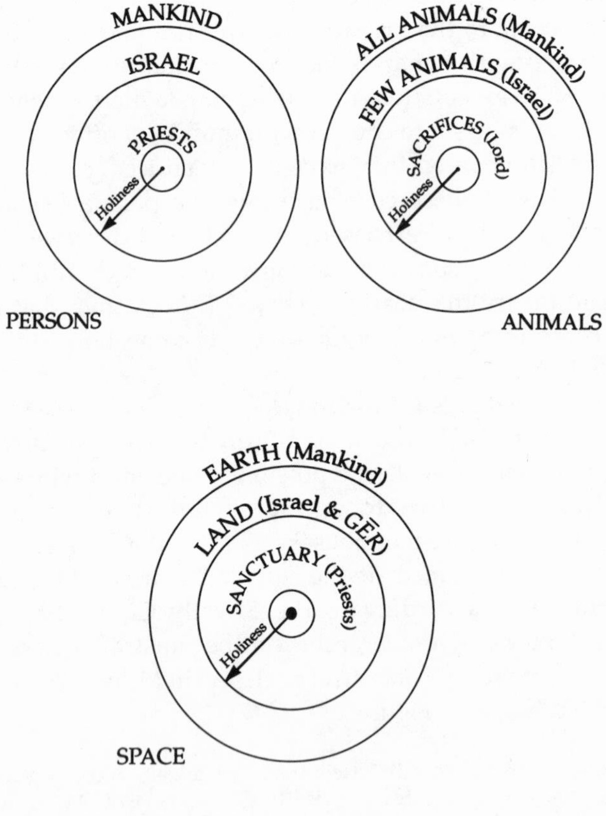

82 Ibid., 718-36.

According to Milgrom, the Israelite layperson can contaminate the sanctuary in three ways: 1) violating prohibitions (e.g., Molech worship, Lev. 20:3), 2) contracting a severe ritual impurity (e.g., becoming a mĕṣōrāᶜ), and 3) failing to purify any ritual impurity (e.g., Num. 19:13, 20).[83] In analyzing the impurity system of the Bible and the Rabbis I am not concerned with impurity of moral trespasses but with ritual impurity, i.e., the state of being unfit to participate in the cult because of an uncleanness of the types mentioned in Leviticus 11-15, all of which are physically purifiable. To blur the distinction between violations of the law and ritual impurity in the Torah is to make a gross error.[84] The penalty for sins such as incest and adultery is kārēt.[85] These cannot possibly be on a par with such impurities as, e.g., menstruation which is purifiable by a simple immersion and waiting for sunset. The impurities of Leviticus 18 are called tôᶜēbot, abominations, and only death can eradicate them.

Furthermore, all violations of prohibitive law automatically defile the sanctuary requiring the inadvertent offender to bring a sacrifice. Pardon is in the hand of God who must consent to forgive the sinner (nislaḥ lô). On the contrary, ritual impurity can be mechanically purified (ṭihēr) by the action of the

83 Ibid., 229; idem, "Israel's Sanctuary: the Priestly Picture of Dorian Gray," *RB* 83 (1976) 390-99. All traces of the notion that demons operating independently from Yahweh cause impurity are ousted by the monotheistic Israelite system. It is man who can cause impurity by his actions. The sacrificial ritual is not an apotropaeic effort to ward off danger to the divine house but rather a means of atonement for man's misdeeds. Nevertheless, in the purification rituals for some severe impurities there are still traces of the ingrained fear of the power of certain impurity sources.

84 Cf. Countryman who states that impurity is a type of sin in one place, 23, and in another, 39, concludes that violations of sexual laws, e.g. adultery, are a combination of purity and property concerns. He concludes that all the laws of the Torah were considered of equal weight, 43. Neusner, *Idea*, 25, says no contrast is made between cultic and ethical impurity and immediately proceeds to distinguish between ritual impurity and sin!

85 D. J. Wold, "The Kareth Penalty in P: Rationale and Cases." *SBL Seminar Papers*, 1 (1979) 1-45.

priest and the prescribed ritual. Indeed, it is not a sin to become ritually impure. Most of the impurities requiring ablutions are inevitable in the normal course of life. However, failure to perform the necessary purifications is considered sin and will contaminate the sanctuary.[86]

Some ritual impurities are potent enough to contaminate the sanctuary from afar, the offender never coming into physical contact with it. This is the reason that severe impurity bearers, e.g., corpses, scale-diseased persons, and persons with abnormal genital discharges, must be expelled from the camp (cf. Num. 5:2). Ritual impurities which contaminate the sacred sphere from afar will contaminate persons and objects by touch.

With the performance of the first purification ritual, the purifying person reduces the impurity's contagion both to the sacred and the common by one degree.[87] For example, the mĕṣōrāʿ automatically contaminates the sanctuary from afar and so must be put outside the camp. However, after the first stage of purification from scale disease, the mĕṣōrāʿ is allowed to enter the camp. Such a person no longer defiles the sanctuary from afar but does contaminate Israelites by touching them. This process will be clearer upon examination of the dynamics of each issue below. In the following diagram (Fig. 2) Milgrom charts the impurity bearers of the Priestly Code noting the mode of contamination, the consequent impurity stages, and purification procedures relating to each one.

It is difficult to extract strands of authorship in the Torah. Nevertheless, if scholarly divisions are correct, one can see a trend toward intensification of the demand for purity. This, I believe, culminates in the halakha of the early Sages. The Priestly Code is primarily concerned that the priests maintain holiness. The Holiness Code emphasizes the ethical aspect of holiness and extends (assuming P is early) the concern to all Israel.[88] It is H

86 Opp. Neusner, *Idea*, 95.

87 Milgrom, *Leviticus*, I, 983.

88 Ibid., 689; I. Knohl, Lecture at the University of California, Berkeley, fall term, 1989.

FIG. 2 THE TABLE OF PURIFICATION PROCEDURES AND EFFECTS

(Copied from J. Milgrom, *Leviticus*, I, 986-87)

	A. Impurity Bearer	B. Duration	C. Purification Stage (days)	Procedures
MAJOR SACRIFICES	1. *mĕṣōrāʿ*, scale-diseased person (Lev 14)	x + 7 (8)	X	
			1st	sp, l, sh, b
			7th	sh, l, b
			8th or [eve]	*ḥaṭṭāʾt* ewe/bird + 3 sacrifices + 2 daubings
	2. Parturient (Lev 12)	7 (14) + 33 (66)	7 (14)	
			7th (14th)	[l, b]
			41st (81st) or [eve]	ḥaṭṭāʾt bird + lamb/bird
	3. *zāb*, person with genital discharges (Lev 15:3–15, 28–30)	x + 7 (8)	x	
			7	
			7th	l, b
			8th or [eve]	ḥaṭṭāʾt bird + bird
	4. Corpse-contaminated priest (Ezek 44:26–27)	7 + 7 (8)	7	[sp on 3rd, 7th]
			7th	[l, b]
			15th or [eve]	ḥaṭṭāʾt (bird?)
	5. Corpse-contaminated Nazirite (Num 6:9–12)	7 (8)	7	[sp on 3rd, 7th]
			7th	sh, [l, b]
			8th or [eve]	ḥaṭṭāʾt + bird + bird + lamb
	6. Person whose impurity is accidentally prolonged (Lev 5:1–13)	x + 1	x	
			xth	[b]
				ḥaṭṭāʾt ewe/bird/
			(x + 1)st or [eve]	semolina

FIG. 2 (Continued)

	7. Corpse-contami-		7	sp on 3rd, 7th
	nated lay person	7	7th	l, b
M	(Num 5: 2–4:19)		7th	eve
I				
N	8. Menstruant	7	7	
O	(Lev 15:19–24)		7th	[l, b]
R			7th	eve
	9. Handler of Red Cow, scapegoat or burnt		P-A	
	ḥaṭṭāʾt (Num 19:7–10;	1	ablution	l, b
E	Lev 16: 27, 28)		eve	[eve]
V			P-A	
E	10. Emits semen		ablution	l, b
N	(Lev 15:16–18)	1	eve	eve
I	11. Carcass-		P-A	
N	contaminated	1	ablution	(l), b
G	(Lev 11:24–40; 22:5)		eve	eve
	12. Secondarily		P-A	
	contaminated (Lev 15; 22:4b–7; Num 19)	1	ablution eve	(l), b eve

Sigla: [ ] reconstructed · eve evening · sh shaving
x indefinite · l laundering · sp sprinkling
b bathing · P-A pre-ablution

which enjoins all Israel to be holy even as God himself is holy (Lev. 19:2).

The Rabbinic System

The Rabbis of the Mishna studied the biblical purity laws to the last detail. They took the laws seriously in theory and, at least in the early period, in practice as well. The Tosefta criticizes the Sages for excessive concern for purity, "The uncleanness of a knife is more grievous to Israelites than murder" (t. Yoma 1:12).[89] This statement is given after a story of a lad who was killed when he was within four cubits of the altar. The Sages make no comment about the stabbed boy's plight but immediately begin to measure to find out what exact area was polluted—the sanctuary or its courts. Even the father of the lad does not grieve but inappropriately proclaims, "His [my] son is still writhing, so the knife has not yet been made unclean." Thus, the knife could be extracted and remain pure because the boy was not yet a corpse. Although the Tosefta is surely exaggerating its story because of its critical stance, it reveals the intense concern of the Sages not to violate the Torah's purity laws.

Nearly 25% of the laws of the Mishna are related to ritual purity, and the Order of Purities, which is devoted to the subject, is probably the oldest of the six orders of the Mishna.[90] A thorough knowledge of purity was a prerequisite for sitting on the Sanhedrin (b. San. 94b; 17a). The teacher Symmachus is praised because he knew 48 reasons for every aspect of ritual purity and its purification (b. Erub. 13b). The Sages like to attribute high purity standards to biblical characters. They said even children in the time of David could understand the laws of

89 Pinchas b. Yair sets forth a progression of attributes, including purity and holiness, for which a Jew should strive. He says heedfulness leads to cleanliness (physical) which leads to purity which leads to pĕrîšût which leads to holiness, on to humility, shunning of sin, saintliness, the Holy Spirit, and resurrection of the dead (b. Sot. 9:15).

90 Neusner, *Idea*, 8.

purity in all their complexities.[91] In Hezekiah's time, everyone "from Dan to Beersheba" was found to be an expert in the laws of ritual purity (b. San. 94b).

In the time of the Second Temple, the cult clearly stood at the center of Jewish life. M. Borg has said that loyalty to the Temple and the Torah accounts for perhaps all Jewish resistance to gentile power.[92] Antiochus' and later Caligula's desecration of the Temple are good examples. Any foreign innovation which defiled the holiness of the cult or the land threatened to bring on a rebellion. This is because the biblical doctrine that God owns the land and the Temple is his house was strongly implanted in the minds of the Jews. Put very simply: defilement pushes God out of his house. Special perquisites from the land are to be kept pure since they support the temple officiants. The people are to be holy as well, some considering it necessary to strive for priestly holiness, since the Holy One lived in their midst.[93]

It seems this striving for increased holiness kept the nation as a whole from heathen culture. Beginning perhaps with the persecution by Antiochus and the subsequent Maccabean victory, spiritual segregation was intensified. The plan of the early Sages was, in Borg's words, to "insulate and isolate the nation from pagan influence."[94] The insider/outsider division became more definite as the religious leaders tried to enforce the purity laws of the national religion.

Immediately after the destruction of 70 C.E. purity matters continued to be primary and maybe even more so in an effort to substitute for the cult itself.[95] The Talmud states, "The priests preserved their status by not passing on to everyone the rules of purity," but that after the destruction of the Temple "purity spread" among the ordinary people (b. Bekh. 30b; y. Shab. 1:3). S. Safrai gives two reasons for the increased concern: 1) to make up

---

91 Mid. Tanh. ed. S. Buber, ḥukat, 106, par. 7.

92 M. Borg, *Conflict, Holiness and Politics*, 53.

93 J. Neusner, *Judaism in the Matrix of Christianity*, 47.

94 Borg, 53.

95 A. Oppenheimer, *The Am ha-Aretz: a Study in the Social History of the Jewish People in the Hellenistic-Roman Period*, 63.

for the Temple's ruin, and 2) to fill the vacuum left in religious life.[96]

Towards the end of the Tannaitic era neglect of the practice of the purity laws sets in. A variety of reasons are possible. There was constant contact between Jew and non-Jew, thus breaking down the barriers the purity rules symbolized. The Temple was becoming a more distant memory and its absence created practical problems: Where was one to get ash of a sacrificially burnt red cow? How was a parturient or a mĕṣōrāʿ to offer the required sacrifices?[97] The Mishna does not answer these questions. Rather, its Sages continue to study the levitical system as if it were still in effect.

Figure 3 below presents the hierarchy of impurity bearers according to Mishna Kelim 1:1-4 beginning with the corpse at the top as the most impure and listing other impure items, ending with the corpse-contaminated person.

Figure 4 charts the purity of space according to the same tractate. Beginning with the Holy of Holies as the most pure of all areas, the mishnaic writer moves outward from it in decreasing levels of holiness until he gets to the whole land of Israel which, although on the bottom of the list, must still maintain a certain level of purity. Below I will set forth general observations about the impurity system of the Mishna under four topics: sources of impurity, items affected by impurity, modes of impurity transfer, and modes of purification.

Sources of impurity are basically those outlined in the Bible: the corpse and its derivatives as well as carcasses, scale disease, and genital discharges. Gentiles are a unique case. In the Bible pagans are metaphorically labelled unclean because of their association with idols. For some Jews of the first century this

---

96 S. Safrai, *The Jewish People in the First Century: Historical Geography, Political History, Social Culture and Religious Life,* Compendium Rerum Iudaicarum ad Novum Testamentum, I:2, 832.

97 Ibid.

FIG. 3 THE MISHNAIC SYSTEM OF UNCLEANNESS (KEL. 1:1-4)

Corpse	(renders unclean by overhang for seven days)
Human Bone	(renders unclean for 7 days)
Mĕṣōrāʿ	(renders unclean by overhang)
Zābâ	(7-day impurity; renders unclean by sexual intercourse)
Zāb	(conveys uncleanness to couch)
Defiled Couch	(touching it requires the same purifications as carrying it)
Defiled Saddle	(unclean under a heavy stone)

Flow, Spit, Semen, and Urine of a Zāb; Menstruant

One Having Intercourse with a Menstruant

Carrion; Purgation water

Corpse-contaminated Person/Object; Purgation Water of Insufficient Quantity for Sprinkling; Miṭṭahēr; Semen

FIG. 4 THE MISHNAIC SYSTEM OF AREAS OF HOLINESS (KEL. 1:6-9)

Holy of Holies	(only the High Priest enters once a year)
Sanctuary	(priests must wash hands/feet before entry)
Area between the Porch and the Altar	(no priests with blemishes or with unloosed hair)
Court of the Women	(no Israelites except as necessary in fulfilling certain rituals)
Court of Israel	(no Israelites still awaiting atonement rites)
Court of Women	(no persons in the status of tĕbûl yôm - those awaiting evening to be totally pure)
Rampart	(no Gentiles or corpse-contaminated persons)
Temple Mount	(no zāb, zābâ, menstruant, or parturient)
Within Jerusalem	(lesser sanctities and second tithe eaten)
Walled Cities	(no mĕṣōrāʿîm or corpses)
Land of Israel	(produces tĕrûmâ, firstfruits, and tithes)

metaphor had been concretized; gentiles were considered ritually unclean.[98]

Items affected by impurity are limited to persons, vessels, clothing, food, and liquid. In certain circumstances, beds and chairs are also affected. Modes of impurity transfer derive from the Bible but are expanded and more specifically defined. After 70 C.E. airborne impurity of any kind was irrelevant since no Temple existed to be vulnerable to it.

Certain items are called by the Rabbis, ʾabôt ṭumʾâ, Fathers of Impurity. These refer to the items the Torah labels ṭāmē: the one who has been contaminated by a corpse, the mĕṣōrāʿ, those with genital discharges, semen, and carcasses. The corpse is called the ʾabî ʾabôt haṭṭumʾâ, the Father of Fathers of Impurity. Any susceptible item which comes into contact with any of these ʾabôt is called an Offspring of Impurity and becomes impure in the first degree. Food and hands which touch items in the first degree become unclean in the second degree. These are the only items which can contract impurity in the second degree. Items with second degree impurity can convey it only to priestly food, tĕrûmâ, sacrifices, qodōšîm, and liquids. Tĕrûmâ is susceptible to impurity up to three removes away from the actual Father of Impurity which was its source; qodōšîm is susceptible even to a fourth remove distant. In the time of R. Yohanan. b. Zakkai (first century Sage), according to R. Booth, it was considered possible for ḥullin, secular food, to be contaminated in the third degree.[99] At the fourth remove away from the source of impurity, liquids, and sacrificial food can still be made unclean (m. Zab. 5:10; m. Yad. 3:1; b. BQ 2b).

---

98 J. Baumgarten in a comment to me states that this metaphor is already concretized by the early second century B.C.E. He points to *Antiquities*, 12. Cf. also b. Shab. 21b which reveals that, according to the Talmud, the primary cause for celebrating Hanukkah is the miraculous increase of the one cruse of oil salvaged from the desecrated Temple. This passage states the cause of the desecration of the rest of the oil supply: "For when the Greeks entered the Temple, they defiled all the oils therein." Thus, only one cruse of oil was considered valid because it had not been contaminated by the touch of Gentiles. Cf. also Acts 10:28.

99 Booth, 177.

Liquids are the transferers par excellence of the impurity system. Even if they are contaminated by an item in the third degree, liquids become unclean in the first degree and also transfer their impurity to the first degree. The Mishna lists the liquids which transfer impurity in this manner: water, dew, oil, wine, milk, blood, and honey (m. Makh. 1:1; 6:4-5).

It is the moistening of food which enables it to receive impurity. This stems from the biblical verse, "If water is put on the seed and any part of their carcass falls on it, it is unclean to you" (Lev. 11:38). Now the Mishna makes it clear that this moistening must have been accomplished with human intention (m. Makh. 1:2; 4:2). For example, wheat in the fields upon which it has rained is not susceptible to impurity even though it is wet, because the rain was not caused by human intention. This is important because otherwise insects would contaminate moistened produce even before it was brought to the storehouse.

Impurity can also be transferred by touch, pressure, and overhang. Merely being in a house with certain sources of impurity can render a susceptible item unclean by the overhang of the roof. Factors to be considered in determining the extent of contamination are: 1) the intensity of the impurity source, 2) the intensity of the contact, and 3) the duration of the exposure.[100]

Depending on the degree of impurity, uncleanness is removed by sacrifices, immersion in water, and waiting for sunset. In the case of the corpse-contaminated person and the mĕṣōrāᶜ, special cultic procedures including the burning of a red cow and a bird rite, respectively, are also required.

It is the claim of this dissertation that the Sages recognize a system in Scripture's purity laws. They develop this notion to its utmost. There is a tendency not only to harmonize traditions but to homogenize them. For example, if the Bible says that the spit of the gonorrheic is defiling, the Rabbis consider all of his fluids to be defiling. If a menstruant must immerse, *a fortiori*, a woman with an abnormal blood flow. This evokes no surprise since in any tradition, a system of rules must be logical in order to be viable.

---

100 Milgrom, *Leviticus*, I, 912.

The Rabbis try to determine underlying principles of the contamination rules of the Torah so that they can determine the furthest effects of contamination on everything from a pot which is overturned to a cloth three handbreadths square.

Other assumptions stem from what Neusner calls the analogical-contrastive method of handling Scripture. According to this approach, if an item is unclean in Scripture, then its opposite is clean. Also, those things which are similar to it are probably also unclean in some way.[101]

In contrast to this extension of the biblical system there is also a rabbinic tendency to limit impurity. Only certain items have the possibility of contracting uncleanness. Persons cannot receive impurity from an item if it is unclean only in the first degree. Vessels cannot become impure unless they are whole and operative containers, and earthenware can receive uncleanness only through its interior (m. Kel. 2:1). Clothing receives uncleanness like rinsable vessels, and in connection with the impurity of discharges it can also transfer impurity by the pressure of the unclean person (See Chapter 6). Hands, if part of a clean body, can contract impurity on their own but only in the second degree. In addition to the limiting of susceptible items, the Rabbis make it very difficult for a person to become an ʾab ṭûmʾâ by restricting the definitions of the impurities. Much of this limiting tendency probably originates in the post-70 C.E. period when it became impossible to purify some of these impurities without the cult.

In Part One below, I analyze the system of impurity of the sectarians at Qumran. I begin with a discussion of exegetical principles and basic doctrines as set forth in the Scrolls (Chapter 1). After presenting the general mindset of the sectarians on matters of impurity, I proceed to recreate the actual system with regard to each type of impurity: corpse, ṣāraʿat, impure flows, semen, carcasses, excrement, and outsiders (Chapter 2). In Part Two, I analyze the rabbinic system of impurity. First, since immersion applies to all impurity bearers, I set forth its biblical

---

101 Neusner, *Purities*, XXII, 133.

basis (Chapter 3). Subsequently, I discuss the three major categories of impurity in the rabbinic impurity system: the corpse (Chapter 4), scale-disease (Chapter 5), and genital discharges (Chapter 6). In each case my contention is the same: the sectarians and the Rabbis are deriving their system from Scripture with a sacred regard for its laws. Violation of the latter must be avoided at all costs and protective regulations introduced where necessary. Stark differences in interpretation between the two groups often co-exist. The sectarians usually increase the stringency of the laws in cases of ambiguity or divergent traditions. On the other hand, it was a continual concern of the Rabbis to limit not extend the restrictions of the Torah whenever possible without incursion of biblical sanctions.

PART ONE

THE IMPURITY SYSTEM OF THE QUMRAN SECTARIES

CHAPTER 1

THE SECTARIAN CONCEPT OF PURITY

With the recent emergence of additional fragments from Cave 4 at Qumran, scholars are re-assessing their positions regarding the purity practices of the Qumran community. The purpose of this chapter is to collect the pertinent data on purity in the sectarian documents and to reconstruct the system as it was envisioned at Qumran. The system was only practiced in part at the Dead Sea commune; full operation would only be possible in the messianic era. After a few preliminary remarks about the sources, I will examine the purity data in two ways: 1) setting forth basic principles which inform the sect's concept of purity in general and 2) examining the dynamics of the system as it relates to specific types of impurity with comparison to other early Jewish traditions. As J. Baumgarten has suggested, "In the end it may well be that the religious laws and practices in the Qumran documents will be more decisive in determining the position of the sect within the spectrum of pre-Christian Jewish movements than any of its theological and messianic speculations."[1]

First, a word about the sources is in order. The most helpful fragments from Cave 4 which discuss purity matters are: 4QThrA1, Ṭaharot A1; 4QMMT, Miqṣat Maᶜaseh ha-Torah; 4QOrdc, *Ordonnances c*; and 4QFl, *Florilegium*. Fragment 4QThrA1 is concerned about the contagion of impure persons. They are warned to keep away even from other impure persons. This as yet unpublished work is to appear in print shortly in two translations, one by J. Baumgarten and one by J. Milgrom.[2] In this dissertation I quote from the manuscript of the latter (9 lines).

Fragment 4QMMT has been presented, although without full text and translation, by E. Qimron and J. Strugnell (1983).[3] It is a halakhic letter from the leader of the sect (possibly the Teacher of Righteousness) to the leader of his opponents (possibly Jonathan or Simon). Qimron and Strugnell have collected and compiled several fragments (nos. 394-399) into one composite work of 120 lines.

M. Baillet was the first to translate (into French) and name 4QOrdc (1982); he also numbers it 514.[4] Subsequently, Milgrom produced another rendering of the same work with translation into English (1991).[5] This 11-line fragment is concerned that unclean persons refrain from eating until after proper ablutions have been made.

Finally, 4QFl, a fragment of 19 lines, was fully published by J. M. Allegro (1968).[6] This text is an eschatological document which looks forward to the re-establishment of the Davidic dynasty in the latter days. The author expects two messiahs: in

---

1 J. Baumgarten, *Studies in Qumran Law*, 12.

2 J. Milgrom, "4QThrA1: an Unpublished Qumran Text on Purities" in *Dead Sea Scrolls Studies*.

3 E. Qimron and J. Strugnell, "An Unpublished Halakhic Letter from Qumran" in *Biblical Archaeology Today*, 400-407.

4 M. Baillet, *Qumran Grotte 4*, III, *DJD* VII, 295-98.

5 J. Milgrom, *Leviticus*, I, 972.

6 J. M. Allegro, *DJD*, I.

addition to the priestly messiah, the writer expects a Messiah of Israel who will interpret the law.

Other pertinent fragments will be noted as needed and the standard sectarian documents will be referred to in conventional fashion:

CD	= The Damascus Rule
1QH	= The Thanksgiving Scroll
1QM	= The War Scroll
1QS	= The Manual of Discipline
1QSa	= The Messianic Rule
11QT	= The Temple Scroll
11QPs	= The Psalms Scroll

The new fragments from Cave 4 reveal a striking affinity to CD and 11QT. They fill in some of the purification procedures missing in the Temple Scroll. M. O. Wise has given proofs of this linkage in his work, *A Critical Study of the Temple Scroll from Qumran Cave 11*.[7] Y. Yadin is confident of this linkage, especially due to the common use of the term עיר המקדש.[8] L. H. Schiffman, on the other hand, has some reservations because the laws in the Temple Scroll regulating the impurity of the corpse are very different from those found in other sectarian documents. While admitting several parallels between the Temple Scroll and other sectarian scrolls from Qumran, Schiffman states, "The laws concerning the impurity of the dead are devoid of any particular characteristics that would be associated with sectarian life as known from the other documents."[9] I would suggest that the reason for this difference lies in the fact that the Temple Scroll sets forth an eschatological ideal and not a rule for the present community (see below). (Schiffman accepts readily the

---

7 M. O. Wise, *A Critical Study of the Temple Scroll from Qumran Cave 11*, 151-53. Wise understands the Temple Scroll to be projecting the rules of the existing community onto a future Temple.

8 Y. Yadin, *The Temple Scroll*, I, 416.

9 L. H. Schiffman, "The Impurity of the Dead in the Temple Scroll" in *Archaeology and History*, ed. L. H. Schiffman, 152.

commonality between 4QMMT and 11QT noting only minor differences.[10])

Much debate has centered over the origin of the Temple Scroll. H. Stegemann insists that the Temple Scroll has no bearing on the community at Qumran since the sect was uninterested in the Temple except as an academic pursuit.[11]

B. A. Levine in an early article points out the difference in the calendar of the Temple Scroll as a reason to presuppose a community other than the Qumran sect behind it, but in a recent article he states that the sectarians did endorse the Temple Scroll even though they did not create it.[12] Yadin, while noting that the Scroll retains earlier traditions, places its redaction in the second century B.C.E. in the Qumran period.[13]

There is no consensus as to the place of origin of the Damascus Rule either. However, P. R. Davies, who has devoted much study to this document, aligns it with the Temple Scroll and states that although its origin was pre-Qumran it was accepted by the sect.[14] I think it is safe to assume for the purposes at hand that, regardless of origin, all of the Scrolls were accepted in some way by the Qumran community. The purity data of all the Scrolls are compatible in most regards.

---

10 L. H. Schiffman, "The Temple Scroll and the Systems of Jewish Law of the Second Temple Period" in *Temple Scroll Studies*, ed. Brooke, 250. Schiffman wishes to see a Sadducean connection: "It is most likely that the sect was founded by disaffected priests who left the Jerusalem Temple after the Maccabean revolt when the Zadokite high priests were displaced by the Hasmoneans," 252.

11 H. Stegemann, "The Literary Composition of the Temple Scroll and Its Status at Qumran" in G. J. Brooke, *Temple Scroll Studies*, 144-145; H. Stegemann, "The Origins of the Temple Scroll," *SVT* 40 (1988) 235-256.

12 B. A. Levine, "The Temple Scroll: Aspects of Its Historical Provenance and Literary Character," *BASOR* 232 (1978) 5-23, esp. 7-11; idem, "A Further Look at the Moʿadim of the *Temple Scroll*" in *Archaeology and History*, ed. L. H. Schiffman, 53.

13 Yadin, I, 390.

14 P. R. Davies, *The Damascus Covenant*, 140; idem, "The Temple Scroll and the Damascus Covenant" in *Temple Scroll Studies*, ed. G. J. Brooke, 209.

In order to put the purity data of the Scrolls into proper perspective, it is necessary to first clarify three basic areas of the sect's ideology: 1) the relationship of the sect to the Temple, 2) the sectarian interpretation of Scripture, and 3) the purity of the common meal. Afterwards, I will examine the specific data of the Scrolls on each impurity bearer in an attempt to construct the purity system the sectarians envisioned.

What was the relationship of the Qumran community to the Temple? It is clear that the Qumran sectarians were disenchanted with the cult at Jerusalem. Scholars have proposed a number of reasons, including: 1) the non-Zadokite priesthood and its laxity in matters of purity, 2) differences over the correct calendar, and 3) the infiltration of Hellenistic practices into Judaism.[15] Nevertheless, the sectarians upheld the importance of the cult and its Jerusalem location albeit not in its present condition.

The Essenes, very likely connected to the Dead Sea sect, are found in Jerusalem as well as in other cities (Wars 5:145; 2:124).[16] Some sent votive offerings to the Temple and maybe even sacrifices (Ant. 18:19). Baumgarten points out that the Essenes' disagreement with the Jerusalem priesthood was not over the existence of the cult at Jerusalem in principle but over its laxity in purity matters. He suggests that the Essenes did sacrifice at the Temple but that they did it separately according to their own rigid standards.[17]

The Damascus Code gives instructions for sending sacrifices to the altar; in particular, they must be sent by ritually clean messengers. However, it is difficult to ascertain the time period to which this refers. It may be referring to an earlier period before the sectarians seceded from the Jerusalem cult or to a future time when proper cultic practice could be restored in

---

15 J. Milik, *Ten Years of Discovery in the Judean Wilderness*, 83.

16 Yadin, I, 398-399.

17 Baumgarten, *Studies*, 62-63, 67. This interpretation is based on Ant. 18:19 in the manuscripts rather than in the Epitome and the Latin version. Baumgarten also cites the Letter of Aristeas 106 which describes special purity standards followed separately by some in Jerusalem.

Jerusalem (CD 11:18-21). It is preceded by an instruction not to offer anything except the burnt offering on the altar on the Sabbath. This clearly was not taking place at Qumran. In any case, the evidence of the Temple Scroll makes it certain that the sectarians did not reject the cult at Jerusalem theologically.

That the Temple remained central in principle is evidenced by the lack of an altar at Qumran. No text mentions a sanctuary at Qumran. Also the interference of the Wicked Priest, whom the sectarians did at first accept, was due to a different calendar not a different altar.[18] The bones of the animals found in Qumran were preserved in jars, not burnt on an altar.[19] Not only the existence of the Temple Scroll but the emphasis on Zion in the War Scroll (1QM 12:12-15) and in the Psalms Scroll (11QPs 12:1-15) is further evidence of the importance of Jerusalem to the sectarians.

Although they disagreed with current Temple practice, the sectarians did not think that their communal meals conducted in ritual purity were equivalent to the sacrifices of the priests in the Temple. Their meals comprised merely a temporary and imperfect substitute.

Some scholars hold the opposite view: the community at Qumran regarded itself as the new Temple. B. Gartner in his work, *The Temple and the Community in Qumran and the New Testament*, was probably the first to promote this view.[20] Also H. W. Kuhn and G. Klinzing state that Qumran saw itself as the eschatological temple.[21] Gartner's work was further supported by E. S. Fiorenza in her comparison of Qumran ideology with the New Testament. Her conclusion is: "The Qumran community's concept of eschatology and its self-understanding as the new

---

18 Ibid., 74.

19 This is in contrast to the practice reflected in the Mishna according to which sacrificial bones were discarded or burnt (m. Ter. 11:5; m. Hul. 9:5; m. Pes. 7:10; cf. b. Pes. 83a).

20 Cambridge: The University Press, 1965, 10-11; 16-46; 44-45.

21 H. W. Kuhn, *Enderwartung und gegen wartiges Heil. Untersuchungen zu den Gemeindeliedern von Qumran (Studien und Untersuchungen zum Neuen Testament*, IV, 185-86; G. Klinzing, *Die Undeutung*, 210.

eschatological temple are central for the theological thinking of Qumran."[22] M. Newton too is influenced by this view in his comparison of the purity concept at Qumran with the letters of Paul. He says that both Paul and "the Qumran covenanters perceive of their respective communities as the Temple."[23] B. Bokser considered the pure meal of the sectarians as a sacred rite substituting for sacrifices at the Temple.[24] Bokser suggests that the pure meal at Qumran was cultic. In other words it was regarded as a sacrificial meal. I agree with Schiffman that there is no reason to regard this meal as cultic. Schiffman compares the meal to that of the Pharisees (See Appendix A) which, although it was not conducted communally, was to be eaten in a state of ritual purity but not considered holy.[25]

To my mind, the discoveries of the Temple Scroll and the Cave 4 fragments reveal a decided interest on the part of the sectarians in the cult, not because they were at present participating in the cult but because they would be at a future time. Their situation is similar to the Rabbis of the Mishna who had no opportunity to effect the sacrifices of the Temple but studied them for future use.

Some scholars say that the laws of the Temple Scroll were mainly projections of the existing community's rules and had little to do with the eschaton. In other words, these laws do not reflect what was anticipated for the future, but rather the Scroll was merely an academic pursuit which combined customs current at Qumran with Scriptural exegesis. Wise says of the Temple

---

22 E. S. Fiorenza, "Cultic Language in Qumran and in the New Testament," *CBQ*, 165. Fiorenza admits, however, that the only clear references to support this are found in the Damascus Rule 3:18-4:10.

23 M. Newton, *The Concept of Purity at Qumran and in the Writings of Paul*, 116. Newton compares the Qumran community to the Holy of Holies at the Temple, 46.

24 B. Bokser, "Philo's Description of Jewish Practices," Protocol of the 30th Colloquy of the Center for Hermeneutical Studies, Berkeley (5 June 1977) 19-27.

25 L. H. Schiffman, "Communal Meals at Qumran," *RQ* 10/37 (1979) 51-52.

Scroll that many of its purity laws did not pertain to entry into the Temple but to eating of the community's food.[26]

The tendency to equate the rules for entry into the Temple in the Temple Scroll and related documents with the current regulations for the community is an inaccurate representation of Qumran ideology. What is missing is the recognition that the sectarians were living in abeyance, as it were. Proper cultic practice was necessary but was temporarily impossible. Why study the rules of Temple practice and sacrifice if these were inoperable? The answer must be that they were expected to be re-established in the future. The same attitude is reflected among the Sages of the Talmud.

Schiffman, in his article, "Purity and Perfection: Exclusion from the Council of the Community in the ***Serekh ha^cEdah,***" demonstrates the parallels between the present practices of the community and those envisioned for the eschaton and concludes that the "life of the sect in the present was to mirror its legislation for the end of days." However, his conclusion is too broad. He says:

> The sect saw itself as constituting a sanctuary through its dedication to a life of holiness and purity. It therefore extended the Temple's legislation regarding the priesthood to the eschatological assembly. It is most probable that the very same regulations were in force in the present age, in which the sect lived in preparation for and in expectation of the dawn of the eschaton.[27]

I think Schiffman is correct about the holy standards for the eschatological assembly, but it is not the case that "the very same regulations" would be considered necessary or even possible in the present.

Wise, too, thinks that the Temple Scroll reflects rules for entering the community at Qumran. He finds support in an unpublished fragment of the Damascus Covenant (4QDb) which

---

26 Wise, *A Critical Study of the Temple Scroll from Cave 11*, 139.

27 L. H. Schiffman, "Purity and Perfection: Exclusion from the Council of the Community in the ***Serekh ha^cEdah***" in *Biblical Archaeology Today*, 385.

bans blind and other handicapped persons from the Temple City but uses the term קהל on occasion instead of עיר המקדש.[28]

The status of the Temple City of the Temple Scroll was not the same as that of the Dead Sea sect at Qumran. Burial rules provide an example. The War Scroll establishes 2000 cubits as the minimum distance away from the camp to bury the dead. The Temple Scroll extends this to 3000 cubits. However, at Qumran, the cemetery was adjacent to the complex. The cemetery is located 4 meters away from the east wall of the complex. Milik describes 110 tombs in orderly rows oriented north to south.[29]

In the Temple Scroll and also in the Damascus Document it is stated that no sexual intercourse is allowed in the Temple City (11QT 45:11-12; CD 12:1-2). Yet, the Scrolls record marriage rules.[30]

As Yadin has pointed out, the lack of installations for impure women prescribed for the Temple City (although they are prescribed for ordinary cities), shows that no women were allowed to reside in the Temple City. The rules notwithstanding, the bones of women have been found at Qumran.[31]

Furthermore, outside of the Temple Scroll, an eschatological document, there is no prescription extant for the division of the Qumran compound into sacred and profane spheres. The graduated purity of the novitiate and the mention by Josephus of senior and junior members (which may refer to the same matter) certainly do not represent a dichotomy of sacred

---

28 Wise, 150.

29 Milik, 47.

30 L. Bennett-Elder, "Female Ascetics in the Late Second Temple Period: Five Provisional Models," AAR National Convention, Kansas City 1991, cites several references in the Scrolls, including 1QSa 1:4-11, CD 4:20, 5:1-10, 16:10-11, 11QT 57:15-19, and 63:10-15, which indicate the presence of women; Milik, 47.

31 Cf. Bennett-Elder, "Female Ascetics," chart entitled "Results of Excavation Reports for Cemeteries at Qumran: Roland de Vaux O. P. and S. H. Steckoll," and Elder's comment, "Of fifty graves at Qumran in which gender designation has been determined, thirty per cent are women and children;" Milik, 47.

and profane statuses.[32] All pure members may touch and/or eat of the טהרה "purity," i.e., pure items such as food, drink, clothing, and vessels.

Furthermore, there is no mention in the Manual of Discipline or in any other non-eschatological text of a three-day purification at Qumran for impurities which are biblically only one-day impurities. Only the Temple City of the Temple Scroll requires this extra stringency of minor impurity bearers (11QT 45:7-12).

As Milgrom has demonstrated, the Qumran community was at present living in the status of the ordinary city of the Temple Scroll.[33] Although corpse-contaminated persons and those with seminal emissions were not allowed in the Temple City (11QT 45:7-10; 49:19-21), they were not expelled from the ordinary city. Milgrom deduces this from the extra ablution required of these persons on the first day of their contamination (11QT 49:17). He suggests that this first-day ablution enables the purifying person to remain within the city.[34] Also, quarantine areas were designated within ordinary cities for certain impurity bearers (11QT 48:14-17), an inconceivable situation for the Temple City.

The War Scroll and the Messianic Rule, on the other hand, refer to the eschatological community. The angels are not present at Qumran, neither is there a war. There will be a battle in the eschaton and at that time the status of the community will be holy like the sacred war camp of Deuteronomy and the holy sanctuary. The Messianic Rule records entrance requirements for the holy messianic community (1QSa 2:4-11; cf. 1QM 7:4-5; 11QT 45:12-14). These cannot be applied to the historical group at Qumran in a wholesale fashion.

The above arguments lead to one conclusion: the sectarians of Qumran regarded themselves as living, not in the sacred status of the Temple of the present or of the future but, in the

---

32 Baumgarten, *Studies*, 94-95.

33 Milgrom, *Leviticus*, I, 968-71.

34 Ibid., 971.

pure status incumbent by the Torah, according to their interpretation, on ordinary Israelites. They believed that in the eschaton there would be a re-established Temple at Jerusalem with an accompanying cult, however, it was impossible to reconstruct a surrogate Temple at Qumran.

Thus, the Qumran sectarians were committed to the cult at Jerusalem, albeit not in its present condition. It was currently considered ineffective because of the invalid genealogy and gross defilement of its priests together with a calendar viewed heretical by the sect, consequently, it had to be temporarily abandoned. It could not be supplanted, however, by a non-biblical replacement. Rather, the sectarians studied its laws for a future when they would again be in effect. For the present, it had to suffice to emphasize the importance of those matters which they could observe at Qumran and leave the re-establishment of the cult to the Messiah.[35]

If one understands this distinction between the present and future statuses of the Qumran community, then Milgrom's suggestion that the Temple City of the Temple Scroll was envisioned on a sacred plane reserved for the eschaton is plausible.[36] The ordinary city of the Temple Scroll reflected the profane status of the community at Qumran. To be sure, high standards of purity were maintained, but the sanctity of the Temple City could not be attained at Qumran.

The Rabbis understand differences in the sanctity of space in terms of three camps: **maḥanēh šekînâ**, the Divine Camp; **maḥaneh leviyyâ**, the Levitical Camp; and **maḥanēh Yiśraʾel**, the Israelite Camp (Sif. Num. 1[4]; t. Kel. BQ 1:12; cf. also m. Kel. 1:8-9; b. Zeb. 116b). The Divine Camp refers to the Temple area only

---

35 Others who support this view are: W. O. McCready, "The Sectarian Status of Qumran: the Temple Scroll," *RQ* 11/2 (1983) 190-191; J. Nolland, "A Misleading Statement of the Essene Attitude to the Temple," *RQ* 9 (1978) 556; J. Murphy-O'Connor states that no community which claimed to observe the law could reject the Temple and that the tithes and firstfruits were sent by the sectaries to the Temple. However, contact was kept to the "indispensable minimum," "The Damascus Document Revisited," *RB* 92 (1985) 236-38.

36 Milgrom, *Leviticus*, I, 968-71.

from the Court of the Israelites inward. The Levitical Camp extends from the Court of the Israelites to the Temple Mount and the Camp of the Israelites from there to the whole area within the walls of Jerusalem.[37]

The equivalent of the rabbinical Divine Camp at Qumran is the whole Temple City. Furthermore, even ordinary cities were to maintain a lesser status of purity equal to that which the Rabbis prescribe for the Camp of the Israelites. Below is a comparison of the two ideologies:

Rabbis	*Qumran*
Temple (Divine Camp)	Temple City
Temple Mount (Levitical Camp)	N/A
Jerusalem (Israelite Camp)	Ordinary City

It is necessary to examine the sectarians' peculiar method of interpreting Scripture in order to understand how they arrived at these conclusions. As Milgrom demonstrates, the Qumran community subscribed to a homogeneous and maximalist interpretation of Scripture. This interpretation was complemented, to be sure, by sectarian traditions, for clearly some of the material of the Scrolls cannot be exegeted from the text. However, the concept that all Israel is to be in a state of ritual purity before eating can be based on Scripture. For example, the laws of Leviticus 11 regarding purity of foods, central at Qumran, are addressed to all Israel, not to priests alone (Lev. 11:2). The commandment to bathe and launder after touching carcasses is also given to all (Lev. 17:14-15). The Pharisees had a similar orientation towards purity. However, they chose to maintain ritual purity within society rather than to secede from it.

---

37 Yadin, I, 278-279.

Milgrom refers to the exegetical technique of homogenization by the Qumran sages.[38] By this he means the method of extending Biblical information about a given item to items which are similar to it. I will quote his definition:

> By this [homogenization] I mean that a law which applies to specific objects, animals, or persons is extended to other members of the same species.[39]

The Rabbis, too, use a method of homogenization or equalization of Scriptural data taking a fact stated about one item as relevant to all similar items; they call it **binyan ʾab**, which has been literally defined as: "a construction of a prototype."[40]

As Milgrom notes, for any group living by Scripture the laws must be cohesive and uncontradictory; both the Rabbis and the sectarians looked forward to a time when the laws would be again in effect. However, there is a difference in the two groups' use of homogenization. For the Rabbis, some laws, although they may be linked in some way to Scripture, are **dĕRabbānan**, i.e., rabbinical enactments which cannot claim the authority of Scripture; for the Dead Sea commune, all sectarian interpretation of the Torah is regarded as Scripture.[41]

I do not think that this is the only difference. The character of the interpretation, too, is different. To be sure, the ambiguity in Scripture lends itself to diverse interpretations. The Rabbis follow the Pharisees, who, unlike the sectarians, refuse to leave society. They wish to alleviate as much as possible the stringencies of the Torah while the sectarians would rather increase them and receive the satisfaction that they have without a doubt kept the Law. The sectarians would rather go beyond the Law excessively than to possibly transgress in one small point. The Rabbis are more practical.

---

38 J. Milgrom, "The Qumran Cult: Its Exegetical Principles: Studies in the Temple Scroll" in *Archaeology and History*, ed. L. H. Schiffman, 171.

39 Ibid., 174-175.

40 D. Boyarin, private communication, fall 1991.

41 Milgrom, "Exegetical Principles," 178.

A clear example of this is the rabbinic limitation of items susceptible to impurity. For the Rabbis, only persons, food, liquids, vessels, and fabrics are susceptible to impurity, even in the house of the dead (Sif. Num. 126 [162]). [In special cases, beds and seats too are susceptible (cf. Chapter 6, below).] At Qumran, stone and wood are also susceptible (11QT 49:11-15). Wood is susceptible, according to the Rabbis, only if it is carved into a usable vessel (m. Kel. 2:1; 15:1; 16:7-8).

Now Milgrom points us to the leniency of the first day ablutions of 4QOrdc as an example of a more lenient stance to purity than the Rabbis.[42] However, by his own admission this first day allowance is only to the profane sphere. The Rabbis, by contrast, allow all impurity in the profane sphere.

Yadin, too, points to a "leniency" at Qumran. He refers to the sectarian interpretation of ʿeṣem ʾādām in Num. 19:16 as "the bone of a dead man." In comparing the biblical with the sectarian rendition of Numbers 19:16, one can see that the sectarians have inserted the word מת, dead, after the word אדם, man, in two places to emphasize that the person must be dead in order to contaminate others:

> Num. 19:16: Whoever in the open field touches one who is slain with a sword, or a dead body, or a bone of a man, or a grave shall be unclean seven days.

> 11QT 50:4-6: And every man in the open field who touches the bone of a dead man, or one who is slain with the sword, or a dead man, or the blood of a dead man, or a grave.

As Yadin suggests, these insertions possibly reflect a polemic against the Pharisaic/rabbinic interpretation according to which the separated bone of a living creature is defiling as well. According to Sifre Numbers, the Torah's double reference to ʿeṣem, bone (Num. 19:16, 18), indicates two different meanings: one reference (v. 16) is to a limb torn from a living body (ʿeṣem ʾādām) while the other reference (v. 18) is to a bone (ʿeṣem) from a

---

42 Milgrom, *Leviticus*, I, 968-71.

dead body (Sif. Num. 127[165]; cf. m. Eduy. 6:3; m. Kel. 1:5; t. Eduy. 2:10). According to the Palestinian Targum on Num. 19:16 the mere fact that the dead body, obviously made up of dead bones, has been declared contaminating in the term, mēt, suggests that the next phrase, ʿeṣem ʾādām, refers to a bone separated from a living creature.[43] Furthermore, without a context indicating otherwise, one would expect the term ʾādām to refer to a living person not a dead one.

I agree with Yadin that Qumran is fighting an opposing view, however, it has nothing to do with leniency. The sectarians regard the rabbinic view preposterous because in their view Scripture is clear that only dead creatures are defiling. Full support for this can be found in the laws concerning unclean animals. Animals convey impurity by contact only if they are dead (Lev. 11:8, 24). Even the eight creepers only contaminate when dead (Lev. 11:31), *a fortiori*, human beings, who are not categorically impure at all. Thus, the sectarians opposed the view of the Sages not because it was harsh but because they considered it unscriptural.

A very stringent example of the sectarians' homogenization of Scripture is found in the case of the mĕṣōrāʿ. The text says the mĕṣōrāʿ must dwell alone, "bādād yēšēb" (Lev. 13:46). The sectarians interpret this to mean that the mĕṣōrāʿ must dwell apart from all other impurity bearers as well (4QThrA1 1-2). This notion is also apparent in the Temple Scroll which establishes separate areas for different impurity bearers outside the Temple City and within the ordinary city (11QT 46:16-18; 48:14-17).

Fragment 4QThrA1 makes it clear that impurity bearers of any type are not to come in contact even with each other and suggests further that if they do make contact, their impurity will increase.[44] Impure individuals who touch mĕṣōrāʿîm, for example, become contaminated further and must bathe and launder before they are allowed to eat. The sectarians interpret the mĕṣōrāʿ's call,

---

43 Yadin, I, 335.

44 J. Milgrom, "4QThrA1: An Unpublished Qumran Text on Purities."

"Impure, impure" (Lev. 13:45), to mean that the měṣōrāᶜ is impure *to the* impure, i.e., to other impure individuals (4QThrA1 3-4).

Not only touching a serious impurity bearer like the měṣōrāᶜ will contaminate an already impure individual, but touching any impurity bearer will add further impurity. This is derived from 4QThrA1 4-5 where the menstruant who touches even an object a zāb has touched becomes even more impure, requiring her to bathe and launder before she is allowed to eat:

> As for the woman who is discharging blood, for seven days she shall not touch a male with a genital flux, or any object [th]at he has either touched, l[ain] upon, or sat on. [And if] she has touched, she shall launder her clothes, bathe, and afterwards she may eat.

This notion of added impurity to an already impure person requiring bathing and laundering before eating stands in direct contrast to the rabbinical impurity system. According to the latter, impure persons only become more impure if they come in contact with pollution greater than what they already bear requiring added purification rituals. For example, a menstruant who buries a corpse must undergo corpse purification as well as menstrual purification. However, if she touches a carcass (an acquisition of lesser impurity than what is already on her), she is not required to observe any additional purification rites.

To summarize the issue of Scriptural interpretation, both the sectarians and the Rabbis regard the text as sacred, both intend to observe it, and both use a homogenization/binyan ʾab technique in their exegesis. However, the sectarians homogenize Scripture in a manner which creates more restriction in almost every case than the Rabbis. If they are going to err they wish to do it on the side of strictness.

On the other hand, it must be kept in mind, when comparing the Qumran material with that of the Rabbis, that Rabbinic halakha as crystallized by Maimonides, or even as reflected in the Talmuds, is not necessarily what it was in the first century. For example, Maimonides says purity was a prerequisite only for the cult, but this was not the consensus in the first century. As Yadin has shown, there are strict rulings in rabbinic literature parallel to many of the Scrolls' rules.[45] However, they are often squelched by majority opinions of the Sages or by later rulings supplanting earlier ones. Thus, when examining rabbinic comparisons to sectarian attitudes, I will use the earliest sources possible.

A final basic principle of the ideology behind the Scrolls is the centrality of the common meal. This meal is referred to as the "purity," and only those who are clean may partake of it (1QS 5:13-14; 6:25; 7:16, 19, 23; Wars 2:129). Josephus states that the sectarians even changed their clothes before eating the common meal (Wars 2:129-31; Ant. 18:18-21).

The term "purity" refers at times to other pure but susceptible items in addition to the common food and drink. In principle, a person who eats or even touches the purity in an unclean condition is expelled from the community. Here again a stringent attitude is apparent. This stands in direct contrast to the belief of many of the early Sages that food to be eaten in ritual purity is invalidated if it comes into contact with impurity, but the unclean person who touched/ate it is not punished (See Appendix A).

According to the Temple Scroll, not only those who are impure but also those in the process of purifying themselves are barred from the common meal:

> And on the seventh day they will be sprinkled a second time and they will bathe and launder their clothes and vessels and become pure at evening to touch any pure item or person that has not been defiled (11QT 49:20-21).

Since the text states that at the end of the seventh day the corpse-contaminated person is free to touch pure food and persons, it must not have been allowed during the purifying week.

According to the newly translated fragment 4QOrdc, all persons who come into contact with impurity (whether they were initially pure, purifying, or already impure) must bathe and

---

45 Ibid., *passim*.

launder before eating. After ablutions, they may eat in accordance with the regulations for their status of purity:[46]

> A man shall not] eat who has not begun to become pure from his sour[c]e. [He indeed shall not continue to eat while] in his initial impurity. And all those "impure of days" shall, on the day of their [he]aling, bathe and launder in water, and become pure. And afterward they may eat their food according to the purity regulations. And he shall not eat while in his initial impurity who has not begun to become pure from his source (4QOrdc 4-7).

Thus, an impure person, e.g., the **zāb**, must bathe and launder before eating. Still, he may not eat of the טהרה, but must eat in accordance with the rules of the **zāb**. So also with the purifying **zāb**. He may eat ordinary food and most likely is allowed in the city, but he still may not eat of the pure meal (11QT 49:20-21). It is in accordance with the strict attitude toward impurity at Qumran that all persons, pure or impure, would be forced to fast who refused to purify after contact with impurity.

The insistence of the Temple Scroll and 4QMMT that the impure person is unclean until his purificatory period is over, i.e., until after sunset on the last day of purification (11QT 45:9-10; 49:20-21; 50:12, 15-16; 51:3, 5; 4QMMT 13-17; 59-67) is curious and probably represents a polemic.[47] The notion stands in direct contrast to the rabbinic concept of **ṭĕbûl yôm** according to which one who has bathed after his impurity is unclean to a lesser degree than before and may touch all but sacred items (m. TY 2:1-2; See Chapter 3, below). Yadin suggests that the repeated emphasis of the Temple Scroll that the purifying person is "unclean until evening" is a polemic against others who accepted the **ṭĕbûl yôm** provision.[48] If Yadin is correct, this reveals an early date for the concept of **ṭĕbûl yôm**.

---

46 Wise misunderstands this phrase and assumes that the text allows the purifying person to eat pure food, 150.

47 Yadin, I, 332; Schiffman, "The Impurity of the Dead," 148; idem, "The Temple Scroll and the Systems of Jewish Law" in *Temple Scroll Studies*, ed. G. J. Brooke, 247.

48 Yadin, I, 331-32.

The insistence on the duration of a person's impurity until evening notwithstanding, the community at Qumran did ascribe some efficacy to the purifying person's initial ablution, albeit not to the extent that the Rabbis did. Purifying persons were most likely allowed into the city after a first-day ablution; they could return home and eat of ordinary food. A supporting example of this in the Temple Scroll is found in the laws of corpse impurity. The Scrolls do not describe installations for corpse-contaminated persons, nor are they expelled from the ordinary city in accordance with Numbers 5:2. Rather, they accord with the situation described in Numbers 19:18 where the corpse-contaminated person is purified "there" at the tent, i.e., within the camp. It seems the corpse-contaminated person is treated like the one purifying from scale disease who, although still impure to a certain degree, is allowed in the city after a first-day ablution (Lev. 14:8).

Fragment 4QThrA1, too, supports the notion that initial ablutions reduce impurity. Although the text gives strict instructions for purifying persons, they are not expelled from the community. Nevertheless, purifying persons were not considered clean, and pure persons could not touch them without contracting impurity (4QThrA1 5-6; cf. 11QT 49:20-21). The purifying zābâ, a woman with an abnormal blood flow, is told to "(strive) with all her might [not] to intermingle (with pure persons) during her seven days in order n[o]t to defile the c[a]mps of the ho[ly ones of] Israel" (4QThrA1 5-6).

The initiation procedure of the novitiate demonstrates the care with which the purity status of the common food was maintained. Only after a year of probation and close examination by a trustworthy member was a candidate allowed to participate in the common meal, and after two years to drink the common drink (1QS 6:17-21). Josephus says candidates were excluded from the "purer waters of sanctification" for a year until they had been tested. His version differs slightly from that of the Manual of Discipline in that after the initial testing year, candidates may eat of the common food and after *two more years* may partake of the common drink (Wars 2:138).

J. Licht has proposed a system at Qumran similar to that of the Pharisees. Since liquid is more susceptible to impurity than solids and is actually a transferer of it (always in the first degree, see Introduction), the candidate is allowed access to it last, only after at least two years.[49] The Pharisees, by contrast, did not meet for common meals but trusted one another to maintain ritual purity at meals in their separate homes.[50]

The life of the sect was sustained both physically and spiritually by this meal. As discussed above, it was not considered a sacrificial meal, but it was one way in which the community could equal the purity status of priests as they ate their tĕrûmôt.[51] The meal at Qumran could not attain a sacral status without the altar and a valid accompanying cult, but it could be as pure as the tĕrûmâ which the laity separated in purity for priestly consumption (Dt. 26:1-15).

Only in this general sense was holiness extended to all the members of the sect. Thus, when the Manual of Discipline states that the sect is "a house of holiness for Aaron being united [so as to constitute] a holy of holies" (1QS 9:6), it is merely using the term "holiness" in a non-technical sense equal to "purity" in order to contrast the purity of the sect with the defiled state of the existing Jerusalem sanctuary.

A final note on exclusion from the "purity" is in order. According to the Manual of Discipline, one was excluded for different lengths of time depending on the nature of the offense. Slandering a fellow member resulted in exclusion for one year; interrupting a fellow member's conversation resulted in exclusion for 10 days (1QS 7:9-10). Deliberate sinners were expelled (1QS 8:22-23); inadvertent sinners were excluded for two years during which time they did penance (1QS 9:2). Pure members were not allowed to touch them or their property or to ask them for advice (1QS 8:23-26). Sinners or ritually unclean

---

49 J. Licht, *Megillat ha-Serakhim*, Appendix.

50 J. Neusner, "The Fellowship (חבורה) in the Second Jewish Commonwealth," *HTR* 53 (1960) 125-42.

51 Milgrom, *Leviticus*, I, 968-71.

persons were not allowed to eat or touch the common meal (1QS 6:17; 8:24).

Thus, the Qumran sect's notion of purity is characterized by 1) an effort to extend the holiness of the Temple to the whole Temple City and require a high level of purity for the ordinary city (the level which the sectarians strove to maintain in the present era), 2) a stringent interpretation of Scripture which homogenized all ambiguous data of the Torah on purity issues to agree with the most demanding relevant text, and 3) an attitude toward community food which required ritual purification before eating. Having set forth these basic principles of the ideology of the sect, I will turn now to the specific data of the Scrolls relating to each impurity bearer.

CHAPTER 2

THE IMPURITY BEARERS

The following is a detailed analysis of the contamination effects of each of the impurity bearers discussed in the Dead Sea Scrolls. Due to the meager amount of material available much will be conjectural. However, I believe there is enough evidence in the texts extant to recreate the system at least in sketch. It will be instructive to compare the information, whenever possible, with relevant parallels from other early Jewish texts.

CORPSE

From the Torah it is clear that the corpse is the most contaminating of all impurities (See below, Chapter 4). At Qumran the dead were separated in a cemetery 4 meters away from the east wall of the complex. They were laid in tombs with their heads to the south.[1] Since the Temple Scroll admonishes not

---

1 J. Milik, *Ten Years of Discovery in the Wilderness of Judea*, 47.

to bury the dead in one's house like the gentiles (11QT 48:11-12), evidently the sect was opposing a common practice.

Yadin refers to Maimonides to show that rabbinic law is lenient with regard to corpse impurity.[2] Maimonides, citing b. RSh 16b, states that corpse impurity applies only to the priests.[3] However, in the Qumran era Jews were much more concerned about corpse impurity (See Chapter 4 below), and neither Maimonides nor the Babylonian Talmud can be cited as proof of an attitude in the first century B.C.E.

Yadin further points out a supposed leniency in the Mishna's allowance of a lost grave in a field (m. Oh. 16). However, this is a concession after the fact. The grave is already in the field, and the present owner is not responsible for that fact. It is important to realize that a grave discovered in a field does contaminate by means of overhang; hence, a house built over such a grave is unclean. The Mishna is lenient only with regard to an upper room, which remains clean as a tent over a tent unless it directly overshadows the grave protruding out over the lower room (m. Oh. 17:5). Additionally, the field in which a grave has accidentally been plowed contaminates for a 100-cubit radius from the grave. The contamination is also by contact and carriage because any part of it may contain a barleycorn's bulk of bone. A field of mourners is not planted or sown, but its dust is clean.[4] The Houses discuss the necessity of examining the soil (m. Oh. 18:4).

In addition, the Mishna gives instructions regarding the purification of one's field if one finds a corpse in it; the corpse is

---

2 Y. Yadin, *The Temple Scroll*, I, 325.

3 *The Code of Maimonides*, X, foodstuffs, 16:9.

4 H. Albeck, *Šiša Sidre Mišna*, VI, 184, explains that śĕdēh bôkîn is a field in which mourners in a funeral procession set down the bier in order to bewail the loss of the loved one. The fear is that some part of the corpse dropped into the field while the mourners were there, thus, the field may be contaminated. The Tosefta uses the terms śĕdēh kûkîn, a field of crypts or ossuaries, instead of śĕdēh bôkîn and identifies the phrase with a field in which graves were accidentally overturned while someone was ploughing in a field (t. Oh. 17:12). The fear is that there are still undiscovered graves in the field.

contaminating and must be removed (m. Oh. 16:3-5). If there are three or more corpses in the field, the area for 20 cubits in any direction away from the bodies is considered a graveyard and must be avoided (m. Oh. 16:3). To purify this area, it is necessary to sift the soil for pieces of bone or other corpse matter (m. Oh. 16:3-4), to replace it entirely with new soil, or to overlay it with paving stones (m. Oh. 18:5).

Schiffman argues that the Tannaim certainly forbade burial within walled cities (m. Kel. 1:7), but he goes on to say, citing y. Erub. 5:3, that Amoraim allowed it except within levitical cities.[5] I am not sure this distinction is valid. The reference to levitical cities is in the context of laws regarding levitical cities, not laws of burial. Schiffman cites the Talmud Yerushalmi (y. Naz. 9:3) to claim that the Amoraim did bury within the city limits. However, the same text supports and explains in detail the Mishna's order to remove graves from inhabited areas. Graves which are discovered in a town are emptied out. Graves surrounded by a town on three or four sides are cleared out. Some discussion arises over a grave surrounded by a town on two parallel sides. According to R. Hisda the grave is cleared out if it is within 70-2/3 cubits of the town. This is a more stringent opinion than that of the Tosefta which unambiguously states that graves surrounded by towns must be cleared out if they are within 50 cubits of the town (t. BB 1:11). R. Aqiba goes so far as to say that even the graves of the king and the prophet are subject to removal (t. BB 1:11). In light of these passages, I do not see the validity of Yadin's claim (Schiffman supports his comments by Yadin's earlier remarks), which he bases on rabbinic literature, that in contrast to the sectarians at Qumran "it is perfectly plain that people used to bury anywhere and everywhere, even inside houses in settled areas." Rabbinic sources do not authorize or imply such indiscriminate burial.

---

5 L. H. Schiffman, "The Impurity of the Dead in the *Temple Scroll*" in *Archaeology and History*, ed. L. H. Schiffman, 137, maintains that the Tannaim allowed random burial outside of walled cities from m. MQ 1:2; Yadin, I, 323.

According to the sect anyone who has had contact with the dead is barred from eating the "purity." Mishna-Tosefta bars any corpse-contaminated person from entering beyond the rampart of the Temple (m. Kel. 1:8), but the sect, trying to maintain the purity of food as if it were tĕrûmâ, bars the corpse-contaminated person even from the communal meal. Likewise, the ḥabērîm, those Sages who agreed to keep strict tithing and ritual purity laws among the Rabbis, bar the corpse-contaminated person, as well as all other impure persons, from eating pure food (See Appendix A).[6]

One can readily see the expansionist interpretation of Scripture in the Temple Scroll's description of items susceptible to corpse contamination. The "tent" of Num. 19:14 is interpreted as a house, a building. Since Verse 18 states that everything in the tent is unclean, the sectarians require the washing of locks, mĕzûzôt, and vessels of all types, even those of wood and stone (11QT 49:12-16).

Not only its contents, but the house itself is unclean for seven days (11QT 49:5-6). Walls, doors, and floors must be scraped (11QT 49:12). The sectarians have firm basis for this interpretation. Scripture states in Num. 19:18 that the tent itself must be sprinkled. Although the early Sages disagreed on this issue, the majority view in the time of the Mishna was that the "tent" and its contents had to be made of an item susceptible to impurity to become impure (See Chapter 4).[7]

The Rabbis enlarge upon the aspect of "tent" to aver that only items unattached to the ground like tents are susceptible to impurity (b. Shab. 81a); permanent structures like houses and other buildings are insusceptible. Also, the Rabbis regard only the items listed in Lev. 11 and Num. 19 as susceptible to impurity, even if they are unattached to the ground. The sectarians, however, include every possibility. From the fact that the stones

---

6 J. Neusner, "The Fellowship (חבורה) in the Second Jewish Commonwealth," *HTR* 53 (1960) 125.

7 Sif. Num. 129 [166], records a discussion between Aqiba and the Sages. Aqiba espouses Qumran's view that all of the contents of the house are impure; Schiffman, "The Impurity of the Dead," 139.

of the house affected by ṣāraʿat are unclean, the sectarians deduce that stone is susceptible to impurity; hence, a stone house or a stone vessel can contract corpse impurity. This is a good example of homogenization.

Some may point to the fact that the Rabbis extend the notion of "tent" to almost any sort of overhang as proof that in this regard Qumran takes a more lenient position. According to the Mishna, even the human body can transfer impurity if it creates an overhang (m. Oh. 6:1). Moreover, an overhang can transmit corpse impurity even if the overhang itself is insusceptible to impurity. The sectarians refer to this overhang only in connection with the house of the dead; they may have extended the principle to other items but there is no evidence of it.

However, the Rabbis so limit the items which can contract impurity that they have in effect neutralized much of the power of corpse contamination according to the plain meaning of Numbers 19. Anyone who touches the house of the dead remains pure because the house, made of stone or wood, is insusceptible to impurity and is hence clean (m. Kel. 2:1, wood must form a usable vessel to be susceptible; m. Oh. 5:5). Unlike Josephus, the sectarians, and the Karaites, the Rabbis do not consider a building to be a "tent." Hence, they insist that the tent itself is sprinkled as an item which has contracted uncleanness (Num. 19:18) only because it is made of fabric, an item susceptible to uncleanness.

Schiffman says that one cannot tell whether or not the sectarians are extending the category of susceptible liquids to anything besides water.[8] I think that it is fairly clear from the prescription to sweep the house of the dead of all oil, wine, and water moisture (11QT 49:11-14) that impure liquid is not restricted by the sect to water. Following J. Baumgarten, even oil is considered a transferer of impurity: if wood, stones, or dust have oil stains on them, they will defile those who touch them (CD 12:15-18).[9] The same principle is operating when senior

---

8 Schiffman, "The Impurity of the Dead," 141.

9 J. Baumgarten's translation, *Studies in Qumran Law*, 91-96; cf. m. Makh. 6:4-5; m. Ter. 11:23; cf. Sifra Shem. Sher. par. 8:1: in the rabbinic

members, who have anointed themselves with oil, touch junior members; they become impure (Wars 2:150).

Further evidence is found in Column 49 of the Temple Scroll. Here the text is explicit that an open vessel in the corpse-contaminated house is unclean. Scholars disagree over the correct translation of מושקה, some translating "drink" and others "moistened food."[10] In any case, the presence of liquid, not necessarily water, is certainly implied.

Schiffman thinks the Scrolls are extending the biblical rule of the susceptibility of open vessels in the tent of the dead to the vessels' contents.[11] I do not think the protection of food and drink inside of vessels is an extension of Scripture but a concern of the priests of the Torah as well as of the sectarians. The concern of both the Bible and the Scrolls was not just the vessel per se but its contents, which could be food for the lay Israelite and more importantly could be sacrificial or priestly food. The Priestly Code makes this clear in a passage relating to vessels and food contaminated by carcasses:

> And if any of them [the carcasses of the eight swarmers] falls into any earthen vessel, all that is in it shall be unclean, and you shall break it. Any food in it which may be eaten, upon which water may come, shall be unclean; and all drink which may be drunk from every such vessel shall be unclean (Lev. 11:33-34).

Nevertheless, the sectarians' expansionist attitude is apparent in this passage in the different rules for the איש טהור and the אדם מישראל. The former is not to eat the contents of even the closed vessel (a more stringent rule than Num. 19:15). The sectarians realize that the clear meaning of the text is to avoid eating the contents of open vessels in a corpse-contaminated tent, however, they expect those really concerned

---

view, dew, water, wine, oil, blood, milk, and bees' honey always become impure in the first degree and can transfer impurity to other items.

10 Yadin, I, 150, following J. Milgrom, "food that has become wet by any fluid"; Schiffman, "Impurity of the Dead," 135, translates "drink."

11 Schiffman, "Impurity of the Dead," 142.

about purity to avoid even the contents of closed vessels in such areas.

The only instance in which a sealed vessel does not protect its contents according to rabbinic rulings is when a person with an impure flow (zāb, zābâ, parturient, or niddâ) shifts it (Sif. Mes. Zab. par. 3:2; b. Git. 61b; b. Nid. 6a; b. Shab. 84b).[12] If, for example, a zāb only touched an earthen vessel on the outside, he would not contaminate it since it only receives uncleanness, according to rabbinic law, via its interior (Sif. Shem. Sher. par. 7:5; Sif. Mes. Zab. par. 3:2). On the other hand, if he shifts it, both the vessel itself and its contents become unclean. Without the intervention of someone with an impure flow, however, a sealed vessel and its contents in the tent of the corpse are completely protected against defilement.[13]

Another stringency at Qumran with regard to corpse uncleanness concerns the woman carrying a dead fetus. According to the Rabbis such a woman, like the woman giving birth, is only impure after the fetus is extracted (m. Hul. 4:3). However, the sectarians considered the woman not only impure but as imparting impurity like a grave (11QT 50:11). As it turns out, the woman contaminates others like a corpse itself, for the same rules applying to a corpse apply to her. Anyone touching her, or in the same house with her even though not making contact, is contaminated for 7 days (11QT 50:13).[14]

Anyone who is contaminated by a corpse can contaminate other persons (Num. 19:22), and hence, the corpse-contaminated person must bathe and launder on the first day in order to remain in the ordinary city. Such an impure person is excluded from the Temple City until completely purified (11QT 49:21).

---

12 Cf. also b. Git. 61b (for the application of the law to the niddâ); b. Nid. 6a; b. Shab. 84b, cf. Soncino note A1.

13 For a good explanation of this, cf. *Enṣyqlopedyah Talmudit*, IX, 599; Maimonides, *Code*, X, couch, 8:1-2, the mĕṣōrāʿ contaminates the one who shifts him/her but does not contaminate others by shifting them. Cf. also Maimonides on m. Zab. 5:6 in *Mišnah ʿim Peruš Mošeh ben Maimon*, vol. 6:2, 685.

14 Yadin, I, 338.

How is one purified from corpse impurity? At Qumran it was impossible because the sectarians did not have the prescribed ashes of a red cow (See Chapter 4 for full discussion of this sacrificial rite). However, like the Rabbis, they expected to renew the correct procedure in the future and, hence, the Temple Scroll describes the process. Following Numbers 19, the corpse-contaminated person or object must be sprinkled with the special ash on Days 3 and 7 of the week-long purification. On the seventh day, the corpse-contaminated person bathes and launders personal clothing, the corpse-contaminated object is washed, and both become clean at sunset.

The sectarians harmonize the purification rites so that the bathing and laundering occur on both days of sprinkling. In addition, the sectarians add a bathing and laundering on the first day. This is nowhere prescribed in the biblical text. The sources indicate that this extra ablution allowed the corpse-contaminated person back into the camp to continue purification. The purifying person was allowed to eat ordinary but not pure food (4QOrdc 4-7; 11QT 49:20-21). There is biblical precedent for this notion by the fact that the corpse-contaminated person is at home while undergoing purification (Num. 19:18).[15] Numbers 5 represents a separate tradition in which the corpse-contaminated person was excluded from the camp. Thus, Numbers 19 provides a basis for the sectarians.

The person purifying from corpse contamination is not allowed in the Temple City, only into the ordinary city. Since in all cases mentioned entry into the Temple City is granted only after the completion of purification, the corpse-contaminated person could only enter the Temple City at the end of purification on the seventh day.

Below are two charts outlining the effect of corpse impurity at Qumran:

---

15 J. Milgrom, "Studies in the Temple Scroll," *JBL* 97 (1978) 515-516.

FIG. 1a: THE CONTAMINATION OF THE CORPSE

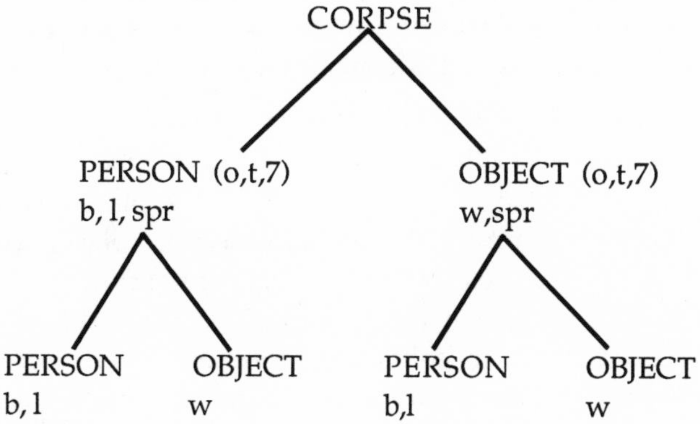

FIG. 1b: THE PURIFICATION OF THE CORPSE-CONTAMINATED

Day	*Purification*	*Allowed Area*
1	b, l	ordinary city
3	b, l, spr	ordinary city
7	b, l, spr, eve	Temple City

References: Num. 19:14-22; 11QT 49:17-21; 50:3-16

MĔṢŌRĀʿ

In this dissertation, I use the biblical term mĕṣōrāʿ to refer to the one who has a scaly affection in the skin (See Chapter 5). The Scrolls use the term מנוגע, a general term meaning "one with an affection." Sometimes the authors use another biblical term צרוע, the Qal passive participle of צרע, the root of mĕṣōrāʿ.

The Temple Scroll states that there is a place east of the Temple City reserved for mĕṣōrāʿîm; two other places were set aside for zābîm, i.e., those with abnormal genital flows, and those who had emitted semen (11QT 46:16-18). Thus, the impurity bearers could have no contact with others, even with other impurity bearers. This separation of impurity bearers from each other is also described by Josephus (Ant. 3:264; Ag. Ap. 1:281).

P. R. Callaway explains that the biblical law to exclude mĕṣōrāʿîm from the camp of the ancient Israelites is transferred at Qumran to the Temple City:

> The temple and its city assume the nimbus and the sanctity of the biblical "camp" mentioned in Deuteronomy 23, Numbers 5, and Leviticus 13.[16]

However, Callaway has not recognized the differences in the "camps" of these three passages: Deuteronomy 23 refers only to the military camp, where greater purity was required; Numbers 5 and Leviticus 13 refer to all Israel (but represent different sources or time periods, see Chapter 4 below). If Callaway is implying that the biblical laws regarding the entire Israelite camp are applied equivalently by the sectarians to the Temple, this would be a restriction of the pentateuchal laws on all Israel to only those who live in the city of the Temple. Rather, the sectarians apply the laws of the biblical Israelite camp to all cities, but the Temple

---

16 P. R. Callaway, "Extending Divine Revelation: Micro-Compositional Strategies in the Temple Scroll" in *Temple Scroll Studies*, ed. G. J. Brooke, 152-53.

City exceeds this status by maintaining purity comparable to that of the biblical sanctuary itself (See Introduction).

The Scrolls, like the Torah and the Mishna, are clear that the mĕṣōrāʿ must remain outside of all walled cities (11QT 48:14; 4QThrA1 1-2; m. Kel. 1:7; cf. Num. 5:2). The residence set up for mĕṣōrāʿîm is 12 cubits northwest of the closest dwelling (4QThrA1 1-2).[17] This is not very far. Hence, the mĕṣōrāʿ must call out in accordance with Lev. 14, "Unclean, unclean," so that others will be warned of approaching impurity and not become contaminated accidentally. Neither pure, purifying, nor impure persons are allowed to eat after touching a person afflicted with ṣāraʿat without first bathing (4QThrA1 3; cf. 11QT 49:19-21).

Indeed, mĕṣōrāʿîm did live outside the city in the first century because, according to the Gospels, this is where they interact with Jesus (Mk. 1:40-45; Lk. 7:22; 17:11-19). On one occasion they meet Jesus as he is entering a city. On another, a mĕṣōrāʿ living in Bethany, a small community just outside Jerusalem, gives Jesus lodging (Mk. 14:3). At least on one occasion, mĕṣōrāʿîm stand at a distance, revealing their hesitation to approach and possibly defile Jesus (Lk. 17:11-19).

4QMMT claims that its opponents allow mĕṣōrāʿîm to touch pure food and, according to Schiffman's interpretation, to enter the Temple.[18] This is certainly a strong accusation in view of the biblical command to exclude mĕṣōrāʿîm not only from the sanctuary but from the whole camp (Num. 5:2). I think the concern is probably just over maintaining the purity of food designated for the Temple. It is hard to imagine that the Jerusalem priests were allowing persons with scale disease to enter the sanctuary.

---

17 For discussion on location of the dwellings for mĕṣōrāʿîm, cf. Yadin, I, 305-07; J. Milgrom, *Leviticus*, I, 806; idem, "4QThrA1: An Unpublished Qumran Text on Purities," forthcoming.

18 L. H. Schiffman, "The Temple Scroll and the Systems of Jewish Law of the Second Temple Period" in *Temple Scroll Studies*, ed. G. J. Brooke, 248.

The sectarians emphasize the biblical command that only a priest can pronounce a person a mĕṣōrāʿ. The Damascus Rule instructs:

> But should there be a case of applying the law of sāraʿat to a man, then the priest shall come and remain in the camp and the guardian shall instruct him in the exact interpretation of the law. Even if the priest is a simpleton, it is he who shall lock up (the mĕṣōrāʿ) for theirs is the judgment (CD 13:5-6).

The notion that the priest should pronounce the impurity and if necessary be instructed beforehand is also reflected in Mishna-Tosefta:

> ...If one is not an expert in them [affections] and their names, he should not examine the affections (t. Neg. 1:1, translation mine).

> They say to him (the priest), "Say, Unclean," and he says, "Unclean"; "Say, Clean," and he says, "Clean" (m. Neg. 3:1).

The similarity of the two approaches notwithstanding, there does seem to be a difference in nuance. The emphasis of the sectarians is on the authority of the priest; the Rabbis emphasize the need and manner of instructing the priest. There may be some silent opposition here, the predecessors of the Rabbis holding that the Sage, because of his instruction, was indispensable to the pronouncement, and the sectarians (many of whom were ex-priests) stressing the priority of the priest in the process.

If a clean person touches a mĕṣōrāʿ he becomes unclean and must bathe and launder before eating (4QThrA1 3). This can be derived from the biblical prescriptions regarding the house affected by ṣāraʿat; all who lie down or eat in such a house are required to bathe and launder (Lev. 13:47). The possibility of coming into contact with a person affected with scale disease is real; the dwelling of the mĕṣōrāʿ is only 18 feet away from the city.

As discussed in Chapter 1, what is new at Qumran in this regard is that persons who are already unclean can become even more impure even if they touch a lighter impurity bearer than themselves.[19] Line 3 of 4QThrA1 states: "[Whoev]er of the impure persons to[uches] him shall bathe in water, launder his clothes, and afterwards he may eat of it (any food). This is what is meant by 'impure (to the) impure he shall call out [Lev. 13:45]' - all the days the [aff]liction is [in him]."

Once healed, the purifying mĕṣōrāᶜ (= miṭṭahēr) is allowed to enter the ordinary city after an initial ablution and to undergo the seven-day purification ritual within the city. However, those who touch the miṭṭahēr will become impure (4QThrA1 9).[20] Furthermore, a miṭṭahēr who becomes even more impure (e.g., by an emission of semen) will contaminate those whom he or she touches as well (l. 8).[21] According to the Temple Scroll the touch of the miṭṭahēr is defiling even without an added impurity (11QT 49:19-21).

In accordance with Leviticus 14, the mĕṣōrāᶜ presumably must remain outside the house for one full week lest sancta (e.g., holy food) become contaminated by means of the overhang of the house. After bathing and laundering on the seventh day, the miṭṭahēr may enter the house and after presenting sacrifices on the eighth day at the Temple becomes completely pure. According to 4QMMT the sect does not allow the miṭṭahēr to eat sacred food until the end of the eighth day (ll. 71-72).[22] Unlike the Rabbis, who refer to three distinct stages of purification for the mĕṣōrāᶜ (m. Neg. 14:3) based on Lev. 14, the Scrolls do not elaborate on this. It is unknown what value, if any, the seventh day ablutions had for the miṭṭahēr.

The Scrolls make it clear that the mĕṣōrāᶜ is in this condition because of sin. In 4QThrA1 the mĕṣōrāᶜ pleads for mercy: "He shall begin to lay his pl[ea]. He shall lie in a [b]ed of sorrow and reside

---

19 Milgrom, "4QThrA1: An Unpublished Qumran Text on Purities."

20 Ibid., see Milgrom's notes.

21 Cf. b. Naz. 66a for the possibility that the semen of a zāb defiles to a greater extent than that of a clean person.

22 E. Qimron and J. Strugnell, "An Unpublished Halakhic Letter from Qumran" in *Biblical Archaeology Today*, 400-407; Milgrom, *Leviticus*, I, 849-50.

in [a dwelling of] sighs" (Line 1).[23] It is well-known that ṣāraʿat was considered a divine curse in the ancient world.[24] The Bible attests to examples of this as well (Num. 12:9-10; 2 Sam. 3:29; 2 Ki. 5:27), but it never presents the underlying ideology in a formal manner. It must be inferred from the examples of the text.

J. Baumgarten and E. Qimron have cited several other texts from Qumran which also indicate that the mĕṣōrāʿ is a sinner. According to Baumgarten's composite text, made up of several fragments of the Damascus Document from Cave 4 (4Q266, 4Q272 and 4Q268), ṣāraʿat is induced by a spirit (evidently evil), רוח (line 4), and is healed when the spirit of life, רוח החיים, returns (line 7).[25]

E. Qimron adds further examples to show that ṣāraʿat is caused by an evil spirit from the Psalms Scroll and the Thanksgiving Scroll.[26] Especially instructive is 1QH 1:32:

> חזקת רוח אנוש לפני נגע ו[נפש עבדכה] טהר֯ת֯ה֯ מרוב עוון
>
> You have strengthened the spirit of a man in front of a plague [of scale disease] and have purified the life of your servant from a multitude of sins.

Baumgarten notes that Frag. 4Q270 of the Damascus Document lists the mĕṣōrāʿ in a catalog of transgressors. This fits well with the penitential tone of the purification rituals from Cave 6 published by M. Baillet.[27]

Thus, I conclude about the mĕṣōrāʿ that only after being forgiven by God, as evidenced by healing, can the purification process begin. The mĕṣōrāʿ can enter the ordinary city after bathing and laundering on the first day of the purification rituals

---

23 Milgrom's translation, "4QThrA1."

24 Cf. Milgrom, *Leviticus*, I, 820-21, for attestations of scale disease as a curse throughout the ancient world.

25 J. Baumgarten, "The 4Q Zadokite Fragments on Skin Disease," *JJS* 41 (1990) 159, 162.

26 E. Qimron, "Notes on the 4Q Zadokite Fragment on Skin Disease," *JJS* 42/2 (1991) 256-259.

27 Baumgarten, "The 4QZadokite Fragments," 162; M. Baillet, *Qumran Grotte 4*, III, *DJD* VII, 262-286.

in accordance with Scripture but must keep away from the members of the community so as not to defile them. After presenting the sacrifices of the eighth day and waiting until sunset, the purified měṣōrāʿ may have access to the Temple City.

Below are two charts outlining the contamination power of the měṣōrāʿ:

FIG. 2a: THE CONTAMINATION OF THE MĚṢŌRĀ‘

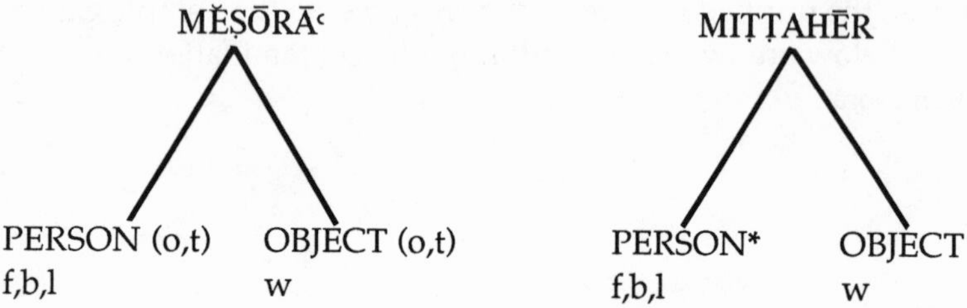

* But, cf. 4QThrA1 9 which regards the person impure only if he or she touches the miṭṭahēr, not vice versa.

FIG. 2b: THE PURIFICATION OF THE MĚṢŌRĀ‘

Day	*Purification*	*Allowed Area*
1	b, l	ordinary city
8	b, l, sacr, eve	Temple City

References: Lev. 13-14; 4QThrA1 1-9; 4QOrdc 4-10; 11QT 46:16-18; 48:14:49:19-21; 4QMMT 71-72

ZĀB/ZĀBÂ/NIDDÂ/YÔLEDET

The **zāb**, a man with an abnormal genital flow (most likely gonorrhea, see Chapter 6 below), was also excluded from the Temple City. Like the **mĕṣōrāᶜ**, a separate dwelling was set up outside the city for the **zāb** until he was healed (11QT 48:14-15). After he is healed, the **zāb** follows the seven-day purification procedure of Leviticus 15 remaining outside the Temple City until this week is fulfilled. He then bathes, launders, and enters the Temple City (11QT 45:15-17). On the eighth day he comes to the Temple to offer the concluding sacrifices (Lev. 15:14).

Objects on which the **zāb** sits or lies are impure and will contaminate others who touch them:

> As for the woman who is discharging blood, for seven days she shall not touch a male with a genital flux, or any object [th]at he has either touched, l[ain] upon, or sat on. [And if] she has touched, she shall launder her clothes, bathe, and afterwards she may eat (4QThrA1 4-5).

This reveals again the stringent homogeneous exegesis of the sectarians. Leviticus 15 is clear that the **zāb**'s bed and chair, because he has lain or sat on them, will contaminate those who touch them (Lev. 15:5-6, 10). However, objects which the **zāb** has merely touched do not have the power to transmit their impurity to others. Again, the sectarians interpret Scripture on the side of strictness.

The **zāb**, like the **mĕṣōrāᶜ**, is probably allowed to enter the ordinary city after his initial ablution, but if pure persons touch him, they must bathe and launder before eating (4QThrA1 9). Line 9 of 4QThrA1 reads:

> [Any]one who touches any of these impure persons during the seven days of [their] purif[ication may n]ot eat, just like one who has become defiled by a corp[se, but must bathe,] launder, and afterwa[rds he may eat.

Thus, the fact that the purifying **zāb** is allowed to enter the ordinary city does not give him access to the pure meal. His impurity is still contagious. Again, one finds stringency at Qumran not lenience.

Curiously, as with the purifying mĕṣōrāʿ, the purifying zāb does not contaminate those whom *he* touches. This is evident from two places in 4QThrA1, line 7 and line 8:

> Line 7: Whoever is counting off (the seven days of purification), whether male or female, must not tou[ch a male during (?)] his fl[ux] (or) a woman during her menstrual infirmity *unless she is purified from her me[nses]* (italics mine).

> Line 8: ...And if he (the male during his seven purificatory days) [has an e]mission of semen, his touch transmits impurity.[28]

Line 7 makes it clear that although purifying persons must not touch a zāb or a niddâ, they may touch a woman who has been purified after menstruation. The fact that purifying persons are allowed to touch the purified niddâ, a completely pure person, suggests that their touch is innocuous; it will not transmit impurity. Line 8 explains that if a purifying person emits semen, thus becoming even more impure, his touch will transmit impurity. The implication is that the purifying person, who has not contracted any additional impurity, will not pollute other persons or objects by touching them.

Thus, the Scrolls distinguish between one who touches the purifying person and one whom the purifying person touches: the former is made impure, the latter is not. This difference is difficult to explain, but Scripture may provide a clue. Leviticus allows the zāb to touch others if he has washed his hands (15:11). The purifying zāb is healed and has washed his whole body, so one would assume no contamination to be involved either way—by his touch or the touch of others on him. However, maybe the Scrolls expect the purifying zāb, like the zāb, to wash his hands before touching other persons. Perhaps this provision, although unstated in the Scrolls, is what made the touch of the purifying

28 Milgrom, "4QThrA1."

zāb innocuous. Those who touch him, however, would still contract impurity.

The impurity of the zābâ, a woman with an extended flow of blood outside of her menstrual period, and the menstruant is equated at Qumran with that of the zāb. These impurities are referred to as one type of uncleanness in 4QThrA1 7, and Line 8 is explicit that menstrual blood is equivalent to genital flux:

> For behold the blo[od of] the menstruant is equivalent to the genital flux; so (too) the one who touches it (the blood)....

The Scrolls do not refer anywhere to a difference in status between the zābâ and the niddâ, even though the latter is less impure according to Scripture (See Chapter 6). According to the Torah, the zābâ is banned from the camp until she is healed (Num. 5:2), those who touch her must bathe and launder (Lev. 15:7, 27), and she must bring a sacrifice after she is healed (Lev. 15:29). By contrast, those who touch the niddâ merely bathe (Lev. 15:19). Also, the zābâ's purificatory week begins only after her flow has stopped; the niddâ is only unclean for a total of 7 days.

Thus the laws regarding genital flows provide yet another example of the equalizing tendency of the sectarians. The one who emits semen, however, is not considered as impure as the menstruant (see below).[29]

Although the Scrolls do not yield information on the yôledet, we can assume that she is at least as impure as the niddâ based on Scripture. According to Leviticus, the impurity of the parturient in the first 1-2 weeks after childbirth is equal to that of the niddâ: "...She [the parturient] shall be impure for seven days; she shall be impure as during the period of her menstrual infirmity" (Lev. 12:2, tr. Milgrom). Hence the yôledet in her first stage of impurity and the niddâ are in the same category. It is not clear whether or not the sectarians would allow the yôledet to eat pure food in her second stage of impurity.

---

29 Milgrom gives Scriptural basis for the notion that vaginal blood is more contaminating than semen. See his comments on Lev. 15:22-23, *Leviticus*, I, 938-940.

The purifying zābâ, who has been healed and is going through purification, like the purifying zāb, is probably allowed access to the ordinary city if she first bathes and launders (4QOrdc 5-6). The laws for the purifying zāb (above) would naturally apply to the purifying zābâ as well.

The niddâ is contaminating to the members of the community and is probably quarantined for the entire seven days of her impurity (11QT 48:14-17). She is most likely releaesd after immersion at the end of the week. Fragment 4QThrA1 stresses the contamination of the niddâ and the need for her to keep away from other unclean persons :

> However, she [the niddâ] should (strive) with all her might [not] to intermingle (with pure persons) during her seven days in order n[o]t to defile the c[a]mps of the ho[ly ones of] Israel (4QThrA1 5-6).[30]

The niddâ must perform ablutions after her menstrual week in order to eat (cf. 4QOrdc 5-6).

In fact, as discussed above (Chapter 1), the menstruant, while still impure, will contract even greater impurity if she touches any other impurity bearer. She must immerse in order to eat even though she is still impure. This requirement on impurity bearers to bathe and launder because of contact with additional impurity of any degree is not found to my knowledge anywhere in rabbinic literature.

One major difference must be noted between the status of the zāb and ritually impure women. According to the Temple Scroll, women are not allowed in the Temple City. Yadin deduces this from the lack of constructed areas provided for them; all of

30 Some may raise an issue here: Why is the niddâ warned in Ṭaharot not to come in contact with other people if, as the Temple Scroll states, she is quarantined? I do not think that there is any real issue here. Each document is merely stressing the severity of the contamination from a different perspective: the Temple Scroll, by describing the quarantine areas and their function, and Ṭaharot, by emphasizing the responsibility on the woman to separate herself from the rest of the community during menstruation.

the isolated residences for those expelled from the Temple City are for men: **měṣōrāʿîm**, **zābîm**, and men who have emitted semen.[31] Women are not banished from the Temple City because they are not residents to begin with. Thus, although there were women at Qumran, they will not be able to live in the sanctuary city of the messianic age but must reside in ordinary cities (cf. 11QT 48:14-17).[32] The notion that women should be isolated during their menstrual impurity may also be present in the records of Josephus and the Mishna (Ant. 3:261; m. Nid. 7:4).

As discussed in detail in Chapter 6 below, the Rabbis discuss at length the parameters of the impurity of genital flows. However, unlike the sectarians' rigid interpretation, the Rabbis, in effect, limit the contamination of the **zāb**. Lev. 15:10 is clear that everything under the **zāb** is impure and will transmit impurity. The Rabbis limit this impurity to only the items singled out in the chapter: the **zāb**'s bed, chair, and saddle (See full text and explanation in Chapter 6). The sectarians consider any object the **zāb** has touched to be contaminated. Additionally, that item will contaminate anyone who touches it (4QThrA1 4-5).

Thus, as noted in other areas, the sectarians are much more extreme than the Rabbis. Unlike the sectarians, the Rabbis do not expel women from Jerusalem. In fact there was a Court of the Women at the Temple. However, quarantine for women during menstruation may have been in effect in Jerusalem in the first century (Ant. 3:261; m. Nid. 7:4). Finally, there is nothing in rabbinic literature stipulating that impurity bearers will increase their impurity by touching one with a flow.

Below are outlines charting the contamination extent and purification stages of the **zāb**, **zābâ**, **yôledet**, and **niddâ** according to the Scrolls:

---

31 Yadin, I, 224.

32 L. Bennett-Elder cites passages from the Scrolls which imply that there were women at Qumran, "Female Ascetics in the Late Second Temple Period: Five Provisional Models," AAR National Convention, 1991. These passages include, among others, 1QSa 1:4-11; CD 4:20, 7:4, 16:10-11; Temple Scroll fragment 57:15-19.

FIG. 3a: THE CONTAMINATION OF THE ZĀB/ZĀBÂ/NIDDÂ/YÔLEDET

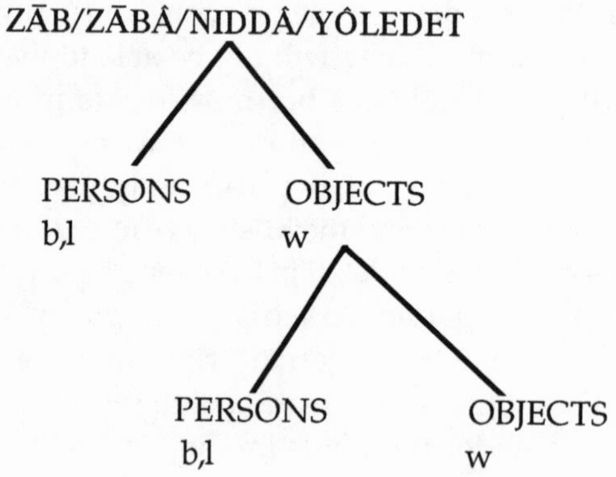

FIG. 3b: THE PURIFICATION OF THE ZĀB/ZĀBÂ

Day	*Purification*	*Allowed Area*
1	b, l	ordinary city
7	b, l	Temple city (zāb only)
8	sacr	Temple (zāb only)

FIG. 3c: THE PURIFICATION OF THE YÔLEDET (FIRST STAGE) AND THE NIDDÂ

Day	*Purification*	*Allowed Area*
7 Days	none	quarantined within or banished from ordinary city
Day 7	b, l, eve	ordinary city

References: 4QThrA1 4-9; 4QOrdc 5-6; 11QT 45:15-17; 48:14-17; Lev. 15:14-15, 29-30

SEMEN

Sexual intercourse is forbidden in the Temple City and those who engage in it cannot enter the holy city for three days (11QT 45:11-12; CD 12:1-2). C. Rabin relegated this law to pilgrims during the festivals, not to residents of the city.[33] However, as Yadin has explained, this ruling is modeled after the laws for the Israelites encamped at the foot of Mt. Sinai who had to refrain from sexual intercourse for the three-day period before God revealed Himself to them.[34] In typical fashion the sectarians have found all of the Pentateuchal information on the subject and homogenized all the laws to agree with the strictest case.

Also the man who has a nocturnal emission is considered impure (11QT 46:16-18). Indeed, this impurity can occur within the Temple City. Like the soldiers of the Deuteronomic War Camp (Dt. 23:10) this man is expelled from the Temple City until he is pure. However, according to the sectarians, the man is expelled from the city for three days, a notable increase over Deuteronomy.

To purify from an emission of semen, a man must bathe and launder on the first day. At this point he is allowed to enter the ordinary city. If he bathes and launders again on the third day he will have reduced his impurity altogether and can enter the Temple City.

The Temple Scroll makes a curious distinction. The text states that one who has had a nocturnal emission is forbidden to enter the Temple, whereas the man who has had sexual intercourse cannot enter the Temple City. It is clear, as Yadin has demonstrated, that the one who has a nocturnal emission cannot remain in the Temple City. It appears that the Scroll is making a distinction between the sanctity of the Temple and that of the Temple City. The Temple Scroll insists that no uncleanness can be tolerated in the Temple City: "...Everything that is in it [the Temple City] shall be pure" (11QT 47:5-6). In fact, special areas

33 C. Rabin, *Qumran Studies.*

34 Yadin, I, 135.

were to be constructed outside of the Temple City for those who were purifying from a nocturnal emission. Evidently, they were to stay there until cleansed:

> And you shall make three places to the east of the city, separated one from another, into which shall come the lepers and the people who have a discharge and the men who have had a (nocturnal) emission (11QT 46:16-18, tr. Yadin).

Nevertheless, the questions remains, why does the Temple Scroll restrict the one who has had a nocturnal emission only from the Temple instead of the Temple City (11QT 45:7-8)? Scholars have offered various interpretations.[35] Milgrom may have a solution: It is clear from the above passages that anyone who has emitted semen is barred from the whole Temple City. However, in column 45 the Scroll excludes the man who has had a nocturnal emission only from the Temple because he is already in the Temple City. He became impure inside the city and will have to be purified outside of it, but the Scroll wants to make sure that while still in the city, the man does not enter the Temple. The man engaged in sexual intercourse, however, is told not to come into the Temple City; everyone knows that sexual intercourse takes place outside the holy city.[36]

As to the contamination power of the one who has emitted semen, Scripture implies that it is at a lesser degree than the other impurities. However, if semen is emitted during one's purification period, the combined impurity is now severe enough to defile by touch.[37] According to Leviticus, only that which is in direct contact with semen is rendered impure (15:17). In other

---

35 Cf. P. R. Davies, "The Temple Scroll and the Damascus Covenant" in *Temple Scroll Studies*, ed. G. J. Brooke, 208: "The reason for this law can be explained from the extent of the Temple in 11QT, according to which, as Maier has shown, the outer court of the Temple includes the major part of the city. Most of those living in Jerusalem were therefore living in the Temple precincts, even if these precincts were not as yet architecturally realized. In a literal sense, the city - or most of it - was the city of the sanctuary!"

36 J. Milgrom, "Studies in the Temple Scroll," *JBL* 97 (1978) 517.

37 Milgrom, "4QThrA1."

words, semen impurity can combine with an already existing impurity, e.g., the impurity of a person in the process of purification, to cause pollution even where there is no direct contact with the semen itself.

In comparison with rabbinic interpretation, the sect is not lenient with regard to this impurity. First, it has turned a one-day impurity into a three-day impurity, at least with regard to the Temple City. This is, as noted above, a more stringent position than that required for the holy War Camp of the Pentateuch. And secondly, the sect makes no provisions for the ṭĕbûl yôm, one who has immersed after impurity and is merely waiting for sunset to be allowed to touch pure food and persons. According to the sectarians, the impurity bearer remains unclean until sunset. The Rabbis, by contrast, allow the one who has emitted semen, as well as other impurity bearers, to have free mobility within Jerusalem and access to all food except that which is to be eaten in a state of purity.

Below are charts outlining the impurity of the one who emits semen:

FIG. 4a: THE CONTAMINATION OF SEMEN

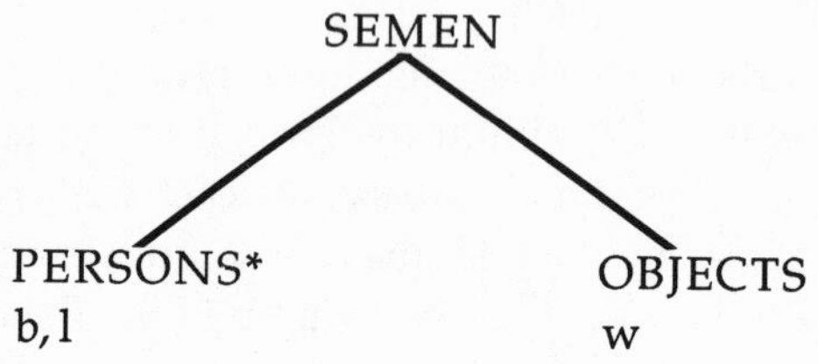

* In combination with other impurities, those with seminal emissions will transmit impurity by touch (4QThrA1 8).

FIG. 4b: THE PURIFICATION OF ONE WHO HAS CONTACTED SEMEN

Day	*Purification*	*Allowed Area*
1	b, l	ordinary city
3	b, l, eve	Temple city

References: Lev. 15:16-18; 11QT 45:11-12; CD 12:1-2

CARCASSES

The Torah rules that eating a **nĕbēlâ**, an animal which has not been slaughtered correctly, renders one impure.[38] Leviticus 17:15 reads:

> And every person that eats what dies of itself or what is torn by beasts, whether he is a native or a sojourner, shall wash his clothes, and bathe himself in water, and be unclean until the evening; then he shall be clean.

The Temple Scroll combines this ruling with Deuteronomy 14:21 which reads as follows:

> You shall not eat anything that dies of itself; you may give it to the alien who is within your towns, that he may eat it, or you may sell it to a foreigner; for you are a people holy to the LORD your God (11QT 52:19-21).

The result, according to the Temple Scroll, is that a **nĕbēlâ**, may not be eaten but can be sold to a foreigner (11QT 48:6).

However, there is some confusion among the documents as to what to do with unclean carcasses. The Damascus Rule forbids selling a **nĕbēlâ** to a foreigner (CD 12:8-9). A similar confusion is evident among the Rabbis. Some Sages allow it and some forbid it (m. AZ 1:5-6).[39]

In accordance with Leviticus 17:3, all sacrificial animals in the Temple City must be first offered as sacrifices before they can be eaten. In fact, all clean animals eaten within a radius of a three-day journey from the Temple must first be slaughtered within the City and offered as sacrifices (11QT 52:13-16).

In accordance with sacrificial rules, no blemished animals could be offered at the Temple and, hence, were not allowed to be eaten in the vicinity of the Temple City (11QT 52:17-19). In the ordinary city blemished animals could be eaten. Additionally, all

---

38 Cf. Milgrom, *Leviticus*, I, 681, for a more extended definition.

39 See discussion in L. H. Schiffman, "Legislation Concerning Relations with Non-Jews in the Zadokite Fragments and in Tannaitic Literature," *RQ* 11/43 (1983) 385-87.

vessels made of skins which were brought into the Temple City had to be made of skins of animals which had been slaughtered in the Temple (11QT 47:7-18).

Like other impurity bearers, one who touches or carries a **nĕbēlâ** becomes impure, is required to bathe and launder, and at sunset becomes pure (11QT 51:1-5). This contrasts with the rabbinic interpretation of Leviticus 11, as explained below.

According to the Mishna, the carcass of a clean animal is an **ʾab ṭumʿâ** and will convey uncleanness to persons who touch, shift, carry, or eat it (m. Hul. 9:5; m. Zab. 5:3, 8-10; m. Toh. 1:1-4).[40] Those who touch a **nĕbēlâ** need only bathe; they require subsequent laundering only if they carry or eat of the **nĕbēlâ**:

> And if any animal of which you may eat dies, he who touches its carcass shall be unclean until the evening, and he who eats of its carcass shall wash his clothes and be unclean until the evening; he also who carries the carcass shall wash his clothes and be unclean until the evening (Lev. 11:39-40; cf. Lev. 17:15, above.)

The Rabbis note that laundering is not mentioned as a requirement for those who have touched a carcass, and so they do not assume it is necessary:

> Touching does not convey uncleanness to clothes. But would it not follow that since carrying, which is slighter (in conveying uncleanness), does convey uncleanness to clothes, touching, which is more severe (in conveying uncleanness), should definitely convey uncleanness to clothes?! Therefore Scriptures say: "whoever touches shall be unclean until the evening"—to teach us that "he who touches does not make his clothes unclean" (Sifra Shem. Sher. 4:7, tr. Yadin).[41]

---

40 Nevertheless, the carcass of a clean bird is not polluting to those who touch or carry it. Only eating it is polluting (m. Toh. 1:1-2; cf. Lev. 17:15). The Rabbis are sensitive to Scripture's omissions. Only eating forbidden birds is prohibited (Lev. 11:13); touching them is not addressed.

41 Yadin, I, 340.

The sectarians, on the other hand, assume laundering to be necessary even if not explicitly commanded by the text.[42]

The other example of stringency among the sectarians with regard to carcasses is their inclusion of the skin and claws of an animal in their definition of "carcass":

> And whoever carries any part of their bones, or of their carcasses, skin and flesh and nail, shall wash his clothes and bathe in water, and after the going down of the sun he will be clean (11QT 51:4-5, tr. Yadin).

As Yadin notes, the clarification of "carcass" as עור ובשר וצפורן is certainly a polemic in light of several rabbinic passages which exclude such items from carrion contamination.[43] Below are two examples:

> The hide...bones and sinews, horns and hoofs are included together (to make up the quantity that suffices) to convey food-uncleanness but not [to make up the quantity that suffices to convey] carrion-uncleanness (m. Hul. 9:1, tr. Yadin).[44]

> "And everything upon which any part of their carcass falls"; any part of their carcass, not any part of their bones, nor of their teeth

---

42 Cf. the laundering requirement for those who touch what the zāb has touched (4QThrA1 4-5) in contrast to Lev. 15:22-23 which states that only those items the one with an impure flow has lain or sat on contaminate others by touch, cf. Milgrom, *Leviticus*, I, 938-940. Also, the sectarians require laundering for those who touch the object the corpse-contaminated person has touched (11QT 50:8-9), in contrast to Num. 19:31 which states that the person who touches a corpse-contaminated person (JPS) [or object a corpse-contaminated person has touched (RSV)] is unclean but does not mention laundering.

43 Yadin, I, 341.

44 H. Albeck defines the items mentioned in this passage and explains that touching a mere olive's bulk of a carcass is all that is necessary to contract carrion contamination. These items do serve to make up that small amount. However, for contamination resulting from the contact of unclean food with clean foods, an egg's bulk of the unclean food is required. Items such as skin connected to a bone embedded in the flesh (Rambam) can serve to make up this requisite quantity, ***Šiša Sidre Mišna***, V, 140.

nor of their nails nor of their hair shall be unclean (Sifra Shem. Sher. 10:2, tr. Yadin).

The following charts outline the contamination effect of carcasses:

FIG. 5a: THE CONTAMINATION OF CARCASSES

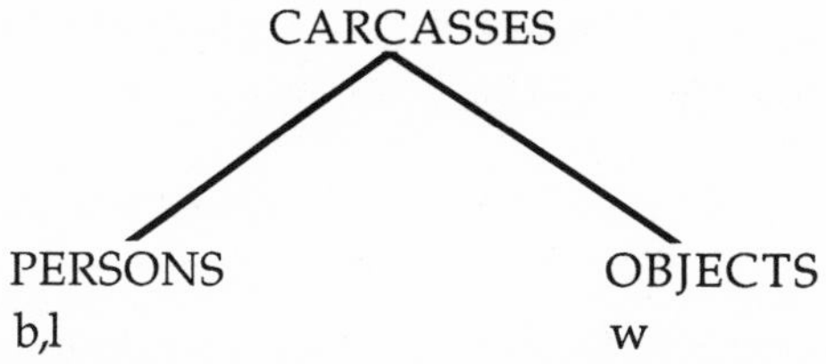

FIG. 5b: THE PURIFICATION OF THE CARCASS-CONTAMINATED

Day	*Purification*	*Allowed Area*
1	b, l	ordinary city
3	b, l, eve	Temple city

References: 11QT 51:1-5; Lev. 11:39

EXCREMENT

The sectarians, unlike the priests of Leviticus and Numbers, regard excrement as defiling. This is obviously taken from the rules for the War Camp of Deuteronomy:

> You shall have a place outside the camp and you shall go out to it; and you shall have a stick with your weapons; and when you sit down outside, you shall dig a hole with it, and turn back and cover up your excrement. Because the LORD your God walks in the midst of your camp, to save you and to give up your enemies before you, therefore your camp must be holy, that he may not see anything indecent among you, and turn away from you (Dt. 23:12-14. Eng.).

Just as the soldiers who are going to battle must take a stick with them to dig a hole to cover their excrement outside the camp, so must the sectarians of the messianic community do likewise. The Temple City, like the War Camp, is holy, thus, defecation must take place outside of its premises.

Josephus says that the Essenes living in Jerusalem did not defecate on the Sabbath:

> But they do not venture to remove any vessel or even to go to stool (on the Sabbath). On other days they dig a trench a foot deep with a mattock...that they may not offend the rays of the deity...when they relieve themselves.... They then replace the excavated soil in the trench. For this they select the more retired spots (Wars 2:147-149).

Urination in the city evidently was allowed, since it is not forbidden by Deuteronomy, and it would have been impossible to avoid for the whole duration of the Sabbath. It is interesting to note that Ezekiel, too, regards excrement defiling (Eze. 4:12-15).[45]

Yadin suggests that the Gate of the Essenes in Jerusalem was used to walk to a latrine area used by the Essenes.[46] The

---

45 Cf. J. Milgrom, "Further Studies in the Temple Scroll," *JQR* 71/2 (1980) 96-97.

46 Yadin, I, 303.

Scrolls support this view by stating that latrines are to be set up 3000 (11QT 46:15-16) or 2000 (1QM 7:3-7) cubits away from the sacred precincts. The purpose given for this distance is so that the act may be done out of sight of the holy area:

> There shall be a space between all their camps and the place of the hand [יד מקום = latrine], about 2000 cubits, and no unseemly evil thing shall be seen in the vicinity of their encampment (1QM 7:6-7).[47]

The Rabbis, on the other hand, do not ascribe to any such view. According to the Mishna, excrement is not ritually impure in any way:

> These do not become unclean and do not impart susceptibility to uncleanness: (1) sweat, (2) stinking pus, (3) excrement, (4) blood which exudes with them and (5) liquid [which is excreted with a stillborn child] at the eighth month (m. Makh. 6:7; cf. also t. Miq. 7:8).[48]

R. Jose goes one step further by asking, "Is excrement impure? Is it not for purposes of cleanliness?" (y. Pes. 7:11). The Babylonian Talmud forbids a Sage to reside in a city without a latrine (b. San. 17b). However, one should not eliminate waste while facing the Temple (b. Ber. 61b). Like the sectarians, there is a concern among the Rabbis to be out of sight of the sanctuary while eliminating waste.

The sect prescribed bathing after relieving oneself. Josephus informs:

> And though this discharge of the excrements is a natural function, they make it a rule to wash themselves after it, as if defiled (Wars 2:148-149).

---

47 The term יד, used here for latrine, is clearly taken from the Deuteronomy passage quoted above, "And you shall have a place, יד, outside of the camp..." (23:12).

48 Even the excrement of the zāb is not impure, Sifra Mes. Zab. par. 1:12-13. By contrast, his urine, being a liquid, is unclean, m. TY 2:1. Urine from clean persons is considered pure, t. Toh. 1:1-2.

Since all of the impurities discussed above require at least one bathing and laundering, it would not be surprising if both were required for this impurity as well. The passage above from Josephus states that the sectarians wash "as if defiled." Hence, the washing probably includes laundering as well as bathing, as it does for other impurities.

The following charts are a guess at the contamination power of excrement:

FIG. 6a: THE CONTAMINATION OF EXCREMENT

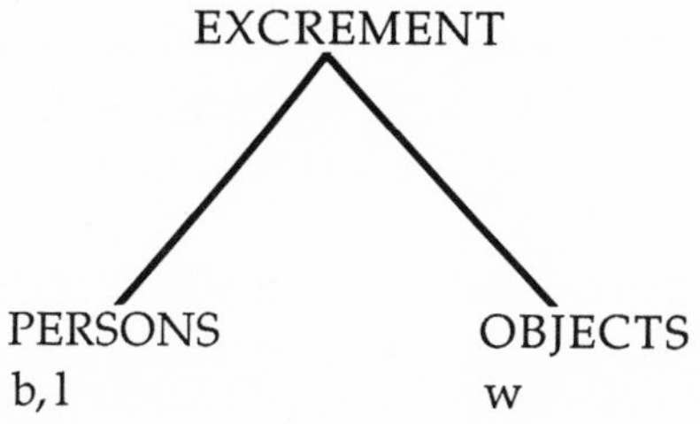

FIG. 6b: THE PURIFICATION OF ONE WHO HAS CONTACTED EXCREMENT

Day	*Purification*	*Allowed Area*
1	b, l	ordinary city Temple City

References: Wars 2:147-149; 11QT 46:13-16; 1QM 7:6-7

OUTSIDERS

At Qumran, contact with outsiders was considered a matter of ritual purity. 4QFlorilegium informs that the Ammonite, Moabite, bastard, alien, and sojourner will never enter the sanctuary again "for my holy ones are there" (vv. 3-4).[49] Josephus states that after contact with outsiders, the Essenes bathed (Wars 2:150); their property as well may have been defiling (1QM 9:8-9). In fact, so as not to contribute to impurity, clean beasts and birds were not to be sold to gentiles (CD 12:8-9), nor were sacrifices to be accepted from them.[50] The Damascus Rule prohibits selling food to gentiles (CD 12:10).

Other groups have considered outsiders defiling. Milgrom refers to Sefer Eldad Ha-Dani, which describes the view of the Ethiopian Jews: "one who touches a person of another religion or any defiling object (or person) may not eat anything until evening and must be quarantined for the entire day. In the evening he immerses himself in water and becomes pure."[51] Also, the Melchisedecitae, a Christian sect in Phrygia, avoided outsiders and refused to take anything from them.[52]

G. Alon has done a considerable amount of work on the rabbinic view of outsiders. In his article, "The Levitical Uncleanness of Gentiles," Alon maintains that the gentile was considered ritually impure in Second Temple times because of the ancient association of gentiles with the uncleanness of idolatry. He states that the Eighteen Decrees of the Sages of the mid-first

---

49 The term gēr should be translated according to its meaning in the Torah, "resident alien," not as Baumgarten, "proselyte," *Studies in Qumran Law*, 75.

50 Schiffman, "Legislation," 385, cites m. AZ 1:5 as proof that the early Sages, too, refused to sell clean fowl to Gentiles for fear that they might sacrifice them to idols. However, there is a difference of opinion and marked lenience with regard to the selling of cattle and sheep to Gentiles in the Mishna, cf. m. AZ 1:6; m. Pes. 4:3. On rejecting sacrifices from Gentiles, cf. Qimron and Strugnell, "An Unpublished Halakhic Letter from Qumran," 401.

51 *Sefer Eldad Hadani, Kitbe R. Abraham Epstein,* I, 173.

52 Baumgarten, *Studies*, 97.

century, which include a statement that the gentile defiles like a zāb (b. Shab. 17b; b. AZ 36b; y. Shab. 1:3), merely re-confirm that the status of the gentile is impure:

> This decree serves only to confirm the fact that it developed organically from a given basic conception which existed in the nation from early times, even though not all agreed to it, nor did the practice at all times conform to it, nor did the Sages rule according to it.[53]

Thus, from ancient times some Jews regarded gentiles levitically impure as did the sectarians. The Eighteen Decrees merely establish this notion as a ruling.

Perhaps the strongest support Alon presents for his argument is the following:

> Gentiles and a resident alien do not defile by reason of a flux, but although they do not defile because of a flux, they are unclean in all respects like those who suffer a flux, and heave offering is burnt on their account...(t. Zab. 2:1; Sifra Mes. Zab. par. 1:1, tr. Alon).

Supporting his claim further, Alon points to the fact that immersion is required of proselytes, at least in Second Temple times. He regards this as an obvious purification from gentile uncleanness.[54] He cites the view of the Hillelites:

> He that separates himself from the foreskin is as one who separates himself from a grave (m. Pes. 8:8).

Alon is correct that in many places the Rabbis claim that gentiles are not subject to the Jewish laws of impurity (corpse, t. Oh. 1:4; ṣāraʿat, m. Neg. 3:1; 11:1; 12:1; impure flows, Sifra Mes. Zab. par. 1:1; b. Nid. 34a; semen, Sif. Dt. on 23:11; m. Miq. 8:4, b. Nid. 34b). They are "outside the pale" and cannot participate in the normal cycle of impurity according to the Jewish definition.

---

53 G. Alon, *Jews, Judaism and the Classical World*, 147-148; cf. also *The Babylonian Talmud*, ed. I. Epstein, on b. Shab. 17b, III, 72; I. Halevi, *Dorot ha-Rišonim*, I, 3, 591-93; I. H. Weiss, *Dor, Dor v'Dor Šav*, I, 129.

54 Alon, 173.

Thus, Alon has a basis for stating that the uncleanness of the gentile is inherent, i.e., not due to any of the impurities of Leviticus 11-15, but just due to the fact that one is a gentile.

Nevertheless, the view that gentiles are ritually defiling cannot represent the attitude of the majority of the Sages. Indeed, the Torah does not propound such a notion. With the known social and economic contact which existed between gentile and Jew in the Talmudic period, it is hard to accept that gentiles would have been regarded as categorically impure.[55] In fact, the Talmud exhorts Jews to befriend gentiles: support their poor, visit their sick, and bury their dead (b. Git. 61a).

There are other problems with Alon's approach. According to the Talmud, **tĕrûmâ** and **qodōšîm** are not burned on account of contact with a gentile (b. Nid. 34a). Also, as scholars have pointed out, if the gentile really defiled as a **zāb**, the proselyte would never be allowed to eat of the passover meal, since **zābîm** cannot be considered pure without atoning sacrifices (Lev. 15:15).[56] R. Simeon declares that the gentile's uncleanness is only a *rabbinical* law (t. Nid. 9:14; b. Nid. 69b). In other words, it is not on a par with the commandments of the Torah and cannot claim biblical authority.

Nevertheless, we cannot jump to the opposite conclusion—that the Jews did not regard gentiles affected at all by impurity. Surely gentile menstruants and corpses would have been avoided as well as Jewish ones.

What can be concluded from the above passages is meager. It appears that gentiles were not considered subject to the Jewish laws of purity and impurity by Mishna-Tosefta and that at least some of the Sages regarded them inherently impure. However, from the substantial contact known to exist between Jew and gentile, and the laws of the Talmud encouraging this to a certain extent, it must be the case that this notion was not upheld by the majority of the Sages.

---

55 Cf. Y. Cohen, "The Attitude to the Gentile in the Halakhah and in Reality in the Tannaitic Period" (Hebrew).

56 "Goy" in *Enṣyqlopedyah Talmudit*, 324.

It seems logical to assume that in the time of the Second Temple there was a great concern to maintain purity in the Temple and outside it. Gentiles were excluded from the Temple proper and avoided by those wishing to maintain purity standards (cf. Acts 10:38). With the destruction of the Temple (70 C.E.) and the expulsion of Jews from Jerusalem (135 C.E.), the Sages despaired of the re-establishment of the cult. The Jews become dispersed into a gentile world. Surely many of them would consider the notion of inherent impurity of gentiles an unnecessary, unbiblical burden.

In any case, as referenced above, the sectarians living at the turn of the era, did consider the touch of outsiders defiling, but the extent of that contamination remains to be determined. Because of the fact that the sectarians regard it necessary to immerse even after touching a junior member, I would suggest that bathing was necessary after contact with all outsiders, both Jew and gentile. It may even be the case that, just as after other ritual impurities discussed above, laundering too was necessary. The following charts are a guess at the contamination power of outsiders on the basis of the other impurities we have discussed:

FIG. 7a: THE CONTAMINATION OF THE OUTSIDER

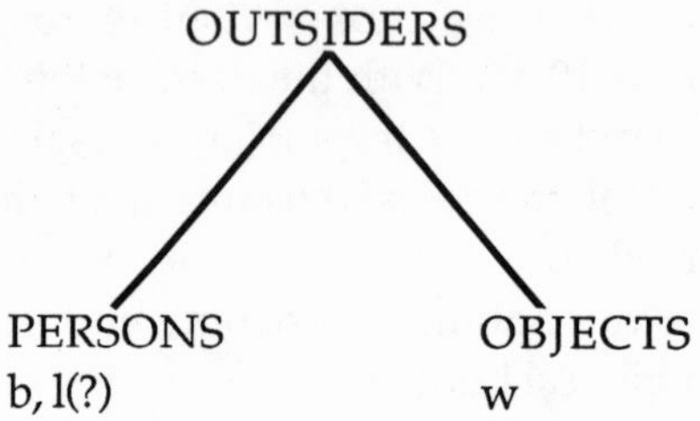

FIG. 7b: THE PURIFICATION OF ONE WHO HAS TOUCHED AN OUTSIDER

Day	*Purification*	*Allowed Area*
1	b, l(?)	ordinary city
3	b, l(?), eve	Temple city

References: 1QM 9:8-9; CD 12:8-10; 4QFl 3-4

In conclusion, the foregoing analysis of the concept of purity at Qumran reveals a stringent attitude on the part of the sectarians. In the comparisons made with rabbinic interpretations of the same purity laws of Scripture, the Rabbis appear more flexible even though they, along with the sectarians, considered the laws sacred and inviolable.

The exegesis of Scripture found in the Scrolls seems overly cautious at times, but the sectarians want to be sure no transgression of the law was made. Where the Torah is ambiguous, the sectarians interpret on the side of severity. Thus, since the text requires bathing after some impurities and bathing and laundering after others, one should bathe and launder after all impurities just in case laundering was intended even when not explicitly stated. According to Scripture, impurity was removed in stages with each purification shedding a layer (cf. the stages of the mĕṣōrāʿ). Hence, in the mind of the sectarians, impurity could also *increase,* according to the Torah, with added impurity contact.

Another example of extreme caution is present in corpse regulations. The corpse conveys impurity by the overhang of a room, but Scripture is silent on the issue of the impurity of a dead fetus. Thus, the cautious sectarian exegetes consider the dead fetus able to transfer impurity just like a corpse, transferring impurity by means of overhang, while it was still within the pregnant woman.

In the laws of the Temple City one finds an even greater extreme. No sexual intercourse would be allowed. No skins or carcasses of non-sacrificial animals would be permitted. No defecation would be allowed. No eating of animals which had not first been offered on the altar would be allowed. Most impurity bearers would have to remain outside the city for a three-day minimum before re-entering the city—an idea unheard of in the purity laws of Leviticus and Numbers.

As discussed above, the laws of the Temple City are not in effect at Qumran; they are studied and reserved for the reinstitution of a pure cult at Jerusalem. There is no question that the biblical division between profane and sacred must be upheld.

Hence the Temple City is credited with an even more stringent status of purity than that observed at Qumran. The purity status of the sectarians at Qumran paralleled that expected of the ordinary city in the messianic era.

The purity code observed at Qumran and that expected of the ordinary cities of the future parallel, in many respects, the purity kept by the Pharisees, or at least those who were ḥabērîm. The ḥabērîm, although not as rigid as the sectarians, are concerned about, e.g., the contamination of the corpse and the menstruant. However, as discussed in the chapters below, the concern of the Sages is to limit, when possible, rather than to increase the laws of purity.

The concern of the sectarians to keep the community meal pure especially reminds one of the ḥabērîm, who bathed before eating and made sure the meal had been harvested, tithed, and prepared in purity. However, the ḥabērîm do not levy penalties for invalidating pure food. The sectarians suspend persons who touch pure food while unclean.

More importantly, the ḥabērîm in their efforts to extend the purity of the priests to the laity remain within society and adhere to the cult in Jerusalem. By contrast, the sectarians establish an isolated and insulated community in the desert in total rejection of the existing priesthood in Jerusalem.

PART TWO

THE IMPURITY SYSTEM OF THE RABBIS

CHAPTER 3

IMMERSION

Scholarly inquiry to date on the subject of immersion in Second Temple times has treated mishnaic rules such as the laws regarding the miqveh or the category of the ṭĕbûl yôm as rabbinic or at most pharisaic anomalies. J. Neusner states:

> The washing in water is not developed [in the Bible] through definition of the nature of the "gathering of water" which is required or involved. On the contrary, water is in no way subject to specification and delimitation, since it does not, in any event, effect purification. Sunset does.... The proposition [of the Mishna] that immersion in a pool effects purification therefore requires the invention of the category of the ṭĕbûl yôm, one who has immersed and awaits sunset for the completion of purification, as specified in various Scriptural verses.[1]

Also, the requirement of immersion for the purification of *all* biblical impurities has been considered a Pharisaic invention. E. P. Sanders states that, except in the case of contact with

---

1 J. Neusner, *A History of the Mishnaic Law of Purities*, XIX, 5.

semen, the Bible requires immersion only for men. He suggests that because women did not participate in the Temple cult, they were not required to bathe after their period of impurity was over:

> During stage one of childbirth-impurity the woman is impure as during menstruation (Lev. 12:2), and at the end she is not required to bathe or to purify herself in any way.... It is probable that, in the first century, when there was a Court of the Women, it was assumed that women bathed after impurity, as did men.... The Bible prescribes bathing for several impurities (e.g. intercourse), and we have just seen that it was extended to other cases (e.g. menstruation) by the Pharisees and probably others.[2]

These claims deserve re-evaluation.

It is my claim that the Pharisees and the Rabbis after them were continuing the biblical tradition. They were concerned not to violate Scripture because of biblical sanctions. Because of difficulties of real life practice the Rabbis even try to limit their obligation at times when the Scripture is ambiguous. At other times they create a "hedge" of extended rules to make sure the biblical laws are not violated. However, at least with regard to immersion, they did not establish any principles without Scriptural warrant.

My working assumption is that the Rabbis were careful exegetes. They tried to explore all of the logical possibilities of the laws discussed below. They knew that these were not just random regulations but that they formed a system based on principles which dictated the law even when it was not spelled out.

The Rabbis are not inventing a new purity system when they, e.g., consider ablutions necessary after menstruation. They are rather reading Scriptural laws as a system. There are gaps in the purity laws of the Torah which must be filled in order to establish the whole system. For example, although it is clear that the mĕṣōrāʿ is a very potent impurity bearer from the isolation and purification rules of Leviticus 13 and 14 (cf. also Num. 5:2), the

---

2 E. P. Sanders, *Jewish Law from Jesus to the Mishnah*, 143, 214.

Torah is silent concerning the ability of the mĕṣōrāʿ to contaminate other persons and objects. Gaps such as this one are filled by the Rabbis in accordance with principles identified in the text itself.

The Rabbis are reading but not inventing Scripture. D. Boyarin, in his work on midrash, explains:

> I will imagine the rabbis as readers doing the best they could to make sense of the Bible for themselves and their times - in short, as readers. It is not exploitation of the text; it is exploitation of the gaps in the text, which are there, as it were precisely to be exploited.[3]

Thus, the Rabbis interpret the gaps in Scripture in a manner consistent with the text and assume that its purity laws constitute a workable system.

By examining the contamination effects and purification procedures, the Rabbis are able to construct a hierarchy of impurities. By comparing passages which treat the same impurity source, mode of contamination, or purification process, one can often assume information explicit in one passage to be implicit in another. This system assumes immersion is necessary after every impurity mentioned in the Priestly Code. It also contains the principles which give birth to the category of the ṭĕbûl yôm and the specifications of the miqveh. Although the Rabbis define these concepts they do not initiate them; they are rooted in Scripture.

In the case of immersion it is possible to infer the need for ablutions for a grave impurity because the Torah requires them for similar but lighter impurities. Scripture explicitly mandates immersion for all of the following impurity bearers:

(1) the mĕṣōrāʿ (Lev. 14:8-9);
(2) the zāb (Lev. 15:13);
(3) the corpse-contaminated person/object (Lev. 22:4-6; Num. 31:23-24);
(4) the one who emits semen (Dt. 23:11; Lev. 15:16);
(5) the one who eats nĕbēlâ or ṭĕrēpâ (Lev. 17:15);

---

3 D. Boyarin, *Intertextuality and the Reading of Midrash*, 45.

(6) those who touch the bed of the zāb (Lev. 15:5) or sit on his chair (Lev. 15:6);
(7) those who touch the zāb (Lev. 15:7-8, 11-12) or that the zāb spits on (Lev. 15:8);
(8) those who carry anything under the zāb (Lev. 15:10);
(9) those who touch the bed/seat of a menstruant or zābâ (Lev. 15:21-22, 25-27).

All of these contaminated persons or objects must be washed in water.

However, the Rabbis require immersion for other impurity bearers as well:

(1) persons/objects who touch or carry unclean carcasses;
(2) all those affected by corpse impurity: the one who gathers the red cow ash, those who touch the water of purgation and persons/objects who touch what the corpse contaminated person has touched;
(3) objects in a house affected by ṣāraʿat;
(4) those who make contact with women with discharges of blood: the parturient, zābâ, and the menstruant.

Scripture does not explicitly require this latter group to wash in water. Scripture merely says these persons and objects are unclean. Following the research of J. Milgrom I want to show that the Rabbis are making a valid, possible interpretation of Scripture when they insist that it mandates the immersion of all of these impurity bearers. The second group is not a list of rabbinic additions to the Bible's impurity list but represents a valid interpretation of Scripture in which all of the purity laws comprise a system. Below I will examine the biblical data on each of the impurity bearers in the second list to see how the rabbinic immersion requirement for each is grounded in Scripture.

UNCLEAN CARCASSES

The Mishna requires immersion for persons or objects who have contacted carcasses of impure animals. In an interesting section about doubts the Mishna discusses the case of a person who touched either the carcass of a šereṣ (one of the eight creeping things which convey impurity to one who touches them according to Lev. 11:29-31) or a frog (which does not transmit impurity by touch) but does not know which was touched and has already prepared food. The answer is that if the individual touched both, he or she must immerse on account of touching the (unclean) creeping thing. However, if the person touched only one carcass, immersed, and then touched the other, he or she may be pure (i.e., the second touch may have only been on the carcass of the frog, not an unclean act). In this case, the doubt of contamination to the food is great enough to consider it still clean:

> The [dead] creeping thing and the [dead] frog in public domain. Someone touched one of them [not knowing which] and prepared clean things and they are eaten. [Then] he immersed, touched the other [carcass], and prepared clean things. Lo, these are clean. If the first remain, these and these remain in suspense. If he did not immerse, meanwhile, the first remain in suspense, and the second are burned (m. Toh. 5:4, translation mine; cf. m. Miq. 10:8).

The important assumption for this discussion is that the Mishna requires immersion after touching unclean carcasses/food.

The Mishna did not invent this requirement; it can be shown to be biblical. Milgrom has made it clear that the phrase, **yiṭmāʾ ʿad-hāʿāreb**, "will be unclean until evening," used several times in Leviticus 11, implies a minimal purification requirement on the impurity bearer: the necessity to bathe.[4] I will list his reasons below and then provide explanation:

1) Ablutions are required for impure vessels (Lev. 11:32), *a fortiori*, impure persons.

2) According to Lev. 11:40 those who eat a carcass are "impure until evening." Comparison with Lev. 17:15 and 22:6, however, reveals that bathing is required.

3) All who carry a carcass are told to launder their clothes (Lev. 11:40). If laundering is required, bathing must be as well.

---

4 Cf. Lev. 11:24, 25, 27, 28, 31, 32, 39, 40 (2x); J. Milgrom, Leviticus, I, 667; D. P. Wright, *The Disposal of Impurity*, 185 n. 38.

To explain in detail, Scripture states that all who touch unclean carcasses will be unclean until the evening (Lev. 11:24, 40). Lev. 11:24 provides the first instance of this phrase:

> And by these you shall become unclean; whoever touches their carcass yiṭmāʾ ʿad-hāʿāreb (shall be unclean until evening).

Milgrom assumes that the phrase yiṭmāʾ ʿad-hāʿāreb implies bathing but not laundering, so that those who touch impure carcasses must bathe but they do not need to launder their clothes. This interpretation can be proven from the fact that objects in contact with impure carcasses must be washed (Lev. 11:32). If objects in contact with a šereṣ must be washed, it stands to reason that persons in contact with impure carcasses, too, must be washed.

Also, support for Milgrom's interpretation is found in the verses about eating carcasses. A comparison of Lev. 11:39-40 with Lev. 17:15 reveals that the former is an abbreviated statement of the full requirement. Let us compare the two passages below:

> And if any animal of which you may eat dies, he who touches its carcass shall be unclean until the evening, and he who eats of its carcass shall wash his clothes, and be unclean until the evening; he also who carries the carcass shall wash his clothes and be unclean until the evening (Lev. 11:39-40).

> And every person that eats what dies of itself or what is torn by beasts, whether he is a native or a sojourner, shall wash his clothes, and bathe himself in water, and be unclean until the evening; then he shall be clean (Lev. 17:15).

Although Leviticus 11:40 only mentions laundering and the fact that the person "yiṭmāʾ ʿad-hāʿāreb, will be unclean until evening," we learn from Lev. 17:15 that the individual is also required to bathe. Thus, it must be the case that Lev. 11:39 is merely an abbreviated version of Lev. 17:15 using the key phrase, "yiṭmāʾ ʿad-hāʿāreb," to indicate the bathing requirement.

Also, with regard to *touching* carcasses, Lev. 11:39 is an abbreviated version of the full requirement. It is clear that

Scripture requires immersion after touching impure carcasses. Lev. 22 clarifies the vague reference in 11 that the individual is "unclean until evening":

> And whoever touches a creeping thing by which he may be made unclean or a man from whom he may take uncleanness, whatever his uncleanness may be—the person who touches any such shall be unclean until the evening and shall not eat of the holy things unless he has bathed his body in water (Lev. 22:5-6).

Here the text states that a priest who touches any of a list of things, including unclean carcasses, is unclean until the evening, and then as clarification it explains that bathing is necessary for him to be purified and allowed to officiate again as a priest.

Finally, the text requires those who carry a carcass to launder their clothes. Since carrying a carcass brings one into more intense contact with the impure item than merely touching it, one can infer that bathing was assumed to be necessary for those who carry a carcass since it is required for those who merely touch a carcass.[5] If the claim is accepted that the phrase, "**yiṭmāʾ ʿad-hāʿāreb,**" indicates the bathing requirement, the system's logic begins to emerge. Carrying and eating are more intense modes of contamination than touching. This notion becomes more pronounced in Leviticus 15 where the pressure (application of greater weight) of the impure person (in effect causing him or her to be borne or carried by the pure item) on a clean bed or seat results in greater contamination than mere touching (see Chapter 6 below). The increased intensity of eating over touching is evident also in the impurity of the person who not only enters a house affected with scale disease but stays and eats a piece of bread or lies down (Lev. 14:46-47). Thus, the carriage of a carcass is regarded contaminating enough to require the basic bathing requirement as well as the added purification of laundering.

---

5 Cf. Milgrom, *Leviticus*, I, 667; opp. the sectarians who assume laundering as well as bathing is required for purification, 11QT 51:2-3.

To summarize, although some verses explicitly state the bathing requirement (Lev. 17:15; 22:6), others abbreviate the law by using the phrase, yiṭmāʾ ʿad-hāʿāreb (Lev. 11:24, 40). The fact that bathing after touching impure carcasses is not always verbalized means nothing. It seems the priestly writer at times felt it unnecessary to spell out the immersion requirement and simply wrote yiṭmāʾ ʿad-hāʿāreb.

I find no basis for assuming that laundering is necessary unless it is explicitly prescribed. The cases in which laundering is stated to be necessary (e.g., after carrying or eating a carcass) are clear examples of more intense transmission of impurity than that of the cases where laundering is not mentioned (e.g., touching carcasses).

Thus, the Rabbis do not assume by Lev. 11:40 that bathing is unnecessary for those who touch nĕbēlâ just because it is not mentioned. Rather they interpret the text as follows: since those who touch nĕbēlâ are said to be unclean, they must bathe. Just the fact that they are unclean indicates that they must bathe. Laundering, on the other hand, is specifically prescribed for the one who eats or carries a carcass in addition to the general, minimal bathing requirement for all unclean persons/objects. As the Mekhilta states categorically:

> In the Torah, there is no laundering that does not require [bodily] immersion (Mekh. Baḥodeš 3, Lauterbach, 212)

CORPSE

Anyone who touches the red cow ash or purgation water becomes impure. The Bible distinctly states that the priest in charge of the rite and the one who burns the red cow are both unclean and must bathe and launder their clothes (Num. 19:7-8). The one who gathers the ash, however, is told to launder his clothes but is not told to bathe (Num. 19:10). The Rabbis assume that he is supposed to bathe as well as launder.

From the above discussion on unclean carcasses it is evident that when the text requires laundering it assumes bathing as well. Another such example is found in the area of corpse impurity. Numbers 31:24 reads:

> You [the corpse-contaminated person] must wash your clothes on the seventh day, and you shall be clean; and afterward you shall come into the camp.

Although Num. 31:24 does not mention specifically the requirement to bathe, it does mention laundering. Because of the added requirement to launder, bathing too must be necessary. This claim is fully justified by Num. 19:19:

> And the clean person shall sprinkle upon the unclean (the corpse-contaminated person) on the third day and on the seventh day; thus on the seventh day he shall cleanse him, and he shall wash his clothes and bathe himself in water, and at evening he shall be clean.

Hence, Numbers 31:24 has merely abbreviated the purification requirement for those impure by contact with the slain. It is clear from Num. 19:19 that bathing is necessary as well as laundering. The Rabbis are treating all of these purification laws as a system in which bathing is necessary if one is unclean and for more severe impurities laundering is necessary as well.

The one who touches anything which a corpse-contaminated person/object has touched must bathe. The Mishna is clear that those who touch a corpse can contaminate as ʾabôt ṭumʾâ, thus contaminating persons as well as susceptible objects, and that these persons/objects will contaminate other susceptible objects (m. Oh. 1:1-4).

In this regard, the Rabbis were reading, not extending, Scripture. They understood Num. 19:22 as follows:

> And whatever the unclean person touches shall be unclean; and the soul that touches it [what the unclean person touches] shall be unclean until evening.

Now, even modern translations differ on the antecedent of "it." The Revised Standard Version and King James Version translate "it"; the Jewish Publication Society "him." The problem is that the Hebrew does not have either "him" or "it." Where the Rabbis understand, "the soul that touches it shall be unclean until evening," the Hebrew has only "hannepeš hannōgaʿat tiṭmāʾ ʿad hāʿāreb." Thus, the rabbinic notion is founded on a plausible reading of Scripture.

AFFECTED HOUSE

R. Meir assumes that it is general knowledge that the contents of a house affected by ṣāraʿat can be merely immersed and then rendered clean after sunset. This is not explicitly stated in the Bible but, as demonstrated below, the Rabbis have valid reasons for interpreting Scripture in this manner. The Sages were discussing the problem of such a house contaminating wood and clothing. R. Meir's challenge reveals that all the Sages agreed on the necessity of immersing the contents of the house:

> Said R. Meir: "And what of his property does it render unclean? If you say, his wooden objects and his clothing and his metal objects—he immerses them and they are clean" (m. Neg. 12:5).

The Rabbis are interpreting according to the same principle discussed earlier that if something is said to be unclean it automatically must be washed whether or not "rāḥaṣ bammayim" is stated in the text. That persons and objects in such a house are made unclean after the priest pronounces the house itself unclean is clear from Leviticus:

> Then the priest shall command that they empty the house before the priest goes to examine the disease, lest all that is in the house be declared unclean; and afterward the priest shall go in to see the house. Moreover he who enters the house while it is shut up [after the priest's inspection] shall be unclean until the evening (Lev. 14:36, 46).

Additionally, the Rabbis insist that those who remain a while in such a house, to lie down or to eat, are even more contaminated than the one who has been in the house only momentarily. The Mishna states:

> He who entered a house afflicted with plague, with his garments over his shoulder, and his sandals and rings in his hands—he and they are unclean forthwith. He was dressed in his garments, with his sandals on his feet and his rings on his fingers—he is unclean forthwith. But they are unclean until he will remain for a time sufficient to eat a piece of bread...(m. Neg. 13:9; cf. Sifra Mes. Neg. 5:4-11).

The notion that lying down and eating are more intense modes of contamination is derived directly from Scripture:

> And he who lies down in the house shall wash his clothes; and he who eats in the [affected] house shall wash his clothes (Lev. 14:47).

Thus, Scripture requires laundering in addition to bathing for those who remain long enough to lie down or eat in the house affected by ṣāraᶜat.

DISCHARGES OF BLOOD

Neither the zābâ, the parturient, nor the menstruant is told in Scripture to immerse. The Rabbis, on the other hand, clearly require immersion as evident in several passages (m. Nid. 4:3; 10:8; m. Miq. 8:1, 5; 5:5). My claim is that the Rabbis are not extending Scripture's laws to require immersion for women with impure flows but that this is already a plausible reading of Scripture. I disagree with those scholars who suggest that, according to Scripture, only men require immersion for sexual discharges.[6]

E. P. Sanders understands the biblical bathing requirement to apply only to those impurity bearers who are explicitly

---

6 S. Cohen, "Menstruants and the Sacred in Judaism and Christianity" in *Women's History and Ancient History*, ed. S. B. Pomeroy, 275; M. Selvidge, *Woman, Cult, and Miracle Recital*, 55. Cohen also errs in failing to notice any reference to immersion for menstruants in the Mishna, 277.

commanded in the text. He claims the Rabbis have extended this concern to women with impure flows. He explains his reasoning as follows:

> With the construction of the large Court of the Women, it was an obvious step to say that women, after impurity because of menstruation or some other flow of blood, should bathe just as did men who touched their beds.[7]

Sanders suggests that the Sages have introduced the requirement for the menstruant to bathe due to a historical shift in conditions, i.e., the construction of the Court of the Women in the Temple. He explains that the Bible does not require impure women to bathe because they did not participate in the Temple cult.

However, contrary to Sanders' claim, women do participate in the cult to some degree; after her period of impurity the parturient brings her own sacrifice to the Temple (Lev. 12:6). Also, as Sanders concedes, the Torah does require the woman who has had sexual intercourse to bathe (Lev. 15:18).

The foundation of the argument that Scripture requires the zābâ, the parturient, and the menstruant to bathe rests on contamination effects and purification rituals which are explicit in the Torah. From this given data it is apparent that these persons are much more potent impurity bearers than some others who are explicitly told to bathe. For example, all of these women are impure for at least seven days, and the text states that the menstruant and the zābâ contaminate their beds and seats so that even those items can convey impurity to clean persons (Lev. 15:19-23; 26-27). The zābâ and parturient are required to bring a sacrifice (Lev. 12:6; 15:29). By contrast, the man who emits semen is only unclean one day (Lev. 15:16). Further, he does not make his bed or seat a generative source of impurity and does not offer a sacrifice. As discussed in greater detail in Chapter 6, by its very nature blood which flows from the vagina is a more contaminating item than semen. However, the text states plainly

---

7 Sanders, 214.

that the man who emits semen must bathe (15:16). If he must bathe, *a fortiori*, the parturient, zābâ, and menstruant must bathe.

Another proof that these impure women must bathe is the fact that those who touch their beds or seats must bathe (15:21, 27). If the one who is contaminated secondarily by touching the bed or seat of the unclean woman must bathe, *a fortiori*, the woman herself, who contaminated the bed or seat in the first place, must bathe.

Finally, the members of the Qumran community certainly assumed that the Torah required immersion for women with flows, just as it was required for all male impurity bearers:

> And all those "[im]pure of days" on the day of their he[aling] shall bathe, and launder in water, and become pure. And afterward they may eat their food according to the reg[ulations] (4QOrdc 8-10, tr. Milgrom).[8]

Thus, the Rabbis are interpreting Scripture in a systemic manner in which some impurities are more severe than others and therefore convey impurity more extensively. However, all impurities require at least immersion for purification. The notion that immersion is required after every impurity described in Scripture is considered biblical by the Sages.

Sanders has argued that the Rabbis have made up rules extending the purification laws of Scripture to women with flows (see above). It is true that the Sages on occasion add regulations of their own to Scripture. They refer to these additional instructions as "dĕRabbānan," rabbinical enactments, to distinguish their origin and authority from that of Scripture. However, the

---

8 Translation by Milgrom, *Leviticus*, I, 972. The claim of Cohen, 278, that the "men of Qumran lived in an exclusively male community far removed from any contact with the pollutions of the world, especially women" is controverted by the research of L. Bennett-Elder who provides numerous citations (several are cited above in the notes to Chapter 2) from the Qumran literature to demonstrate the presence of females, cf. "Female Ascetics in the Late Second Temple Period: Five Provisional Models," AAR National Convention, 1991. Cohen is following L. H. Schiffman, "Exclusions from the Sanctuary and the City of the Sanctuary in the Temple Scroll, " *HAR* 9 (1985) 301-20.

immersion requirement of women with flows is never placed in this category. It is not considered a rabbinic addition to Scripture; it represents Scripture itself.

The concept of the ṭĕbûl yôm is commonly considered to be a rabbinic notion. The idea is that one who immerses after any impurity, even though still waiting for evening for complete purification, is unclean only to the second degree, potentially defiling only to food to be eaten in purity and sancta. The fluids of the individual, or ṭĕbûl yôm, are unclean only in the third degree, dangerous only to sancta (m. TY 4:1-3; 3:6; 2:1-3; t. TY 1:3; Sifra Shem. Sher. 8:9).

The Rabbis are credited with the innovation of the effectiveness of ablution because they are intent on defining Scripture as clearly as possible. The Sages' description of the rite for the one purifying from scale disease is probably the best example of the notion that ablutions remove layers of impurity:

> He [the priest] came to shave the leper. He passed a razor over all of his flesh. And he washed his garments and immersed. He is clean so far as rendering unclean through entry, and lo, he renders unclean like an insect. He enters inside the wall, is separated from his house seven days [Lev. 14:8], and is prohibited from sexual intercourse. On the seventh day he shaves the second shaving, as [in the manner of] the first shaving. He washed his garments and immersed. He is [now] clean so far as rendering unclean like an insect. And lo, he is one who has immersed [on the selfsame day]: he eats [second] tithe. [Once] his sun has set: he eats heave offering. [Once] he has brought his atonement offering [on the eighth day], he eats holy things. It comes out that there are three [stages of] purifications in regard to a leper, and three [stages of] purifications in regard to one who gives birth (m. Neg. 14:2-3).

Thus, the Sages describe three stages of purification, which are delineated by ablutions, for both the mĕṣōrāʿ and for the parturient (cf. m. Nid. 4:3).

The Bible nowhere mentions the category of ṭĕbûl yôm. J. Neusner has noted the biblical stress on the fact that after immersion, an individual is *unclean*, not partially clean, until evening. Consequently, he refuses to ascribe to the biblical writer any notion that ordinary water had a purgative effect. He declares that this is purely a rabbinic invention with the advent of the immersion pool:

> Scripture is unambiguous about the status of that which has been put in water. It is unclean until the evening. It is the principle, surely deriving from the period before the turn of the first century, that the immersion pool of forty seahs of still water effects purification, which much later raises the ambiguity.[9]

And also:

> It is perfectly clear, therefore, that ordinary water is distinguished from spring water or living water and is not understood as a substance capable of purifying anything from uncleanness.... Leviticus is clear that the spring (running water) does purify; other water does not.[10]

Neusner also points out that the Bible, unlike the Rabbis, does not specify the necessary amount of ordinary water to be used. He claims that this is because in the biblical view ordinary water cannot purify.[11]

Accordingly, for Neusner the Bible mandates only spring water for purification; ordinary water needs to be combined with the requirement for sunset for it to have any effect. In Neusner's view the Rabbinic notion of **ṭĕbûl yôm** is in no way founded on Scripture but rather stands in contradistinction to it. Neusner states that it is the Rabbis who have decided that a pool of naturally standing (not drawn) water can purify when according to the biblical view it cannot. To accept these statements is to claim that the Rabbis are intentionally innovating principles contrary to Scripture. Neusner is aware of this implication for he says sources of uncleanness are derived from Scripture but loci of uncleanness and modes of purification are not.[12]

---

9 Neusner, *Purities*, XIX, 99-100.

10 Ibid., 4.

11 Ibid., 4-5, 99; XXII, 85.

12 Ibid., XXII, 26.

D. P. Wright, too, declares that water on its own has no purgative value in the biblical system. His arguments are paraphrased below:[13]

1) The Bible never points out a separate priestly status for those who have bathed but not yet waited for sunset.

2) Ablution is tightly bound up with the prescription to wait for evening. It is even assumed if the text reads only "yiṭmāʾ ʿad-hāʿāreb" omitting "wĕrāḥaṣ bammayim."

3) Deuteronomy 23:11 states that one with a seminal emission must bathe "towards" evening and then may re-enter the camp. Thus, in this case the two requirements take effect at almost the same time.

4) Other rituals (e.g., the sprinkling rites for the corpse-contaminated person) do not have individual effect but contribute collectively to the larger goal of purification.

These cogent arguments seem to be conclusive, but there are instances in which ablutions are not tightly bound up with the requirement to wait for evening and in which they do mark a different degree in a person's impurity status. One example is the case of the one purifying from ṣāraʿat. Leviticus 14:8 reads:

> And he who is to be cleansed [from ṣāraʿat] shall wash his clothes, and shave off all his hair, and bathe himself in water, and he shall be clean; and after that he shall come into the camp, but he shall dwell outside his tent seven days.

Here there is no command to wait for evening. The first day rites of the one purifying from ṣāraʿat, the miṭṭahēr, end with bathing after which he or she is re-admitted to the camp. The individual is said to be ṭāhôr, clean! It is clear that this does not mean totally clean because the miṭṭahēr still cannot go home (Lev. 14:8). Probably, although no longer a threat to the sanctuary (from afar), the miṭṭahēr might still defile sacred food by overhang and

13 D. P. Wright, *Disposal*, 220-222 n. 105.

will also defile other persons by touch. Thus, until the end of the seventh day, the miṭṭahēr must stay out in the open.[14]

After seven days in this status, the miṭṭahēr undergoes another purification rite including shaving all body hair, laundering personal clothes, and bathing, and then he or she is allowed entry into the house.[15] The impure individual is again said to be clean (Lev. 14:9). Milgrom has shown that this purification completely takes away the overhang potency of the miṭṭahēr, who will no longer contaminate ordinary persons/objects even by touch; the individual can only convey impurity via direct contact with sacred food and objects. Milgrom states: "The person need no longer remain outside his tent but can now enter it...for he no longer contaminates sancta by overhang only by touch."[16] This last vestige of contamination potential is removed by the sacrifices on the eighth day (Lev. 14:10-32).

Nowhere in the biblical account is there a requirement on the miṭṭahēr to wait for evening before proceeding to a lower stage of impurity. The individual is allowed to re-enter the camp after bathing (Lev. 14:8). As Milgrom has stated, "Clearly, he does not make his way into the camp after dark."[17]

Milgrom has systematically applied the principle that ablutions reduce impurity by one degree to all impurity bearers in the Priestly Code charting the results in three comprehensive tables.[18] [The first table is reproduced above, Introduction, Figure 2.] He concludes that already in the Priestly system

---

14 Milgrom, *Leviticus*, I, 843, supports his argument by reference to newly discovered Dead Sea Scroll fragments. However, the Mishna regards the miṭṭahēr innocuous to both sacred and profane items via overhang: "He renders unclean like an insect" (m. Neg. 14:2). Cf. also Wright, *Disposal*, 213; m. Kel. 1:4; m. Neg. 13:17.

15 Milgrom, *Leviticus*, I, 843, claims that Scripture's repetition of the command to shave all body hair includes that of the private parts. The Rabbis understand this repetition to exclude that of private parts (Sifra Mes. Neg. 2:2).

16 Milgrom, *Leviticus*, I, 844, 993.

17 Ibid., 842.

18 Ibid., 986-91; cf. also 957-68, for a full discussion of the effect of ablutions in the Priestly system.

ordinary impurities are neutralized by ablutions, which remove the threat of contamination to the profane world, and sunset, which removes the danger to sancta. For severe impurities the threat to the sacred realm can be removed only by sacrifices; sunset is not enough.

The status of the ṭĕbûl yôm is the same as that of the miṭṭahēr on the seventh day. The individual does not affect ordinary persons or objects but does remain a threat to the sacred. In fact, the Rabbis point out that it is only the performance of ablutions which reduces the impurity of the miṭṭahēr and makes admittance to the camp possible. Commenting on Lev. 14:8, the Rabbis state:

> The washing of his body hinders him from coming inside the camp, but the birds [observance of the required bird rite] do not hinder him from coming into the camp (Sifra Mes. Neg. par. 2:10).

Another biblical example of water acting as a purgative agent without evening is the zāb's rinsing of hands. If a zāb washes his hands before making contact with clean persons, the latter are not affected by his impurity (Lev. 15:11). Certainly, this act does not change the zāb's status, but it has an effect of its own without extraneous rites. The ṭĕbûl yôm is in a similar situation. Although still regarded unclean with respect to sancta, this partially pure individual will not affect clean persons/objects because of his or her initial immersion. (It is of interest that the Rabbis understand the zāb's "handwashing" to include all visible body parts, excluding private parts, interpreting it as almost a full immersion, Sifra Mes. Zab. 4:5).

Other examples of the purifying power of immersion can be found in the account of the sacrificial rites of Yom Kippur. The one who lets the scapegoat go merely launders and bathes and "afterward he may come into the camp" (Lev. 16:26). The same is stated about the one who burns the ḥaṭṭāʾt sacrifices (Lev. 16:28). Although he has become impure, washings alone serve to re-admit him to the camp.[19] Therefore, although there is no explicit

---

19 Ibid., 1050-51.

category of ṭĕbûl yôm in the Bible, the principle is in operation with several impurity bearers.

In response to Neusner's argument that ordinary water is not specified in the Bible because it did not purify, it should be noted that neither is the measure of spring water prescribed. The amount of water is not specified because probably any amount which serves to cover the whole body will suffice. I make this deduction, as did the Rabbis, from the much repeated law to bathe *the body* in water (Lev. 14:9; 15:16; 16:4, 26, 28; 22:6; cf. below Sifra Mes. Zab. 6:3).

Neusner on occasion argues that proof the Rabbis are often not exegeting Scripture but are propounding notions of their own is the differences in the various sects' decisions. Above (see Introduction) I took issue with this viewpoint stating that it is the Torah which is ambiguous and gapped and which provides the groundwork for various interpretations. Groups like the Rabbis or the sectarians filled these gaps only by recourse to Scripture itself. They would not knowingly propound a human notion against what they believed to be divinely appointed in the Torah. Nevertheless, because of the ambiguity in the Torah itself, their interpretations often differ.

In the case of the ṭĕbûl yôm, the Qumran sectarians provide a substantial parallel for the rabbinic argument that immersion is effective to some degree without sunset. Both the sectarians and the Sages agree that ablutions do reduce impurity to some extent even without sunset. I have noted above (Chapter 1) that a first day ablution may, in the view of the yaḥad, serve to restore a corpse-contaminated person to the camp (11QT 49:16-17; 50:10-14; IQM 14:2-3). The same holds true for lighter impurity bearers. For example, the man with a flow of semen is required to bathe twice in order to enter the Temple City; the first ablution probably allows him to re-establish contact with profane persons/objects (11QT 45:7-10).[20]

---

20 J. Milgrom, "Studies in the Temple Scroll," *JBL* 97 (1978) 513-514; *Leviticus*, I, 970-71.

Therefore, although by definition the Qumran sectarians and the Sages represent opposing systems, they agree on the effectiveness of ablutions without sunset. This is because both groups are carefully reading the same biblical text and they are reading it as a system.

Finally, let us raise the question, where did the requirement of an immersion pool containing 40 seahs of undrawn water originate? Certainly it is not a prescription of the Torah. Neusner suggests that the advent of the miqveh is what brought about the notion that ablutions were effective.[21] Now, it has been demonstrated that the effectiveness of ablutions is biblical, but what brought about the advent of the miqveh?

Neusner does not answer this question but he does explain that the Rabbis wanted to create a contrasting analogue to Scripture's spring water: a still pool. He states that the Rabbis are constructing a mirror image of Scripture to reflect their changed situation—a Jewish community without the Temple which is trying to keep the table at home pure:

> The Mishnaic system to begin with thus provides a mode of purification different from that specified in the Written Torah for the Temple, but analogous to that suitable for the Temple.... They bathe not in running water, in anticipation of the end of days and for the sake of eschatological purity, but in still water, to attain the cleanness appropriate to the eternal Temple, the cycle of cleanness and the perpetual sacrifice.... As sun sets, bringing purification for the Temple, so rain falls, bringing purification for the Table.[22]

There are some problems with this approach. First of all, Scripture only explicitly requires bathing in spring water for the zāb, one of the most potent of all impurity bearers (Lev. 15:13).[23]

---

21 Neusner, *Purities*, XIX, 4-5, 99; XXII, 85.

22 Ibid., XXII, 87.

23 Milgrom, *Leviticus*, I, 924, believes that spring water is also required for the ablutions of the zābâ and the menstruant. He points to the fact that Leviticus 15 begins with instructions regarding the zāb, including the command for him to bathe in spring water. The other persons with flows discussed in the chapter, the menstruant and the zābâ, are not given any instructions regarding ablutions. Milgrom claims that the pericopes

Can we use this extreme example to infer spring water is prescribed for purification of all impurity bearers? Even in the case of the zāb, spring water alone does not effect purification; his sacrifices on the following day complete the process.

More importantly, the writer of Leviticus is clear that both water in a spring or in a *cistern* (obviously still) cannot be contaminated:

> Nevertheless a spring or a cistern holding water shall be clean; but whatever touches their carcass [of one of the eight creepers] shall be unclean (Lev. 11:36).

I claim that *this* is the fact which makes both types of water perfect agents for purification: neither can become impure.

The Rabbis notice that just two verses prior (Lev. 11:36), the Torah states that drink in a *vessel* is susceptible to uncleanness:

> Any food in it [an earthen vessel into which one of the eight creepers has fallen] which may be eaten, upon which water may come, shall be unclean; and all drink which may be drunk from every such vessel shall be unclean (Lev. 11:34).

Hence, the question is: What is the difference in a vessel and a cistern? The Rabbis distinguish the two by saying that the cistern is embedded in the ground whereas the kĕlî, a vessel, is detached from the ground:

> Might one say that if it [water] is in cisterns, pits, and caves, it imparts susceptibility to uncleanness? Scripture says, "In...a vessel it will be unclean." Just as a vessel is distinctive in that it is

---

on the menstruant and the zābâ are abbreviated versions of that of the zāb. Thus, information not stated explicitly about the menstruant and the zābâ, including purification instructions, can be assumed, albeit cautiously, from the information given concerning the zāb at the beginning of the chapter. Also, the parturient, since she is likened to the menstruant (Lev. 12:2), can logically be assumed to require purifications by spring water as well. However, as Milgrom is well aware, this was not the understanding of the Rabbis, for whom the immersion pool of 40 seahs of water sufficed for the purification of the menstruant and the parturient (m. Zab. 5; m. Nid. 4:3; m. Miq. 8:1). The zāb and the zābâ, by contrast, could only be purified by water as it was flowing from its source.

> detached from the ground, so anything which is detached from the ground [imparts susceptibility to uncleanness]. I thereby include water which one drew [with a utensil used] for kneading and for rinsing utensils, which is detached from the ground. And I thereby exclude water which is in cisterns, pits, and caves, which is not detached from the ground" (Sifra Shem. Sher. par. 8:2).

This passage from the Sifra leads us to examine another curiosity: the notion that drawn water is invalid for immersion. Although drawn water can be added to the 40 seahs [= ca. 500 litres] required for the miqveh, it cannot make up more than three logs [= .9 litres] of the principal amount:[24]

> Two weavers came from the dung gate in Jerusalem and gave testimony in the name of Shemaiah and Abtalion: "Three logs [= 36 qabs] of drawn water invalidate an immersion pool." And sages confirmed their report (m. Ed. 1:3; cf. m. Miq. 4:4).

Nevertheless, the question remains, what is the difference between the quality of water which is drawn by a vessel and water which is in a cistern? Why is one subject to impurity and the other not? The answer lies in the manner in which the cistern or vessel is filled with water. The contaminated vessel of Lev. 11:34 was clearly filled by humans, whereas the spring or cistern of Lev. 11:36 was provided directly by Heaven.

This is the reason an immersion pool is invalidated if filled with water drawn from a vessel: it must be filled directly by a source of water, for example, by falling rain or by water channeled through a conduit from a spring. There can be no use of extraneous vessels to separate water from its source to create pools for immersion.

The Sifra confirms that only water directly in contact with its source is insusceptible to impurity and can function as a purification agent, even for impure water:

---

24 "Weights and Measures," *EJ*, XVI, 380, 387-88; E. Netzer, "Ritual Baths in Jericho," *Jerusalem Cathedra* 2 (1982) 107, but other estimates range from 250-1000 litres, cf. "Mikveh" in *EJ*, XI, 1536; cf. also S. Rattray, "The Biblical Measures of Capacity" in Milgrom, *Leviticus*, I, 900.

> Just as...water, which returns to its source to become clean, imparts susceptibility to uncleanness to seeds... (Sifra Shem. Sher. 11:7).

> Just as a spring is made by nature (lit. "by the hands of Heaven"), so an immersion-pool is to be made by nature. If you then wish to add, "Just as a spring does not involve human agency, so an immersion-pool should not involve human agency...," Scripture says, "cistern" (Sifra Shem. Sher. par. 9:1).

The rationale is clear: only water given directly by Heaven can purify. Human intervention will neutralize this purifying power. Thus, it is allowed for humans to make the cisterns, but only Heaven can fill them.

In a forthcoming article entitled, "Two Biblical Hebrew Priestly Terms: šeqeṣ and ṭāmēʾ," Milgrom discusses the origins of the priestly view that only water from its source is insusceptible to impurity.[25] In his analysis of the two terms for impure animals, šeqeṣ and ṭāmēʾ, Milgrom discovers that the former, reserved for fish and fowl in Leviticus 11, denotes less contamination than the latter. The sea creatures designated unclean in Leviticus 11 only convey uncleanness to those who eat them (Lev. 11:9-23). Milgrom claims that the reason for this lesser impurity is because fish and fowl originate from the waters (Gen. 1:20) in the priestly account of creation, and water from its source according to the Priestly Code is not subject to impurity but is rather an agent of purification (Lev. 11:32, 36).

In any case, the Rabbis of the Mishna certainly interpreted the Torah in this manner, for they regard the sea and its creatures and fowl free from impurity by touch. Utensils from the hides of sea creatures are pure (m. Kel. 17:13; m. Neg. 11:1). The Sifra points out that the hides of sea creatures are insusceptible to impurity because ʿôr in Lev. 11:32 (which provides a list of items susceptible to impurity) refers only to the hides of land animals (Sifra Shem. Sher. par. 6:9-10; cf. also m. Miq. 6:7). According to Milgrom, the Mishna regards those who eat shrimp, a forbidden food, a minor threat to the sanctuary as

---

25 J. Milgrom, "Two Biblical Hebrew Priestly Terms: šeqeṣ and ṭāmēʾ" in S. Gevirtz Memorial Volume, forthcoming.

compared to those who eat pork.[26] The Mishna states clearly that the carcasses of unclean fowl (unlike those of swine) do not contaminate persons except by ingestion (m. Toh. 1:1; m. Zab. 5:9).

The Rabbis do appear to notice the presence of these ideas in the priestly account of creation: 1) the notion that water from its source does not defile and, therefore, 2) creatures who live or originate in such water are pure. The Mishna states:

> Everything created on Days One, Three and Six are subject to uncleanness but in the items created on Days Two [water division], Four [heavenly bodies] and Five [fish and fowl] no uncleanness inheres (m. Kel. 17:14).

Archaeological work supports the notion that only water channelled directly from its source can fill a valid miqveh. Sanders has surveyed the extant findings on immersion pools and concludes that three types of miqvāʾôt existed in the first century.[27] First, there were pools built below the level of a spring and fed by an aqueduct, for example, the Hasmonean and Herodian palaces at Jericho. Second, some miqvāʾôt were connected by pipe to a second, unstepped pool. If it was necessary to add water to the miqveh, one could add drawn water if it was mixed with some undrawn water of the reservoir pool. The latter water purified the former. Sanders refers to the Mishna:

> They clean immersion pools: a higher pool by the lower pool, and a distant by a nearby [pool]. How so? One brings a pipe of earthenware or lead, and puts his hand under it until it is filled with water, and draws it along and makes it touch. Even by as much as a hair's breadth suffices. [If] the upper one contains forty seahs [of fit water], and in the lower pool there is nothing—one draws [water and carries it] on the shoulder and puts it into the upper one, until there will descend into the lower one forty seahs (m. Miq. 6:8).

---

26 Ibid.

27 Sanders, 218-219.

Third, there were single miqvāʾôt unconnected to either a storage pool or a source of running water. Although these miqvāʾôt are numerous in the Upper City of Jerusalem, they would have been considered invalid by the authors of the Mishna. Sanders suggests that the wealthy residents of the Upper City, in opposition to Pharisaic rules, merely had their servants empty and refill these pools as needed.[28] Thus, difficulties aside, the understanding of the Mishna, and probably the early Pharisees, was that only water which has come directly from its natural source without first being drawn into vessels is valid for purification.

Finally, the issue of size must be addressed. Why does the miqveh have to hold a certain capacity? Again the answer is derived from Scripture. The Torah states in connection with the man who has had an emission of semen that he must bathe his whole body:

> And if a man has an emission of semen, he shall bathe his whole body in water, and be unclean until the evening (Lev. 15:16).

The Rabbis prescribe a quantity of water for the miqveh which will, in fact, cover the whole body of one immersing in it:

> "...he shall bathe his whole body in water": even in the water of an immersion pool [and not necessarily in running water]. "...he shall bathe his whole body in water": it must be water of sufficient volume to cover his whole body. And how much is that volume? A cubit by a cubit by three cubits, so you turn out to give the requisite volume water of an immersion pool at forty seahs (Sifra Mes. Zab. 6:3).

Because of their constant concern of transgressing Scriptural commands, the Sages do not leave the possibility of insufficient water open for question; they define the amount. If there is any doubt as to whether or not a biblically impure person has immersed, or if sufficient water was used, the individual is

28 Ibid., 220.

considered unclean, since this is a doubt about a biblical command (m. Miq. 2:1).

In addition, the yaḥad interpreted Scripture similarly to the Rabbis with regard to the immersion pool. Many such pools dating back to the Second Temple period have been found at Qumran as well as in other parts of Israel.[29] The Damascus Covenant is clear that the pool must contain enough water to cover the person:

> No man shall bathe in dirty water or in an amount too shallow to cover a man. He shall not purify himself with water contained in a vessel. And as for the water of every rock pool too shallow to cover a man, if an unclean man touches it, he renders its water as unclean as water contained in a vessel (CD 10:11-13).

This passage also supports the rabbinic notion that water drawn by a utensil is invalid. The Mishna states that this was already assumed by Hillel and Shammai (m. Eduy. 1:3). Hence, the immersion pool is not a rabbinic innovation; the Rabbis merely limit the definition of such so as not to transgress Scriptural commands.

In summary, the foregoing investigation of the rabbinic laws of immersion revealed biblical roots at every turn. First, assuming that the biblical laws comprise a system, I reiterate the claim that ablutions are required by Scripture after every impurity. Following, not initiating, this system, the Rabbis support the laws of immersion as shown above. The theory that these laws are implicit, if not explicit, already in Scripture is supported by the Dead Sea Scrolls.

Secondly, I examined the concept of ṭĕbûl yôm to see if it was purely a rabbinic invention and found that the notion of ablutions effective before sunset is in fact in Scripture. Prime examples of this are the cases of the mĕṣōrāʿ, the zāb, and those contaminated in the Yom Kippur rites, all of which shed a certain layer of impurity after ablutions but before sunset. Although not required to immerse, the zāb may touch profane persons/objects

29 Ibid., 214 n. 28, 217.

only if he first washes his hands; this, too, supports the effectiveness of ordinary water without sunset. Also, I noted that the capacity of ordinary water to purify is reflected at Qumran and I concluded that both the Rabbis and the sectarians must have derived this from Scripture.

Finally, I discussed the origin of the miqveh and concluded that, although it has been defined and restricted by the Rabbis, this too rests on Scriptural foundations. The Mishna's careful definitions are based on Scriptural principles such as the insusceptibility of water in a spring or cistern and the need to cover the whole body with water for proper purification. Again these requirements are reflected at Qumran.

I conclude that the Rabbis of Mishna-Tosefta were not interested in revamping Scripture or reversing its principles. They were rather reading the text as a workable system, one that had worked and which they hoped would be in effect again in the future.

The Bible is clear that severe sanctions apply if impurity is allowed to enter the realm of the sacred, hence, purification rites had to be followed. The Rabbis also designate as impure items which were doubtfully clean according to Scripture, and they developed a large corpus of regulations which created a "hedge" protecting the biblical commands. The rabbinic regulations with regard to immersion do not contradict biblical principles, rather, they were established to support them.

Thus, in an effort to create a more completely defined system, the Rabbis do extend Scripture's principles and thereby add many supporting rules. However, when one realizes that the authors of the Mishna were late second century sages who were concerned to reconstruct the cultic system from a text they considered sacred, there is simply no basis, at least from the laws of immersion, for the claim that they were interested in introducing new principles unfounded on or contrary to the biblical text.

CHAPTER 4

CORPSE IMPURITY

A major fallacy in the method of examination of mishnaic thought particularly on the subject of ritual purity has been the isolation of the Sages from their biblical roots. The presence of a system in the biblical laws and the fact that the Rabbis inherited that system is necessary for correct interpretation of their writings. In this chapter I will focus on those biblical rules regarding corpse impurity and related sacrificial laws to see what the Rabbis innovated in this regard and what was simply part of the system they inherited.

To state my conclusions in advance, 1) much of what scholars label rabbinic innovation is inherent in the biblical text; 2) the Rabbis meticulously define biblical principles regarding corpse impurity but they do not reverse biblical law; and 3) biblical sanctions create the necessity to carefully define corpse impurity.

In order to clarify the task ahead, I will begin by describing generally Mishna Tractates Ohalot and Para which focus on corpse impurity. The former includes hair-splitting definitions of corpse matter, "tents," and graveyards. The example below is typical:

> [After agreeing that a bone the size of a barleycorn contaminates by contact the sages debate as follows:] A bone the size of a barleycorn which was divided into two [parts] - R. Aqiba declares unclean. And R. Yohanan b. Nuri declares clean. Said R. Yohanan b. Nuri, "They spoke not of *bones* the size of a barleycorn but a *bone* the size of a barleycorn." ...A quarter-kab of crushed bones in any one of which there is not a bone the size of a barleycorn - R. Simeon declares clean. And sages declare unclean (m. Oh. 2:7).

The large part of Ohalot is interested in the matter of "tents," containers housing corpse matter. Based on Num. 19:11 in which a person dead in a tent contaminates everything inside it, the Sages define "tent" as any container of corpse matter. They establish what can prevent corpse contamination in a tent (e.g., sealed vessels) and what can transfer it (e.g., a hole, another tent). The difficult question is: To what extent are the Rabbis stating obvious deductions from the text or even actual Second Temple practice and what is innovation?

Tractate Para presents a detailed description of the rite of the red cow which was burnt to create purification ashes for the corpse-contaminated. As in Ohalot, the laws of corpse impurity are explicitly defined.

J. Neusner suggests that Para is an example of the Rabbis formulating principles of their own agenda from the biblical text. Once firmly rooted in Scripture these principles could easily apply to other areas of life. Is this the case with Para?

What can be said about the plethora of laws and discussions in Ohalot and Para? There is no doubt that the Rabbis have extended the simple meaning of the text, but to what extent? and why? If one regards the biblical laws of corpse impurity as comprising a system, it becomes clear that much of what scholars have labelled extension or innovation is inherent in the biblical text, the Sages' inherited tradition. In this chapter I will evaluate some of the claims made by E. P. Sanders and J. Neusner that the

Rabbis are diverging from Scriptural principles either by unwarranted extensions or by outright contradiction.

There is no question that the corpse is the most potent source of impurity in the biblical worldview. One is contaminated by coming into contact with not only the corpse but the corpse-contaminated person/object. In what follows I will examine the contamination power of a corpse with relation to the sanctuary, the priests, laity, and objects. Afterwards, I will discuss the procedure for purification.

The sanctuary in the biblical view is the most holy place in the community for the presence of God abides there. Hence, it is the place in the land most vulnerable to impurity. In the case of corpse contamination, the sanctuary is polluted only if the specified purification rite is not observed.[1] Otherwise, no sacrifice is required.

The personnel connected to the sanctuary must maintain a higher level of purity than ordinary Israelites. The high priest cannot have any contact with death; he is not even allowed to bury his parents. All other priests can attend the burial of immediate relatives only (i.e., those listed in Lev. 21:2-3), although they will be polluted and have to undergo purification rituals.

All Israelites incur a seven-day contamination after touching even a bone of a corpse (Num. 19:11, 16, 18). A person who enters a tent which overhangs a corpse automatically contracts a seven-day impurity, even though he or she does not touch the dead (Num. 19:14).

The practical consequences of this type of impurity are as follows. Such a person is barred from all sacred areas and objects including sacrificial food. If impure at the time of Passover, the individual must wait one month and eat the sacrifice in a pure condition (Num. 9:10-11). Any person or object touching the corpse-contaminated person also becomes unclean, but only for one day.

---

1 Num. 19:13; J. Milgrom, "Israel's Sanctuary: the Priestly Picture of Dorian Gray," *RB* 83 (1976) 390-99.

Although the Torah provides no examples of persons banished from the community for seven days after burying someone, Numbers 5 does exclude the corpse-contaminated from the camp. Scholars have offered various explanations for this seeming incongruence. J. Milgrom detects two traditions at work: 1) P1, a strand of the Priestly Code, allows the corpse-contaminated to remain at home. Milgrom points us to Num. 19:18 where the defiled person is undergoing purification "there" at home; and 2) another tradition excludes the corpse-contaminated individual from the community entirely. Along with the general exclusion in Num. 5, Chapter 31 insists that all contaminated soldiers be purified outside of the war camp (Num. 31:19, 24). Milgrom identifies these traditions as either P2, an older strand of the Priestly Code, or as H, the Holiness Code.[2]

D. P. Wright, while recognizing the different attitudes in the text, explains that they apply to different situations. He says the strict view of Num. 5 and 31 reflects the "wilderness camp ideal" when Israel is a transitory group; the more lenient view applies to Israel's sedentary situation in the Land of Canaan.[3]

Wright describes the wilderness camp as "a hybrid cross of a regular community and a war camp."[4] The military was required to keep a strict purity code. In the tents of the troops, separated from the congregation for an upcoming battle, a high level of purity had to be maintained because God himself led the battle and resided in the camp (Dt. 23:14). Human excrement had to be buried outside the military camp (Dt. 23:12-13). A soldier who had had a nocturnal emission had to purify himself (Dt. 23:10-11). Sexual intercourse disqualified a soldier from serving unless he purified himself (1 Sam. 21:4-7; 2 Sam. 11:11).[5]

---

2 J. Milgrom, *Leviticus*, I, 997-99.

3 D. P. Wright, "Purification from Corpse Contamination in Numbers xxxi, 19-24," *VT* 35 (1985) 215; idem, *The Disposal of Impurity*, 171.

4 Wright, *Disposal*, 171.

5 David is allowed to take the holy bread because he and his men are sanctified for a holy mission, Wright, *Disposal*, 171. Cf. also "War, Ideas of" in *IDB*, ed. E. S. Burke, IV, 803; G. von Rad, *Der Heilige Krieg*.

The wilderness camp is not the same as the war camp because the laws of Numbers 5 and 31 exclude only a few impurity bearers: the mĕṣōrāʿ, the corpse-contaminated person, and those with abnormal flows. Additionally, the text addresses both men and women (Num. 5:2).

Nevertheless, the wilderness camp was required to keep a stronger connection to the sanctuary than the regular community settled in all parts of Canaan. A comparison of Leviticus 17 and Deuteronomy 12 reveals this difference. In the wilderness all animals which could be sacrificed had to be offered first on the altar, and then they could be taken home and eaten (Lev. 17:3-4). However, after occupying the land of Canaan, Israelites merely drained the blood of edible animals, and then they were allowed to eat them. The animals did not have to be brought to the sanctuary (Dt. 12:21-24).

Since the laws of Numbers 5 and 31 appear in the context of the wilderness experience (Numbers 5 appears in the text right after a long description of the arrangement of the camp of the Israelites in the wilderness; Numbers 31 also describes an episode in the wilderness), one can assume that the banishment of the corpse-contaminated applied to all persons only in this time period. Numbers 19 reflects either a later time period when the Israelites had settled in the Land of Canaan (Wright) or a different tradition entirely (Milgrom).

Objects too are subject to contamination by contact with death. Any vessel which touches a corpse or is in a tent containing a corpse becomes impure. If it is made of clay, it must be broken unless it is sealed. Objects made of other materials are unclean for seven days and must undergo purification rites (see below). This distinction may be based on the porous nature of earthenware which might absorb some impurity which water could not expunge.[6] A curious distinction applies to a vessel within a tent housing a corpse. If it has a lid, its contents remains clean (Num. 19:18) although the vessel itself apparently must be purified like everything else inside such a tent (Num. 19:18).

---

6 G. B. Gray, *Numbers*, ICC, 40.

The Book of Numbers outlines a specific ritual which is necessary to purify those contaminated by a corpse. A mixture of special ashes and spring water (mayim ḥayyîm; cf. Dt. 6:1, not stored or drawn) is sprinkled on the polluted person/object on the third and seventh days of uncleanness (Num. 19:18-19). Corpse-contaminated individuals must bathe and launder their clothes at the end of the seven days (Num. 19:19).[7]

These ashes are obtained by the slaughter and sacrifice of an unblemished red cow outside the camp. The priest sprinkles some of its blood toward the tabernacle seven times and then burns the animal completely. Next, cedarwood, hyssop, and scarlet wool are thrown into the conflagration. The ashes are then collected and deposited in a clean place outside the camp. It is of note that the priest who threw the cedarwood, hyssop, and wool onto the burning cow, the person who burned the cow, and the one who collected the ash must all bathe and launder their clothes before reentering the camp (Num. 19:21).[8] After some of the ashes have been mixed with fresh water, any clean person may sprinkle the mixture on corpse-contaminated persons or objects using a sprig of hyssop. This person will be required to bathe and launder as well. An individual who merely touched but did not sprinkle the water of purgation must bathe but need not launder (Num. 19:21).

Objects too are apparently sprinkled with the special ash/water mixture on the third and seventh days of their uncleanness. Numbers 19 refers to the sprinkling of everything within the tent of the corpse. Chapter 31 adds that all vessels which can withstand it must be purified by fire as well (Num. 31:23).[9] This passage is interested primarily in purification after

---

7 Wright, "Purification," 219 n. 18.

8 It is true, nevertheless, that not all persons involved in the rite are contaminated. The red cow is potent only after it is burnt. Thus, neither the one who slaughters it nor the priest who consecrates the blood by sprinkling it toward the sanctuary are made unclean, J. Milgrom, "The Paradox of the Red Cow (Num. XIX)," *VT* 31 (1981) 67.

9 Num. 19:22; D. J. Wold, "The Kareth Penalty in P: Rationale and Cases," *SBL Seminar Papers*, 16 (1979) 1-45.

battle and the resulting contact with the slain. Soldiers must remain outside the camp for seven days and then be purified with their captives on Days 3 and 7.

The text gives further instructions concerning objects. All which cannot go through the fire must be passed through water (**heʿevîr bammayim**) (Num. 31:23). This water is not the special purgation water since this is not a sprinkling but an immersion ritual.[10] It appears that **bammayim** parallels **baʾēš** as a generic term.[11] D. Wright notes that this immersion ritual for corpse-contaminated objects corresponds to the bathing a corpse-contaminated person does at the end of his seven-day impurity. The addition of fire into the purification for corpse-contaminated objects accords with the status of corpse impurity: the most potent of all impurities requires fire, the most intense purifier.[12]

In comparing Figure 1 below by D. P. Wright with my diagram in Figure 2, one can see the differences in contamination according to the priestly and rabbinic systems.[13] The comparison might be somewhat misleading because it seems that the Rabbis have extended corpse impurity several removes beyond the original priestly intention. However, one should remember that the Rabbis regard only certain items to even be susceptible to impurity and some are only susceptible in certain degrees, therefore the chart represents a reduction rather than an extension of the potency of the corpse-contaminated. (See Introduction for further information on susceptible items and degrees in the rabbinic system.) By contrast, the Bible explicitly states that all objects can be affected (Lev. 11:35).

The chart diagramming the rabbinic view (Fig. 2) assumes certain hermeneutical principles which are peculiar to corpse impurity. Since the Bible is clear that both the corpse and the corpse-contaminated individual defile persons and objects (Num. 19:14), the Rabbis consider both to be **ʾabôt ṭumʾâ**. However, since

---

10 Wright, "Purification," 219; Gray, 423.

11 For references regarding the assumption of Num. 19 in Num. 31, cf. Wright, "Purification," 214 and references cited there in note 4.

12 Wright, "Purification," 214 n 3.

13 Wright, *Disposal*, 197.

FIG. 1 THE CONTAMINATION OF THE CORPSE IN THE BIBLICAL SYSTEM

(Copied from D. P. Wright, *The Disposal of Impurity*, 197)

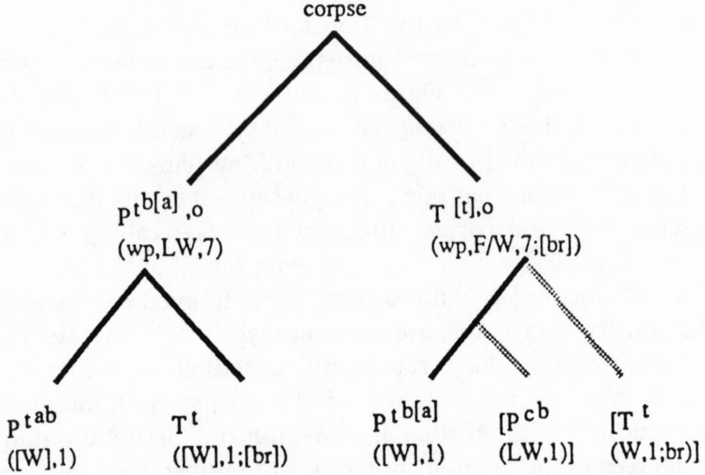

FIG. 2 THE CONTAMINATION OF THE CORPSE IN THE RABBINIC SYSTEM

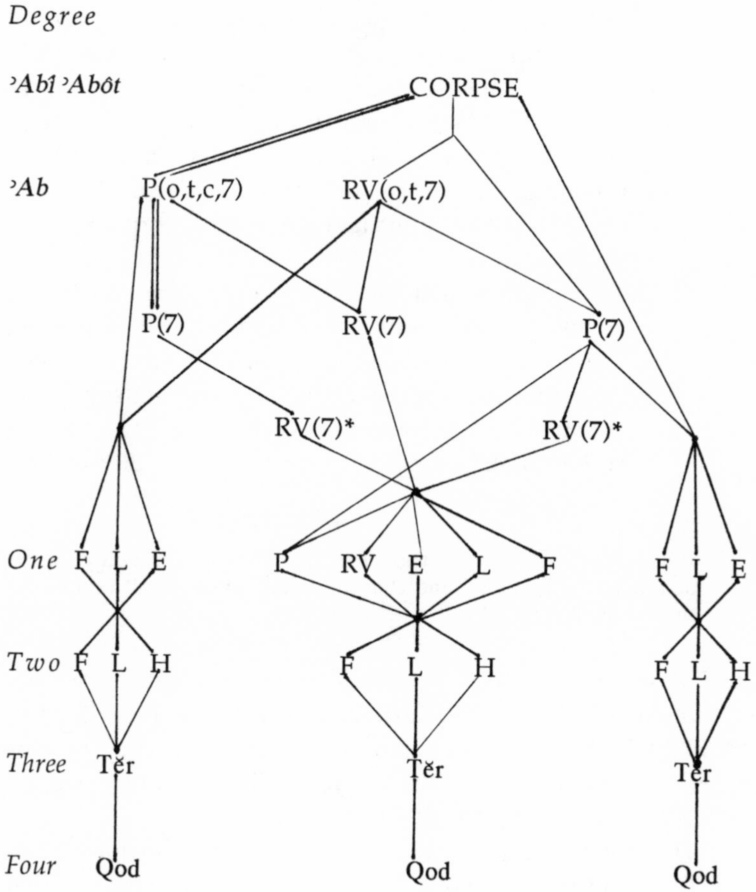

References:
Branch 1: b. AZ 37b; b. Naz. 42b, 49b; cf. m. Zab. 5:10
Branch 2: m. Oh. 1:1-3; b. Shab. 17a; b. BK 2ab; b. Pes. 14a
Branch 3: Num. 19:14-18

* The Palestinian Talmud does not ascribe this extra level of potency to the corpse-contaminated person (y. Naz. 7:4).

the corpse is the source of the impurity of these ʾabôt ṭumʾâ, it must be regarded at a more intense level of impurity. Hence, it is called ʾabî ʾabôt ṭumʾâ, the Father of Fathers of Impurity.

Since the Torah uses the participle nōgēaʿ to describe the contact between a pure person and one who is contaminated by a corpse (Num. 19:22), some Rabbis of the Talmud suggest that the reference is to contact which occurs at the same time the corpse-contaminated is in contact with the corpse. In this case the individual touching the corpse-contaminated person becomes unclean seven days as if he or she had touched the corpse itself (b. Naz. 42b; b. AZ 37b).

Rinsable vessels which touch the corpse are considered contaminating like the corpse itself and will infect both persons and other rinsable vessels with seven-day uncleanness. (Earthenware cannot become ʾabôt ṭumʾâ or contract seven-day uncleanness; it must be broken when it becomes unclean.) This is derived from the Torah by analogy with the sword of Numbers 19:

> Whoever in the open field touches one who is slain with a sword, or a dead body, or a bone of a man, or a grave, shall be unclean seven days (Num. 19:16).

The Rabbis understand this verse to signify that the sword has the same degree of impurity as the slain person (b. Hul. 2b-3a; b. Pes. 14ab), because the mention of the sword would otherwise be superfluous. Why mention the sword at all if it is not to signify that it has a special impurity status?

This must be the logic behind the Mishna in Ohalot 1:1-3 as well. There the Mishna explains that the corpse is so impure that it can transmit impurity to several removes away from itself. The corpse contaminates to two degrees removed from itself (persons touching it and vessels which they touch) and to three removes (vessels touching it and persons touching those vessels and then other vessels which the persons touch). The Mishna goes on to state that the corpse can contaminate even to four degrees away from itself:

> Four are unclean through a corpse. Three are unclean with the uncleanness of seven [days], and one is unclean with the uncleanness [that passes at] evening.... Utensils which touch the corpse, and a man [who touches] utensils, and utensils [which touch] man are unclean with the uncleanness of seven [days]. The fourth, whether man or utensils, is unclean with the uncleanness that passes in the evening.

This passage reveals that utensils are even more vulnerable to corpse impurity than people because they can transmit impurity to further degrees than humans can.

The Sifra reveals that these conclusions of the Mishna are the direct results of exegesis of Scripture:

> "And everything that the unclean person touches becomes unclean" [Num. 19:22]. Why? This is said because it [Scripture] says, "[touches] the slain with a sword" [Num. 19:16]. So the Scripture comes to teach about the sword that it is unclean with seven-day uncleanness and the one who is touching it is unclean with seven-day uncleanness. So we learn about vessels and man. But where do we learn about [contamination from the corpse to] vessels to man to [other] vessels? Scripture teaches, "You will wash your clothes" (Num. 31:24). So we learn about [contamination from the corpse to] vessels to man to [other] vessels. You may say, "Where do we learn about [contamination from the corpse to] vessels to [other] vessels?" It is an *a fortiori* argument: Just as vessels in contact with a person who is touching [other] vessels in contact with the dead are unclean, vessels in contact with [other] vessels which are in contact with the dead should logically be unclean. You may say, "How do we know [the corpse can contaminate] vessels [to contaminate] man?" It is an *a fortiori* argument: If vessels in contact with a person who is touching [other] vessels in contact with the dead are unclean, vessels in contact with the person who is touching the dead should logically be unclean. Or you may say, "How can a man receive uncleanness from the dead to contaminate his fellowman with seven-day uncleanness?" It is an argument *a fortiori* : Just as vessels that do not contaminate on top of a bed or chair, but they receive uncleanness from the dead to contaminate persons with seven-day uncleanness, is it not logical that a person that does contaminate on top of a bed or chair would receive uncleanness from the dead to contaminate his fellowman with seven-day uncleanness? The Scripture says, "The person who is touching the corpse-contaminated will become unclean until evening." He is defiled with every uncleanness and does not

> receive uncleanness from the dead to contaminate his fellowman with seven-day uncleanness (Sif. Num. 130[168]).

The Sifra accepts all but this last proposition (that persons who have touched a corpse can make other persons unclean with seven-day uncleanness) as a correct understanding of Scripture. The extra contamination of vessels in contact with a corpse is clearly derived from the sword of Numbers 19:16.

Thus, the sword which has slain a human being takes on the same degree of defilement as the corpse. Likewise, all metal vessels which come into contact with the corpse take on the same degree of contamination as the corpse. Hence, persons and objects which touch them will become unclean seven days as if they had touched the corpse itself. The Babylonian Talmud explains further:

> For the Divine Law said, "...one that is slain by the sword," intimating, the sword is as the slain; hence it is a principal defilement (b. Pes. 14ab).

As the Mishna and Sifra state, all susceptible vessels (except earthenware) which touch the corpse-contaminated person become unclean for seven days. This notion is derived from Scripture which ascribes a seven-day uncleanness to both corpse-contaminated persons and their clothing:

> You must wash your clothes on the seventh day, and you shall be clean; and afterward you shall come into the camp (Num. 31:24).

All items contaminated with seven-day uncleanness can impart impurity to all susceptible items to the first degree. Further transmission will only affect food, liquids, hands, and sancta.[14]

---

14 Maimonides states that these degrees of impurity for rinsable vessels are in effect only with regard to tĕrûmâ and qodōšîm, but that normally only the one who is made unclean directly by the corpse (via touch, carriage, or overhang) or the corpse-contaminated (by touch) is impure, *Code*, X, corpse 5:5. Nevertheless, neither the Mishna nor the Babylonian Talmud references quoted above make any such distinction. Maimonides is following the Palestinian Talmud (y. Naz. 7:4).

Although he realizes that clarification of the biblical passages is in order, E. P. Sanders lists four areas in which the Sages have extended Scripture beyond its bounds, in his words: "to discussion of situations not envisaged in the Bible at all."[15]

1. Corpse impurity can escape through a hole (m. Oh. 13:1, 4; 15:8; t. Oh. 14:4).

2. All entrances are impure unless there was intention to carry the corpse out through one of them, in which case only that entrance is impure (m. Oh. 7:3; t. Oh. 8:7).

3. People should not walk over ground containing corpse matter; examination of the ground is necessary (m. Oh. 18:1-2, 6; t. Oh. 16:6).

4. Whatever overshadows a corpse is impure and whatever the corpse overshadows is impure (m. Oh. 3:1; 6:1; 11:4-6; t. Oh. 5:5).

While it is obvious that the Mishna has extended the biblical material beyond the pĕšaṭ of the text, it is also the case that a careful, systemic reading of the text provides the basis for much that has been considered rabbinic innovation by modern scholars.

Let us examine the list above: With reference to No. 1 the Bible does assume that impurity in general can travel through the air. In the words of J. Milgrom, "For both Israel and her neighbors impurity was a physical substance, an aerial miasma which possessed magnetic attraction for the realm of the sacred."[16] Milgrom cites several examples of impurities which pollute the sanctuary even though the impurity bearer does not enter the sacred precincts:

> [The Molech worshipper:] I myself [the LORD] will set my face against that man...because he has given one of his children to Molech, defiling my sanctuary and profaning my holy name (Lev. 20:3).
>
> [Those with flows:] Thus [by purification as commanded throughout Leviticus 15] you shall keep the people of Israel

---

15 E. P. Sanders, *Jewish Law from Jesus to the Mishnah,* 186.

16 Milgrom, "Israel's Sanctuary," 392.

> separate from their uncleanness, lest they die in their uncleanness by defiling my tabernacle that is in their midst (Lev. 15:31).

As Milgrom notes, the Israelite is forbidden access to the altar, shrine, and adytum. Thus, the impurity has polluted the sanctuary from afar; it has travelled through the air.[17] Milgrom presents a graduated list of impurity effects on the sanctuary. Inadvertent misdemeanors of an individual contaminate the altar (Lev. 4:25; 9:9-14). Inadvertent misdemeanors of the high priest or the whole community contaminate the shrine (Lev. 4:5-7, 16-18, 25). Intentional misdemeanors penetrate even into the adytum (Num. 15:27-31; cf. Isa. 37:16).[18]

A third example is even more appropriate for this discussion of corpse impurity. The corpse-contaminated person who does not purify pollutes the sanctuary:

> Whoever touches a dead person, the body of any man who has died, and does not cleanse himself, defiles the tabernacle of the LORD, and that person shall be cut off from Israel...(Num. 19:13).

Another example of the travel of corpse impurity is found in regard to the house of the dead. Impurity travels from the corpse to other persons in the room without direct contact, merely via the overhang of the ceiling (Num. 19:14). The same holds true for the house affected with ṣāraʿat (Lev. 14: 36, 46).

Finally, the particular notion that corpse impurity can escape from or fill a container, be it a house or a vessel, is clearly implied in Num. 19:14-15. In a corpse-contaminated house only vessels which have lids on them will protect their contents. The reason is obvious: corpse impurity will not be able to penetrate the vessel. If it is unsealed, the corpse impurity in the house will fill it.

J. Neusner describes the rabbinic notion of uncleanness as follows:

---

17 Ibid., 394.

18 Ibid., 393.

> The conception of uncleanness seems to involve a kind of invisible, dense, and heavy gaseous substance, which will flow out of the specified substances if not contained by a barrier of some sort, but which, if contained by a wall, will then not evaporate upward.[19]

This definition would have been endorsed by the priests of Leviticus and Numbers. Although the Rabbis consider corpse-impure persons dangerous to the sanctuary only if they physically enter it, one can see that their general concept of uncleanness as a penetrating gas rests on biblical premises.

The Rabbis understand corpse impurity to escape through holes only because the aerial character of this and other severe impurities 1) has already been established in Scripture and 2) represents the basic understanding of impurity dynamics held by most people of that day.[20] However, they introduce a limiting aspect. Corpse impurity is nowhere in rabbinic literature said to affect the sanctuary from afar and its aerial quality is in fact limited to vertical motion. Mishna-Tosefta confirms this claim:

> The uncleanness is in the wall [corpse matter is in the wall of a house], and its place is a cubic handbreadth—all the upper rooms which are on top of it are clean. A second wall [corpse matter is in another wall]—uncleanness breaks forth and ascends, breaks forth and descends. [Corpse matter is in or under] a solid tomb monument—he who touches it from the sides is clean, because the uncleanness breaks forth and ascends, breaks forth and descends. If the place of the uncleanness was a cubic handbreadth, he that touches it in any place is unclean, because it is like a sealed grave (m. Oh. 7:1, bracketed comments mine; cf. also t. Oh. 5:5; 6:2).

---

19 J. Neusner, *History of the Mishnaic Law of Purities*, I, 47.

20 Cf. R. Parker, *Miasma*. Especially instructive is Parker's chapter on birth and death, 32-73. Immediately at death, the corpse's impurity fills the house, requiring those in it to bathe. This impurity traveled even into the water supply requiring the residents to fetch water from elsewhere. If death occurred in a public area, all those in the vicinity would be affected by the impurity. Parker states that impurity was believed to spread even along family ties, contaminating relatives which were miles away from the corpse, cf. esp. 35, 38-40.

According to this passage, if a person touches the side of something which has corpse matter under it, for example, a monument on a tomb, he or she remains pure. However, people who walk over a coffin will become impure, because they will cross paths with corpse impurity as it spurts upward and downward, but not sideways, from the corpse.

No. 2 on Sanders' list introduces the element of intention into the situation at No. 1. Sanders, following Neusner, insists that intention does not play a part in the biblical laws of purity, and that it is a new principle created by the Rabbis: "The idea of human intention, greatly and correctly emphasized by Neusner, is original to the Pharisees as far as we know."[21] This cannot be the case.

Neusner states that Jewish law is "radically revised" by certain conceptions including the notion of human intention in the period after 70 C.E.[22] He makes it very clear that this advent is not due to the destruction of the Temple which certainly collapsed the cult and disillusioned many people. Rather, the rise of human intention was due, in Neusner's opinion, to the logical outgrowth of the laws the Sages had already developed by that time.[23]

Neusner claims that the great emphasis of many of the tractates of the Order of Tohorot on human intention is a reaction to the prior notion that purification must be brought about by natural means. He says the logic unfolds as follows: since purification must be done in a natural pool of water unaffected by human agency, contamination can be, by contrast, subject to the human will. Neusner calls this contrastive logic:

> The development at the time of Yavneh of the notion that human intention is essential in the process by which something becomes susceptible to uncleanness is the result of contrastive, as against analogical, thinking.

21 Sanders, 187; Neusner, *Purities*, XXII, 182.

22 Neusner, *Purities*, XXII, 182.

23 Ibid., 188.

Thus, as a reaction against the exclusion of man from the process of purification, the Sages began to develop the notion of human intention as effective in bringing about or in preventing contamination.

Supporting his case, Neusner points to Aqiba in the early second century who distinguishes between water which is drawn from a well and water which comes up accidentally, stating that only in the former case can water make items susceptible to uncleanness, i.e., only when it is acted upon deliberately by man. Neusner claims that, in contrast to Scripture, the Mishna wants to know, what can man do?[24]

H. Eilberg-Schwartz follows this line of thinking in his monograph, *The Human Will in Judaism: the Mishnah's Philosophy of Intention*. He insists that the biblical purity and sacrificial laws do not address the notion of intention: "Leviticus does not specify any legal consequences for the mere intention of doing something wrong."[25] The priest does not spoil the rite unless he does something improperly; mere wrong intention is not harmful. In fact, Eilberg-Schwartz says, "The biblical rules of purity do not place any stress at all on human intention."[26]

Eilberg-Schwartz claims that the Mishna does draw from biblical strands to develop its concept of intention but these derive from other parts of the Bible, most notably from the creation stories of Genesis 1 and 2. Just as God classified his creation into distinct categories and commanded Adam to continue the job by naming the animals, so the Mishna emphasizes the continuing opportunity humanity has to classify creation and thereby determine whether or not it is brought into the realm of susceptibility to impurity.[27] Eilberg-Schwartz also notes

---

24 Ibid., 187, 285, 290. In Neusner's view, Paul drops an early hint of the development to come when he says nothing is unclean unless one thinks it is so (Ro. 14:14), cf. J. Neusner, *The Idea of Purity in Ancient Judaism*, 59.

25 H. Eilberg-Schwartz, *The Human Will in Judaism: the Mishnah's Philosophy of Intention*, 224 n 24.

26 Ibid., 101, 173.

27 Ibid., 103.

passages, mostly from the Writings and the Prophets, which emphasize the power of the human will, however as stated above, he emphasizes that the *priestly* writers were only interested in observing proper rites, not in the intention behind the deed.

According to Eilberg-Schwartz, the Bible does know of human intention but sees it usually as a negative trait in people which rebels against God. The Mishna, on the other hand, encourages human will as part of God's plan: humanity should continue to classify and categorize creation, finishing the job God began in the beginning.[28]

There is no question that the Mishna is interested in analyzing the concept of human intention in detail but the Rabbis of Yavneh did not invent the category.[29] The priestly writers, concerned with sacrificial rites and purity codes, do recognize the power of the human will. It does matter what the intention of a person is before committing an action. The priestly writer of Numbers 15:27-31 differentiates between the sinner who has transgressed intentionally and therefore deserves death and the one who has inadvertently transgressed and may bring a sacrifice to be reinstated into the community. Sacrifices are for unintentional transgressions, not for willful violations of the law (Lev. 4:2, 13, 22; 5:18; Num. 5:22-31).[30]

---

28 Ibid., 102.

29 J. Milgrom citing b. BQ 26b, points out that the Rabbis understand their concept of inadvertence to be based on Scripture, *Leviticus*, I, 487.

30 Cf. the encroacher on sancta who is killed because the sin is intentional, cf. J. Milgrom, *Studies in Levitical Terminology*, 20-21; idem, "Sancta Contagion and Altar/City Asylum" *SVT* 32 (1981) 278-310. But cf. Lev. 5:20-27 where one person has dissembled to another in a certain matter, e.g., has stolen or withheld what rightfully belongs to the other. The misdeed is clearly known to the offender who has intentionally transgressed. Yet this offense is allowed to be expiated by a sacrifice. This passage seems to defy the whole system (cf. Num. 15:24-30). Milgrom has explained that this provision for sins requiring restitution is probably instituted in order to encourage the voluntary surrender of illegally acquired goods, *Cult and Conscience*, 124. Arguing from ancient Near East parallels as well as biblical examples, Milgrom argues that the confession of the transgressor is the key which makes sacrifice in ths case effective. In

Perhaps the most obvious example in the Torah of the power of intention is found in the case of homicide. A person who accidentally kills another person may find asylum in a refuge city (Num. 35:22-25). If the act was intentional, however, the murderer must be slain (Ex. 21:12-14; Num. 35:20-21; Dt. 19:1-7).

Further, the matter of consecrating sacred gifts rests on the intention of the donor for the Bible as well as for the Rabbis. Because of the mere intention of the offerer to sanctify the gift, it becomes "most sacred" even before it is brought to the sanctuary. Leviticus 6:18 reads:

> This is the ritual of the purification offering: the purification offering shall be slaughtered before the Lord, at the spot where the burnt offering is slaughtered; it is most sacred (tr. Milgrom).

Thus, the sanctity of the offering begins before it is burnt on the altar, even before it is slaughtered, at the moment the offerer designates it to be sacred.[31]

Another example of profane goods being sanctified by the intention of the owner is found in the matter of setting aside tĕrûmâ, a gift dedicated to the sanctuary. From the time the offerer sets aside a gift to the sanctuary, it becomes sacred. Deuteronomy 26:14 reveals that the tĕrûmâ is called qōdeš even while it is still in the offerer's house. This principle is exemplified by Micah's mother who consecrated her silver by stating her own intention that it be sculptured into an idol (Jud. 17:3). Thus, the intention of the donor expressed orally was enough to ensure the sanctity status of an offering.

The above examples should confirm that the presence or absence of human intention is indeed a deciding factor in the laws of the Torah. That the Rabbis apply this principle to the laws of corpse impurity should come as no surprise.

---

every example of deliberate sin in the Bible, confession is required (Lev. 5:5; 16:21; 26:40; Num. 5: 6-7). Milgrom claims that repentance, confession, and restoration of goods with the 20% penalty retroactively turns these intentional sins into unintentional sins which can be removed by atoning sacrifices.

31 J. Milgrom, *Studies in Cultic Theology and Terminology*, 160-62.

The concern in No. 3 of Sanders' list regarding treading on corpse matter is addressed already in Numbers 19:16, which specifies contact with graves and bones in an open field (not a graveyard) as contaminating for seven days. The question of examining such an area to avoid corpse matter had to have been important already in biblical times.

The final item on Sanders' list concerns overshadowing. Here Sanders fails to see the connection between Numbers 19 and the principle of corpse contamination by overshadowing.[32] Without this connection the Sages could never have extended the definition of overshadowing as they did. Num. 19:14 reads:

> This is the law when a man dies in a tent: every one who comes into the tent, and every one who is in the tent, shall be unclean seven days.

It is because the overshadowing of the tent transfers the impurity of the corpse to everything else under the overhang that those in the room with the corpse become impure. Thus, rabbinic notions of overhang (suggesting that an overhang over corpse matter of even trees, persons, and awnings can convey corpse impurity) are in principle anchored in Scripture.

Another example of overhang impurity in the Bible can be extracted from the case of the mĕṣōrāᶜ. This potent impurity bearer, like the corpse, is excluded from the camp (Num. 5:2). After healing and an initial purification rite, the individual may be re-admitted but only to open areas within the camp—not to his or her tent (Lev. 14:8). The most logical explanation for this is that the mĕṣōrāᶜ will contaminate by means of the overhang of the tent. This interpretation is supported by the example of the house affected by the same disease (ṣāraᶜat). Such a house contaminates everything in it (Lev. 14:36, 46-47). Comparing the red cow rite with the purification rites of the mĕṣōrāᶜ, scholars have demonstrated the similarities between the effects of the corpse and those of the mĕṣōrāᶜ, a sort of living corpse.[33] Thus, although

32 Sanders, 232.

33 Milgrom, *Leviticus*, I, 819.

the material of Leviticus and Numbers does not dictate that the Sages should develop further the particular notion of overhang it does assume this principle.

One other item Sanders designates as a post-biblical innovation is the necessity for handling priestly food in purity (discussed above in Chapter 1). He writes, "...the Pharisees extended the biblical law by deciding they would keep the priests' food from ever contracting corpse-impurity."[34] However, the purity of holy food from harvest is not a rabbinic innovation but a requirement of Deuteronomy 26:14 in which the harvester must swear, when presenting his tithe to the priest, "I have not eaten (of the tithe) while I was mourning, or removed any of it while I was unclean, or offered any of it to the dead...."

With regard to all of the items above I submit that there is firm basis in Scripture for the *principles* and sometimes even the details involved. Instead of a severance from Scripture the Sages show a dependence on it.

The foregoing argument, although intent on uncovering the biblical basis of much of what has been labeled rabbinic extension, is not blind to the fact that the Mishna is not merely a commentary on Leviticus and Numbers. Certainly the Rabbis had their own motives for selecting and expanding the material they did. Purity concerns in Second Temple times and after were a high priority matter.

Groups such as the Essenes and the Pharisees had taken it upon themselves to eat in purity like the priests ate their sacrificial prebends. This was an effort to extend the holiness of the Temple to the secular world in order to be close to God and insulated from pagan influences. The sectarians at Qumran chose to be physically isolated from what they considered a corrupt society. The Pharisees, rather, tried to protect holiness within society.

One can apply Mary Douglas' group and grid structure here. Douglas says that a society's image of itself is mirrored in

---

34 Sanders, 232; cf. 198-199.

its treatment of the physical body.[35] When the group is threatened, it will intensify its purity code. These rules are called the "grid" or classification system of the group. The Pharisees were born out of intense Hellenistic pressure on Judaism; they represent a strong group - a group with strong social pressure on its members, and a strong grid - a well-defined set of purity laws. Douglas presents the Israelites as a persecuted minority carefully maintaining physical purity codes on an individual as well as a societal level:

> The Israelites were always in their history a hard-pressed minority. In their beliefs all the bodily issues were polluting, blood, pus, excreta, semen, etc. The threatened boundaries of their body politic would be well-mirrored in their care for the integrity, unity and purity of the physical body.[36]

If ancient Israel is an example of a group clinging to its purity codes as it experiences outside pressure, the Jews of Hellenistic times are an even more appropriate example.

However, Douglas' sociological explanation is inadequate and even inaccurate. First of all, it is not the case that all flows from the body are impure. No purity laws are prescribed for saliva (except for that of some already impure persons, Lev. 15), sweat, urine, or non-genital blood. Not everything which crosses the body's boundaries is impure and thus the model of body boundaries for those of society is not accurate. Some further explanation is needed.

It would be more correct to state that persecution brought about the Pharisaic emphasis on purity in the manner prescribed by the Torah. The Torah was considered the only effective weapon against Hellenism. The purity rituals of Leviticus and Numbers, not just those which categorically pertain to body boundaries, define the way to holiness. As stated in Scripture,

---

35 M. Douglas, *Purity and Danger*; idem, *Natural Symbols: Explorations in Cosmology*, 82.

36 Douglas, *Purity and Danger*, 124.

observance of these laws ensured God's continued presence among the people and their right to the holy land:

> You shall not defile the land in which you live, in the midst of which I dwell; for I the LORD dwell in the midst of the people of Israel (Num. 35:34).

Only God's presence and his power, activated by the holiness of Israel, would be able to counter the increasing pressure of Hellenistic ideas and customs weakening the purity of Judaism.[37] One might also say that the temptation of participating in the gymnasium and achieving status in the polis, both contingent on accepting pagan practices, had to be countered with tangible, positive efforts confirming and reinforcing the rightness of Judaism over the prevalent idolatry.

It is important to bear in mind that this "quest for holiness," using M. Borg's terms, could only follow guideposts dictated by Scripture. The Bible is insistent that God's people be "holy," meaning "set apart," even as Yahweh himself is set apart. In Leviticus and Numbers specific laws are set in motion which define the holy life. Some Jews would interpret these laws as applying only to the priests; Pharisees intent on insulating Israel from pagan influence by encouraging them to be more holy interpreted many of these laws as applicable to all Israel.

Furthermore, D. Boyarin probes deeper into the Jewish struggle against Hellenism. The impact of Greek allegory on Jewish interpretation of Scripture was monumental. As Hellenists emphasized that true meaning was located in the spiritual realm, some Jews like Philo began interpreting Scripture in a similar way. Indeed, Paul regards the literal understanding of Scripture as superseded by a symbolic interpretation of it which points to and culminates in the advent of Jesus Christ.

Thus, as certain Jews in the Second Temple period emphasized a spiritual/allegorical interpretation of the text over its literal meaning, the Pharisees and their rabbinic successors focused on the physical body of the Jew as the true identifier of

---

37 M. Borg, *Conflict, Holiness and Politics*, 56, 58-59.

God's elect.[38] The purity laws of the body were emphasized because they plainly distinguished Israel from non-Israel and defined Israel as physical and dependent on history and genealogy not on a universal, spiritual idea.

Nevertheless, this emphasis on the body is not according to a sociological norm in which all body orifices must be guarded with restrictive rules corresponding to those imposed on Jewish society in general. Rather, the rules can only be defined according to the sacred text of the Torah.

Thus, although Pharisees emphasized the importance of the purity of physical Jews and included all Israel in this concern, they would not overturn a biblical principle to support their agenda. In this regard I disagree with J. Neusner.

A clear indication that Neusner has over-extended the issue is his analysis of Tractate Para. Neusner claims that the Rabbis reverse the meaning of the biblical red cow rite to fit their agenda of extending holiness to the realm outside of the cult. This claim of reversal is unnecessary. The rabbinic declaration that this rite conducted outside of the Temple is sacred is also the position of Scripture.

The point at issue is this: Neusner says the biblical rite was conducted in a state of impurity and thus contaminated the participants. The paradox is that the ashes of this unclean cow purify the corpse-contaminated. Neusner attributes to the Rabbis the reversal of this "biblical" idea stating that the Mishna knows the rite is profane but twists the text in order to create a holy rite and hence a prime example of what the Rabbis wish to support: cleanness outside of the cult. With regard to the biblical rite Neusner says,

> A rite performed outside of the Temple is by definition not subject to the Temple's rules and is not going to be clean. The priestly

---

38 D. Boyarin, "Behold Israel according to the Flesh," I, 2, 5; "Behold Israel according to the Flesh, II: Death, History and the Erotic Life of God and Israel," 4, 12. Philo is only one example of the many Hellenistic Jews existing in the Second Temple period, D. Winston, "Philo and the Contemplative Life" in *Jewish Spirituality from the Bible through the Middle Ages*, ed. A. Green, 198-231.

> author assumes the rite produces uncleanness, is conducted outside of the realm of cleanness, and therefore does not involve the keeping of the Levitical rules of cleanness required for participation in the Temple cult. By contrast Mishna-Tosefta Parah is chiefly interested in that very matter. An important body of opinion in our tractate demands a degree of cleanness higher than that required for the Temple cult itself.[39]

Let us look at Neusner's proof texts. He lists several including m. Par. 2:3 and 4:1. In each case the Sages insist on a high degree of purity for the red cow rite, but R. Eliezer claims that this is not necessary since the rite is not in the Temple. Neusner claims that R. Eliezer is stating the logical understanding of Scripture, but the Sages wish to intensify the purity required for the rite because they want to see purity in effect outside the Temple and hence in the world of ordinary not just priestly Jews.

Neusner describes the rite as the Sages construct it and points to the fact that none of these men ever saw the actual rite and are therefore constructing it in accordance with how they think it should have been. This turns out to be as much of a replication of sacrifices in the Temple as possible. Neusner interprets: "The rite of the cow is done in the profane world, outside the cult, *as if* it were done in the sacred world constituted by the Temple itself."[40]

A careful examination of the relevant Scriptural passages will reveal whether or not the priestly writers intended the rite to take place in the profane world. J. Milgrom in his article, "The Paradox of the Red Cow," has made it clear that the red cow ritual was a sacrificial rite—a ḥaṭṭāʾt, and as such it had to be conducted in purity. He translates Num. 19:9b:

> [The ash shall be] preserved by the Israelite community for waters of lustration. It is a ḥaṭṭāʾt.

---

39 Neusner, *Purities*, X, 222-223.

40 Ibid., 225.

The ḥaṭṭā't was one of five types of offerings defined in the first seven chapters of Leviticus. Many translate it "sin offering," but this has been proven incorrect.[41] Milgrom, who prefers "purification offering," has pointed out that many of the circumstances requiring ḥaṭṭā't offerings have nothing to do with violations of the law but do in some way involve pollution, e.g., the woman after childbirth (Lev. 12:6) and the occasion of building a new altar (Ex. 29:36f.; Lev. 8:15). Also, from the point of view of grammar, Milgrom argues that the word derives not from the paʿal conjugation meaning "to sin" but from the piʿel meaning "to cleanse, decontaminate."

In any case, Leviticus describes two kinds of ḥaṭṭā't offerings. In one, the blood of the animal is daubed on the sacrificial altar and then the flesh is eaten by the priests (Lev. 6:19). In the second, the blood is daubed on the inner incense altar as well as sprinkled before the veil before the ark; the pollution has penetrated the shrine. This second type is not eaten but burned outside the camp (Lev. 4:11-12, 21). The first type is for purgation on behalf of individuals while the second is for sins of the priests or the congregation as a whole. These are more serious since they endanger the purity of the sanctuary.[42]

Ḥaṭṭā't offerings, which are sacrificed outside the camp must be taken to a clean place (Lev. 4:12). Also, the ḥaṭṭā't contaminates the one who burns it, forcing that person to bathe and launder his clothes (Lev. 16:28). On those occasions on which the ḥaṭṭā't is not burned outside the camp, its flesh makes whatever touches it holy (Lev. 6:20). If this is true for the ḥaṭṭā't for less dangerous impurity, it is certainly true for the ḥaṭṭā't for more severe impurity.

These instructions certainly do correspond with the Numbers 19 prescription of the red cow rite. The cow is burned outside the camp following the procedure for the ḥaṭṭā't offered

---

41 J. Milgrom, "Sin Offering or Purification Offering?" *VT* 21 (1971) 237.

42 J. Milgrom, "Two Kinds of Ḥaṭṭā't," *VT* 26 (1976) 333.

for more serious pollutions, and those who handle its ash become impure.

Milgrom provides additional proof that this rite is a sacrifice from the sprinkling of blood toward the sanctuary. According to Milgrom, it is the blood of a ḥaṭṭā'ṭ which purges sancta of impurity. Milgrom states, "Its [the blood of the ḥaṭṭā'ṭ] placement on the horns of the altar (Lev. iv 4,7,18,25,30,34), in the shrine (Lev. iv 6,17) or in the adytum (Lev. xvi 14) is what purges these sacred objects of their accumulated impurities."[43] Usually, the blood of the animal is placed on the altar, in the shrine, or in the adytum to purify these items. However, since the blood is needed in the case of the red cow to empower its ashes to purify the corpse-contaminated, after the sprinkling toward the sanctuary, the blood of the animal is burnt with it. Sprinkling of blood toward the sanctuary is a symbolic gesture; it is as if it were sprinkled on the altar itself.[44]

Milgrom also points to the parallel rite of sevenfold sprinkling with ḥaṭṭā'ṭ blood on the altar to cleanse it. This act cleanses the altar and reconsecrates it to function again as a purgation agent (Ex. 29:36-37; Lev. 16:19).[45] Similarly, by sprinkling it toward the sanctuary seven times, the blood of the red cow is consecrated so that its presence in the ash may render it an effective purgative for the corpse-contaminated.

Thus, after examining the biblical information regarding the red cow rite, it becomes clear that the Sages did not add greater sanctity to the rite but rather they inherited such regard for it from their tradition as explicitly described in Scripture. In Tractate Para it is R. Eliezer that is in opposition to the accepted interpretation of Scripture. The Sages assume the sanctity of the rite.

Other early interpreters also considered the red cow rite a sacrifice. The author of Hebrews chooses the red cow sacrifice to be a prime source of metaphor for the superior sacrifice of Christ.

---

43 Milgrom, *Leviticus*, 63.

44 Ibid., 66, n 14.

45 Milgrom, "Paradox," 66.

Unless this rite was considered a sacrifice, the metaphor is certainly poor (Heb. 9:13-14). If the rite is understood as a sacrifice, it is inconceivable that it would be conducted in impurity.

To encapsulate my disagreement with Neusner that the Rabbis reverse the meaning of the rite by insisting it must be conducted in a clean place, I find that this principle is essential for a correct understanding of the biblical text. The fact that it takes place outside the camp does not suggest an unclean place, cf. Lev. 4:12. Since the personnel handling the red cow become unclean, they must have been clean when the rite began. Finally, the fact that those who handle the ash must purify does not mean that "the rules which govern rites in the Temple simply do not apply to the rite of the burning of the cow."[46] To the contrary, the rules of Lev. 16:28 are in effect because the burning is that of a ḥaṭṭāʾt for severe impurity.

I conclude, as with other matters of corpse impurity, that the mishnaic system builds directly on the foundation laid down by Scripture. If one understands the sacrificial system of Scripture, one will recognize the sanctity and power inherent in the ḥaṭṭāʾt of the red cow.

Having established the strong biblical foundation for the rabbinic understanding of corpse impurity, I will proceed to perhaps the most crucial issue: If the Rabbis are not elaborating on new principles what is the purpose of all of this data on corpse impurity? Why is there such concern to define corpse impurity so meticulously? A. Büchler said only the priests shared this concern.[47] J. Neusner, following G. Alon, states that lay Pharisees are trying to extend priestly holiness to themselves.[48]

---

46 Neusner, *Purities*, X, 222-223.

47 A. Büchler, *Der galiläische ʿAm haʿAreṣ in des zweiten Jahrhunderts*, 154-155, 162.

48 G. Alon, *Jews, Judaism and the Classical World*, 233; J. Neusner, *From Politics to Piety: the Emergence of Pharisaic Judaism*, 83; "The Fellowship (חבורה) in the Second Jewish Commonwealth," *HTR* 53 (1960) 126-127.

Sanders claims that these lay Pharisees were not concerned about themselves becoming corpse-impure but rather for priests to even accidentally become impure. However, their careful definition of corpse impurity led them to avoid the "new" sources themselves. Sanders says, "They (the Pharisees) first extended corpse impurity and then tried to avoid contracting it from their new sources as a kind of gesture toward living like priests."[49] Sanders is suggesting that the Pharisees are concerned to avoid only their rules of corpse impurity not the biblical, priestly rules of corpse impurity. Again, "The extremely careful definition of where corpse impurity is and is not probably encouraged caution."[50] This is a sort of backwards logic where the rules create the need for avoidance.

If one understands the biblical purity system which the Pharisees and later the Sages of the Mishna must have inherited there is a much more straightforward answer to these convolutions of logic. To begin with, the Pharisees were a group which considered the cult and its officiants ordained by God and which participated regularly in the life of the Temple. These zealous Jews even increased their own purity concerns to include some priestly ones, thereby acquiring for themselves more holiness. Laws had to be defined so as not to desecrate consecrated food, objects, area, and personnel.

The later Sages who were responsible for the Mishna did not live in a cult-centered community and had never even seen the Temple in operation. Nevertheless, they fully expected the sanctuary to be rebuilt in the future. The biblical laws of purity had to be studied carefully so they could once again be put into effect.

Thus, in determining the presence of Scripture in the corpse laws of the Mishna it really does not matter what data goes back to Second Temple times. The reason for concern for corpse impurity remains the same whether this is a present (Pharisees) or future (for a third temple) issue. I submit that the Sages are

---

49 Sanders, 166.

50 Ibid., 187.

concerned because they do not want to incur biblical penalties by failing to purify from impurity.

What are the specific biblical restrictions on corpse-impure persons? In addition to the danger of invalidating priests or priestly food by contact, these persons are under severe personal restrictions:

1. They may not offer anything at the Temple and/or eat a sacrifice (Lev. 7:19-20; Num. 9:7-11).
2. They may not celebrate the Passover (Num. 9:7-11; 2 Chr. 30:3).
3. They may not handle holy food of any type (e.g. tithes, tĕrûmâ, ḥallâ, etc.) (Lev. 7:19; Dt. 26:14).
4. They must purify (Num. 19:13, 20).

The practical inconvenience of these restrictions would make it impossible to celebrate any of the pilgrimage feasts or to separate tithes of any kind while impure from corpse impurity.

More importantly, if these laws are not observed, the penalty is death:

> Lev. 7:21: And if any one touches an unclean thing, whether the uncleanness of man or an unclean beast or any unclean abomination, and then eats of the flesh of the sacrifice of the LORD's peace offerings, that person shall be cut off from his people (= death by divine agency).

> Lev. 15:31: Thus you shall keep the people of Israel separate from their uncleanness, lest they die in their uncleanness by defiling my tabernacle that is in their midst.

> Num. 19:13: Whoever touches a dead person, the body of any man who has died, and does not cleanse himself, defiles the tabernacle of the LORD, and that person shall be cut off from Israel (= death by divine agency).

It is these biblical sanctions which provide the impetus for the Pharisees and the Rabbis to extend the laws to the degree evident in the Mishna.

No matter what the date of the rabbinic rules concerning corpse impurity, one of two principles is in operation: 1) Corpse impurity was a large concern in Second Temple times (see below), and its parameters were defined carefully so as not to incur it even accidentally and then violate the sanctity of consecrated items. Indeed, many simply did not want to become impure even if they were not planning to visit the Temple or come into contact with sacred persons/items. 2) The Sages of the Mishna, although not possessed of a sanctuary, still had to clarify the biblical laws so that they could be applied again in a future Temple. Some might add a third principle, the mere pursuit of academics, but that still does not provide a reason to study the laws of corpse impurity in particular.

Sometimes the Rabbis limit the extent of corpse contamination, but only when they can do so on the basis of biblical principles. An example is the insistence that only certain substances can be susceptible to corpse contamination (m. Kel. 15:1; cf. Lev. 11:32; Num. 31:20). It is not the intention of the Priestly writer in Lev. 11:32 to limit susceptibility to these substances, rather he presents them as examples only. I infer this because the text reads, "*Kol* kĕlî, *any* object, on which one of them [the eight creepers] falls when it is dead shall be impure...." He is explicit in Lev. 14:36 that everything in the house affected with ṣāraʿat is unclean unless it has been emptied before the priest's declaration. Neither is there a disclaimer with regard to the contents of the tent containing a corpse except for the contents of a sealed vessel. It is noteworthy that the Qumran exegetes differ from the Rabbis here, for they consider every lock and lintel in a corpse-contaminated house impure (11QT 49:13).

Nevertheless, without biblical warrant the Rabbis could not have limited corpse contamination. The Priestly Code does provide such warrant. Leviticus 11:32 and Numbers 31:20 single out particular items which are susceptible to corpse impurity. The Rabbis would clearly like to limit corpse impurity because of the severe biblical restrictions and penalties connected to it but could not do so without this Scriptural support.

Texts from the world of the first century reveal that actual practice in Temple times confirms the Rabbis' concern. I will first discuss the larger Hellenistic world which influenced the Jews and then focus on the particular Jewish world.

Among the Jews' overlords, the Greeks and the Romans, there was a strong concern to avoid corpse impurity. Peristratus demands that the dead be removed from the sacred Island of Delos if their graves were even within sight of the Temple.[51] It is said that a plague afflicted the Delians since they had allowed burial on the island. Artemis, who is immortal, cannot undergo the pollutions of death and hence shuns Hippolytus who must of necessity die. She says the law forbids her to even look at death.[52]

If the sacred area is polluted, the efficacy of the cult is automatically cut off. In the Antigone, birds of prey carrying scraps of a corpse to the altar consequently interrupt the contact between god and man.[53] A certain Coan inscription explains that if the sacred area is polluted, the god's statue must be taken out of the shrine and washed, the shrine purified, and a sacrifice offered.[54]

Humans, too, are affected by the polluting power of death. The personnel dedicated to the gods are defiled by merely gazing at a corpse. In Hellenistic Syria the priest who looks at a corpse is unclean for one day as the following quote explains:

> Those priests who bore the corpse of a Galloi priest of Syria were not allowed to enter the temple for seven days: if any priest looked at a corpse he was impure for that day and could only enter the temple the following day if he was cleansed.[55]

According to a Solon tradition, no priest could attend a funeral.[56] A person who has come into contact with a corpse is barred from sacred precincts and cannot participate in the worship of the gods.[57] Usually the dead were buried outside the city. After the burial, mourners washed themselves. Although the number of

---

51 R. Parker, *Miasma*, 33, 73.
52 Ibid., 33 n 6.
53 Ibid., 33.
54 Ibid., 53.
55 Lucian 2:62, *De Dea Syria*, ed. H. W. Attridge and R. A. Oden, 57.
56 Parker, 36.
57 Ibid., 33-34.

days differs among the sources, there was a waiting period after which a corpse-contaminated person could be considered pure for worship at the shrine. Washing was not enough to reinstate the corpse-contaminated.[58]

Even the house of the dead person contracted serious impurity. Special water vessels stood outside of the house to mark it as a house of death and to provide purification for those visiting it. The water was brought from elsewhere as the supply at the "house of death" was considered polluted. It is possible that houses were even sealed off when death was expected.[59] At Iulis and Athens it was customary to sprinkle the "house of death" with sea water to purify it. Priests at Coan were not allowed to enter the "house of death" for five days after the carrying out of the deceased.[60]

The corpse was washed, anointed, dressed in clean clothes, and laid out in a leaf-strewn bier for viewing. In this way, the corpse was symbolically purified even though everyone around it was defiled. A crown, the symbol of purity, was placed on its head.[61]

If the house of the deceased defiles, *a fortiori*, the tomb. Greeks were afraid to step on a tomb, and if one found a human bone or an uncovered grave in a public place, the area had to be purified.[62]

The Romans, too, feared the contaminating power of death. The Roman high priest, the *Flamen Dialis*, was forbidden, like his Hellenistic counterpart, to look at a corpse.[63] As in India, corpse contamination was assumed to extend along blood ties to near relatives of the dead, even if physically they were many

---

58 Ibid., 34, 37 n 17.

59 Ibid., 35; E. Rohde, *Psyche: The Cult of Souls and Belief in Immortality Among the Greeks*, tr. W. B. Hillis, 188-189 n 38.

60 Parker, 38, 52.

61 Ibid., 35.

62 Ibid., 38-39.

63 Milgrom, *Leviticus*, I, 979.

miles away. The Romans called those affected by this pollution the *familia funesta*.[64]

It should not be surprising then that the Jews of the Second Temple era, surrounded by Hellenistic culture, would adhere to similar laws of corpse impurity of their own and avoid becoming impure as well as circumventing the penalties for lack of purification. Indeed, first century sources confirm this concern even when Jews were not in the Temple area. Let us examine these documents.

Philo explains that those in a house where someone has died cannot touch anything until they have bathed and washed the clothes they are wearing:

> Indeed he [Moses] did not permit even the fully cleansed to enter the temple within seven days and ordered them to purge themselves on the third and seventh. Further too, those who enter a house in which anyone has died are ordered not to touch anything until they have bathed themselves and also washed the clothes which they were wearing. All the vessels and furniture and anything else inside the house, *practically everything*, is held by him to be unclean (*De Specialibus Legibus* 3:206-207).[65]

Thus, according to Philo, a Jew must bathe immediately after contracting corpse-uncleanness even though that will not re-admit him or her to the Temple precincts. To enter the Temple, the individual must have completed the whole seven-day rite. I also note that "practically everything" in the house is made unclean. In Philo's interpretation there is no tendency to limit the impurity, as the Rabbis do, just to certain items.[66]

---

64 Parker, 40.

65 tr. F. H. Colson in LCL, ed. T. E. Page et al., VII, 603-605.

66 The text mentions furniture; this was probably made of wood or stone. Wood was susceptible to impurity only if it formed a usable, whole utensil with a receptacle (m. Kel. 15:1); stone was insusceptible (m. Oh. 5:5) except for the rolling and buttressing stones of a grave (m. Oh. 2:4). Philo's interpretation is quite strict; the Rabbis reveal a limiting tendency. For the rabbinic view of susceptible vessels, see Introduction.

Josephus records the fear of Jews to live in Tiberias, even though Herod offered them grants of houses and land, since the city was built on grave sites:

> For he [Herod] knew that this settlement was contrary to the law and traditions of the Jews because Tiberias was built on the site of tombs that had been obliterated, of which there were many there. And our law declares that such settlers are unclean for seven days (Ant. 18:38).

L. Levine has done a critical study of the many versions of this story in the Talmuds and the Midrash. He concludes that Tiberias did have a problem with impurity because of the presence of graves and that this problem continued through the second century. R. Shimon bar Yohai and probably others at different times tried to decree purification of the city but there was opposition.[67] Thus, it was not for fear of insulting the dead, but from a desire to avoid impurity that Jews would not move to this city.[68]

Josephus, following Numbers 19:13 (cited above), warns that one who does not purify after seven days of corpse impurity must bring a sacrifice to the Temple to atone for this transgression (Ant. 3:262). Thus, even if not planning to visit the Temple, a corpse-contaminated individual had to purify after the week's period of impurity.

Now Sanders has presented arguments to prove the opposite, that corpse purification was not in effect in Second Temple times, and thus subsequently it was not a main concern of the Mishna except as it affected priests.[69] His main argument is that the law of Numbers 5, which requires the corpse-contaminated to be sent out of the camp, would have been impossible to realize considering 1) the number of people involved included relatives, mourners, and friends who would all be corpse-contaminated if they came into the house where the

---

67 L. Levine, "R. Simeon b. Yohai and the Purification of Tiberias: History and Tradition," *HUCA* 49 (1978) 172.

68 Sanders, 188; cf. Alon, 229 n 105 for further arguments.

69 Sanders, 159.

corpse was; 2) the position of Josephus (Ag. Ap. 2:205) who says persons are supposed to join a funeral procession if they pass by one (are all these people to be excluded from the city for a week?); and 3) although the Mishna records much information on corpse impurity, nothing is said of the banishment of corpse-contaminated persons. Sanders says, "This rule was not in effect in the first century, and so fulfilling the positive expectation to tend the dead did not result in the severe inconvenience required by Numbers 5."[70]

Sanders does not note the fact that already in the Priestly material there is a dual conception of the procedure for the corpse-contaminated. The law of Numbers 5 probably refers to the situation of the wilderness camp, but the laws of Numbers 19 assume that the corpse-contaminated is at home (see above). The Qumran documents help to resolve the issue by referring to an ablution required on the first day of corpse impurity:

> As for persons: whoever was in the house and whoever enters the house shall bathe in water and launder his clothes on the first day (11QT 49:16-17; cf. 50:13-14; 1QM 14:2-3).

After this initial bathing the corpse-contaminated person could remain in the city and finish the week's rites.[71] This ablution on the first day is also noted by Philo (see above), although it is nowhere in the biblical text.

The Gospels corroborate the notion that corpse-contaminated individuals were not expelled. Four days after the death of Lazarus his sisters, Mary and Martha, are still at home (Jn. 11:17-19).

Thus, when Sanders claims that the Mishnaic discussions presuppose the corpse-contaminated is at home, he is probably correct.[72] However, this does not annul the necessity for purification procedures; it merely alleviates the difficulties.

---

70 Ibid., 142-143.

71 J. Milgrom, "Studies in the Temple Scroll," *JBL* 97/4 (1978) 515-516.

72 Sanders, 256.

The Gospels, too, may add further evidence that corpse impurity was taken seriously in the first century. Matthew and Luke refer to "white-washed" graves, which may have been those marked with lime so people could avoid them and not contract corpse impurity unnecessarily.[73] The Mishna says Jews would mark graves in blue so as not to become defiled by them (m. MQ 1:2). This practice of marking graves continued well into the rabbinic period (b. MQ 5b). Thus, the concern for contracting corpse impurity continued even when the Temple was only a distant memory.

Also in John, Chapter 10, a priest and a Levite ignore an unfortunate man waylaid by robbers and left "half-dead." Both the priest and the Levite may have been concerned not to contract corpse impurity.[74] The biblical laws do not prohibit a Levite from contracting corpse impurity, but it still resulted in a decided inconvenience.

Both the Gospels and Josephus discuss Pharisees who tried to extend priestly food laws to their own food and thus replicate in their own homes the holiness of the Temple (See Appendix A). For this, they avoided corpse impurity whenever possible. If of necessity (e.g., burial of relatives) they had to handle or mourn the dead, purification had to follow.

What of this purification? Did the Jews of the Second Temple really burn the red cow? It is true that none of the Second Temple documents report the operation of this rite. However, the Mishna in Parah 3:5 claims that a few red cows had been burnt during the time of the two temples. A minimal amount of the ash of one cow mixed with the other ingredients would last a long time. The Palestinian Talmud states that R. Haggai and R. Jeremiah used this ash for corpse purification (y. Ber. 6:10a). Additionally, the Samaritans, who maintained a sacrificial cult

---

73 Mt. 23:27; Lk. 11:44; Maimonides, *Code* X, Corpse 8:9; Eze. 39:15; m. MQ 1:2; E. Feldman, *Biblical and Post-Biblical Defilement and Mourning*, 58 n 200; J. Rothschild, "Tombs of the Sanhedrin," *PEQ* 84 (1952) 24.

74 Feldman, 60 n 210.

on Mt. Gerizim, are reported to have burnt the red cow as late as the 14th century C.E.[75]

The strongest argument that the red cow was actually burnt in Second Temple times is perhaps that of logic. While the Temple stood it is inconceivable that persons who were defiled by contact with a corpse would have been allowed to enter the Temple and offer sacrifices. As stated above, a sacrifice is required if one does *not* purify. With the sanctions against entering the sanctuary in a state of impurity or on contaminating holy food, such behavior would certainly be unacceptable. The Scripture is clear that the unpurified corpse-contaminated person defiles the sanctuary even from afar.[76]

Therefore, from the above first century sources it appears that 1) the Jewish populace at large did avoid corpse impurity whenever possible, 2) purification was assumed to be necessary after contamination, and 3) rules regarding purification were couched in general not sectarian terms by first century Jewish authors. If the average Jew living in Second Temple times, whose tradition was the Bible, was concerned not to trespass biblical regulations concerning corpse impurity, it is not difficult to believe that the meticulous care of the Sages of the Mishna who inherited the traditions of the Pharisees, and who fill 25% of their recorded work with explanations of purity matters, is also based on respect for biblical sanctions.

Sanders points out that R. Judah is alone in thinking that a ḥābēr must not contract corpse impurity; the other Sages disagreed (m. Dem. 2:3). The decision of the Sages is biblical; laity should bury the dead and thus contract corpse impurity. The dissension of R. Judah, however, is understandable. In his day there was no red cow rite and hence no possibility of proper purification. The mere fact that the matter was at issue shows a concern for corpse impurity long after the Temple's demise, but

---

75 J. Bowman, "Did the Qumran Sect Burn the Red Heifer?" *RQ* 1/1 (1958) 78; M. Gaster, *Samaritan Traditions and Law*, 195.

76 Num. 19:13; Milgrom, "Israel's Sanctuary," 390-9.

the Sages' decision reveals a recognition of the futility of keeping pure from corpse impurity at the end of the second century C.E.

In conclusion, it is clear that the Rabbis of the Mishna are analyzing and defining the biblical data on corpse impurity with a clear understanding of the biblical principles involved. They assume a homogeneous system which they examine to include all possible components. This is evident in the many passages which declare that things like the biblically named items also come under the particular ruling, and things bearing opposite characteristics from these items follow an opposite ruling. However, one cannot attribute the whole notion of system to the Rabbis; it is evident already in the Priestly Code.

The Rabbis worked from the biblical text in extracting from the recognized principles of this system as much information as possible. Often they extend the laws beyond Scripture in an effort to make sure the biblical laws are not violated. However, they are not interested in merely adding more restrictions on impure persons, and in some places it is evident that they are attempting to limit the effects of corpse impurity. In any case, the Rabbis would not have considered a reversal of biblical principles, e.g., those behind the red cow rite, to fit their own agenda.

Finally, first century sources as well as the Hellenistic milieu of the Second Temple era corroborate the concern to keep pure from corpse impurity on the part of the average Jew due to biblical and cultural sanctions. Although in the time of the Mishna the red cow was no longer burnt, exegesis continued and this exegesis was based on the biblical text. The writers, many of whom tried to maintain purity on a level greater than that demanded of lay Jews, were very careful to define corpse impurity so as to avoid contracting it whenever possible. In addition, when the Temple would be rebuilt, the laws of the system would be clear to all and the red cow rite could again be put into effect.

CHAPTER 5

THE IMPURITY OF ṢĀRAʿAT

The rabbinic material on ṣāraʿat, the scaly skin disease commonly mistranslated "leprosy," is based directly on the biblical text.[1] There do not seem to be any new principles or underlying agenda in the Mishna's tractate, Negaim, only details and clarifications of Leviticus 13-14. And yet it is not merely a restatement of Scripture; it is a view through a special lens.

In this chapter I will set forth the rabbinic attitude to the scale-diseased person, the mĕṣōrāʿ. Although I agree with the general opinion that this attitude is based on Scripture, the rabbinic interpretation is still unique, e.g., it is not that of Qumran.[2]

---

1 For a good explanation of the disease, how it came to be termed "leprosy," and its decided difference from modern leprosy, see E. V. Hulse, "The Nature of Biblical Leprosy and the Use of Alternative Medical Terms in Modern Translations of the Bible," *PEQ* 107 (1975) 87-105, cf. 91.

2 I would not go so far as to agree with Neusner that in the Mishna tractate of Negaim, "[A]ll we have is a reprise and logical expansion of

To uncover the Sages' attitude one must examine all of the hard data available in the rabbinic sources as well as notice undercurrents: what is selected for discussion, what is emphasized in the discussion, and how Scripture's gaps are filled. Questions I will raise include: What was the rabbinic definition of the disease? What was the contamination power of the mĕṣōrāᶜ? Is the rabbinic interpretation stringent compared with other contemporary Jewish interpretations or lenient? Are there differences among the sources? The Rabbis were very concerned about the contamination of ṣāraᶜat because it is a biblical concern carrying heavy sanctions. First of all, they define the disease as narrowly as possible in an effort to limit the incidence of it. Secondly, according to their interpretation the contamination potency of the confirmed mĕṣōrāᶜ is high, even greater than a simple reading of the Torah requires.

I will begin by presenting the biblical understanding of ṣāraᶜat in order to establish the text which the Rabbis are reading. As with corpse impurity, the biblical text itself, although ambiguous at times, represents a workable system based on specific axioms.

The biblical terms for the disease are ṣāraᶜat or negaᶜ ṣāraᶜat. The word negaᶜ, here translated "affection," literally means "becoming touched" and perhaps reflects the understanding of the neighbors of ancient Israel that skin disease was the result of "becoming touched" by a demon.[3] Ṣāraᶜat is a generic term which refers to certain scaly skin diseases in humans and discolorations (probably due to fungus or mold) in fabrics and houses. Much time and energy has been invested analyzing the meaning of

---

biblical rules," *A History of the Mishnaic Law of Purities*, XXII, 277. A certain slant of interpretation is discernible.

3 J. Milgrom, *Leviticus*, I, 776, notes that in Akkadian the verb "touch" also refers to an attack by demons. Milgrom agrees with K. Elliger, *Leviticus*, HAT, IV, that in the ancient world ṣāraᶜat indicated a demonic attack. In the Bible, however, God is always the author, controller, and healer of the disease.

ṣāraʿat; at present no definitive translation has been accepted by scholars.[4]

The symptoms of ṣāraʿat as recorded in Leviticus include the following: śĕʾēt, discoloration; sappaḥat, scab; baheret, shiny mark (Lev. 13:2).[5] If the affliction had penetrated through the epidermis, causing hair to turn white, this would indicate negaʿ ṣāraʿat.[6] Those certified with the disease were banished from the community. If the disease was evident only on the surface of the skin (evident below the epidermis but not below the dermis), the ailment may be only a minor skin disease like eczema, leukoderma, or psoriasis.[7]

The Camp of Israel had to be kept pure of ṣāraʿat, whether in the form of persons, houses, or fabrics. A person who developed a white baheret, which was not deeper than the skin and in which there was no white hair, was quarantined for one week. If the affection did not improve, the suspected person had to be quarantined for an additional week.[8] After this period of time, the musgār (= quarantined person) was released after bathing and laundering, if the symptoms had faded (13:4-6). If the symptoms remained, the person was certified by the priest as a mĕṣōrāʿ and banished from the camp. Curiously, if the ṣāraʿat had spread over the whole body turning it completely white, the person was declared clean (13:39).

Negaʿ ṣāraʿat could occur spontaneously (13:2-17), or it could follow a boil, šĕḥîn (13:18-23), or burn, mikwat-ʾeš (13:24-28). If the disease broke out on one's head or beard as a neteq, making the

---

4 For a survey of the etymological research on ṣāraʿat, cf. J. F. A. Sawyer, "A note on the Etymology of Ṣāraʿat," *VT* 26 (1976) 241-245; Milgrom, *Leviticus*, I, 775.

5 For identification of terms, cf. J. Wilkinson, "Leprosy and Leviticus: the Problem of Description and Identification," *Scot J Th* 30 (1977) 155-160. For śĕʾēt as discoloration instead of swelling (RSV), cf. Milgrom, *Leviticus*, I, 773, who observes that in verse 3, the sore is *lower* than the skin.

6 "Leprosy" in *EJ*, XI, 33-34.

7 Ibid.

8 If the affection did improve, allowing the person to be released, it is not clear in all cases what the status of the impurity would be at that point, cf. D. P. Wright for full discussion, *The Disposal of Impurity*, 211.

hair yellow and thin, this too would be diagnosed as ṣāraᶜat (13:29-37; cf. 13:42-44, ṣāraᶜat can also break forth on a bald head). The term, neteq, has been identified as "scall" or "scaly rash."[9]

The text is especially interested to describe the affection so that the priest can identify it. J. Wilkinson has outlined five secondary features which would indicate the presence of ṣāraᶜat in the discoloration, scab, shiny mark, or scaly rash.[10]

1. Skin color change
2. Hair color change
3. Infiltration of the skin
4. Extension or spread in the skin
5. Ulceration of the skin ["living (raw) flesh"]

The priest does not identify medical problems but must ascertain the presence/absence of these particular physical signs; this underscores the ritual character of the disease. It is these signs which show, not if an affection is healthy or unhealthy but, "when it is unclean and when it is clean" (Lev. 14:57; cf. 13:59).[11]

Negaᶜ ṣāraᶜat also affects fabric and houses. Evidently this refers to mold on garments and some type of fungus or mildew in houses. Similar quarantine procedures apply for fabric and houses. Evidence of fungus beneath the surface of the walls subject the whole house to a seven-day quarantine. If no improvement is noticed after this time, all objects are taken out of the house, and the priest pronounces it impure. All affected stones are thrown outside the city and replaced (14:40-42). If the disease returned, the house would have to be torn down (14:43-45).

---

9 Milgrom, *Leviticus*, I, 793; Wilkinson, "Description and Identification," 158. According to *Webster's Third International Dictionary*, ed. P. B. Gove, et al., a scall is defined as "scurf or scabby disease esp. of the scalp," 2023.

10 Wilkinson, "Description and Identification," 158, 160, identifies the affection as one in which the hair is torn from the follicles or scalp. The yellow color is typical of *favus*, following Hulse, 99.

11 Ibid., 164, 168. Note that Chapters 13-14, which discuss ṣāraᶜat, are part of a larger section of Leviticus which treats ritual impurities of various types (Chaps. 11-15). See J. Wilkinson, "Leprosy and Leviticus: a Problem of Semantics and Translation," *Scot J Th* 31 (1978) 155 and Milgrom, *Leviticus*, I, 816-20, for more on the ritual nature of ṣāraᶜat.

It is significant that the objects are not retroactively impure although they had been in an impure house; both house and contents are defiled only after the priest's pronouncement. This, too, emphasizes the ritual nature of the impurity. Contact with the mĕṣōrāʿ constitutes no hazard to health.

The symptoms of negaʿ ṣāraʿat do not indicate a physically contagious disease. The procedures espoused in Leviticus 14 do not curtail the spread of the disease or treat it medically; all procedures take place only *after* the person has been healed. Indeed, the priests of Leviticus and Numbers do not handle contagious diseases. Their duty is to preserve the sanctuary from ritual impurity.

Since those affected with ṣāraʿat can contaminate sancta even by being in the same room (see below), they must be banished from sacred places. They must be banished from the entire community as well for they can unknowingly contaminate other Israelites by sharing the same overhang. If the latter enter the sanctuary, they will bring divine wrath on the entire community because the sanctuary has been defiled.[12] As discussed below, the capacity of the mĕṣōrāʿ to contaminate by overhang is explicit in the rabbinic system; it is implicit in the Priestly Code.

Further corroboration of the notion that ṣāraʿat in the Bible was ritually but not necessarily physically contagious is the example of Naaman, the Syrian military commander (2 Ki. 5:1). Although afflicted with ṣāraʿat, Naaman is able to lead an army. Also, the catalog of impurities in Leviticus 11-15, which contains the rules pertaining to ṣāraʿat, discusses only ritual not physical impurities: e.g., those who touch carcasses or persons with genital flows become ritually contaminated, but their health is not endangered. Indeed, in an extensive case of negaʿ ṣāraʿat, in which scales cover one's whole body, the afflicted person is diagnosed pure! (Lev. 13:13)

The Bible does not describe the contamination of the mĕṣōrāʿ. This is probably because it is of no great concern. The

---

12 J. Milgrom, *Studies in Cultic Theology and Terminology*, 80-81.

měṣōrāᶜ is banished, thus, there is no fear of accidentally coming into contact with him or her.[13]

Nevertheless, from the analogy of the instruction for houses affected by ṣāraᶜat in which the contents become impure, it can be inferred that persons affected by ṣāraᶜat contaminate others if present in the same house with them (Lev. 14:36). This is the clear interpretation of Josephus (Ag. Ap. 1:281) and the Rabbis (m. Neg. 13:7-9). Thus, clean persons under the same roof as the měṣōrāᶜ must bathe, and, if they eat food or lay down to rest in that house, they would be required to launder their clothes as well.[14]

If the overhang of the měṣōrāᶜ defiles, *a fortiori*, the touch. Persons touching the měṣōrāᶜ would surely have to bathe and launder their clothes. Objects could be washed or fired unless they were earthenware, in which case they would have to be broken (cf. Lev. 11:33; Num. 31:23).

To understand the possible extent of the defilement caused by the měṣōrāᶜ, see the diagram below prepared by D. P. Wright (Fig. 1).[15] As stated above, the Bible does not offer any explicit information on the contamination of the měṣōrāᶜ. However, since the text does provide information on the contamination power of a house affect by ṣāraᶜat, assumptions can be made about the potency of the měṣōrāᶜ from this and from other relevant biblical data on purity matters. The dashed lines show what can be assumed but not proven.

In Branch 1 Wright distinguishes between the person who is subject to an overhang affected by ṣāraᶜat for a brief period only and one who has either lain or eaten under it. The former is required to bathe; the latter must bathe and launder personal

---

13 According to the sectarians the měṣōraᶜ is confined (11QT 46:16-18; 48:14-15; 4QThrA1 2); the Rabbis allow měṣōraᶜîm to roam freely (Sif. Zut. on Num. 5:2). In both views the měṣōraᶜ must remain outside the city. Cf. Wright, *Disposal*, 20, for definition of bêt haḥopšît.

14 Lev. 14:46-47; Milgrom, *Leviticus*, I, 876.

15 Wright, *Disposal*, 209.

FIG. 1 THE CONTAMINATION OF THE MĔṢŌRĀʿ IN THE BIBLICAL SYSTEM

(Copied from D. P. Wright, *The Disposal of Impurity*, 209)

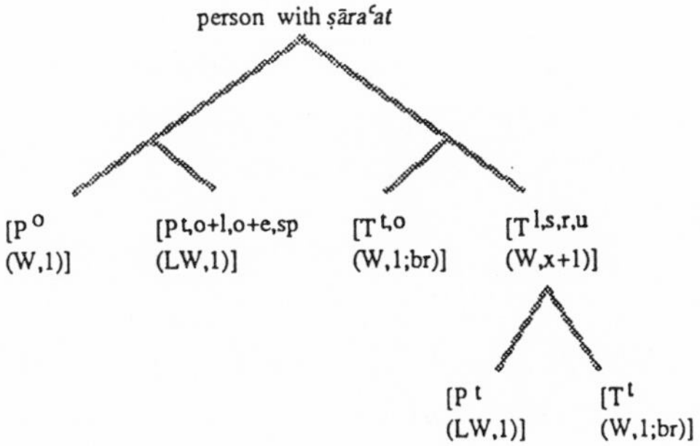

FIG. 2 THE CONTAMINATION OF THE MIṬṬĀHĒR IN THE BIBLICAL SYSTEM

(Copied from D. P. Wright, *The Disposal of Impurity*, 212)

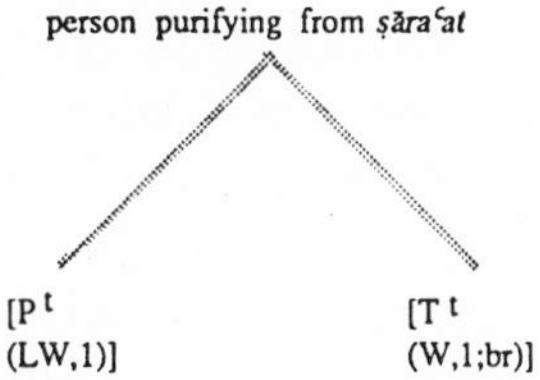

clothes. I am not sure this distinction applies to the biblical system, but it certainly does for the Rabbis (see below).

It is reasonable to assume that the spit of the mĕṣōrāᶜ is defiling. This is because mĕṣōrāᶜîm must cover their mouths. Moreover, because saliva is a pollutant in the case of the zāb, a lesser impurity bearer (Lev. 15:8), it is most likely also a pollutant in the case of the mĕṣōrāᶜ. The breath of the mĕṣōrāᶜ, however, is probably not defiling. Although the Rabbis declare that the breath of the mĕṣōrāᶜ is defiling, in no place does the Bible state that breath is a conveyer of impurity.[16] I will discuss the rabbinic reasoning below.

I question the validity of Branch 2 of Wright's diagram showing the contamination of items on which the mĕṣōrāᶜ has lain, sat, ridden, or has been located. This assumption is based solely on the Mishna, which might be homogenizing the biblical impurity rules more than the original priestly intention. Since ṣāraᶜat is a higher grade of impurity, the Mishna adds to the mĕṣōrāᶜ's contamination possibilities those of the zāb. However, the zāb contaminates primarily by means of his flow, which could easily have had contact with the bed or chair. The mĕṣōrāᶜ's impurity has nothing to do with genital emissions.

Because of the high risk of contaminating clean persons, the mĕṣōrāᶜ must observe special deportment rules, including, wearing torn clothes, covering the upper lip, and allowing the hair to hang loosely. In addition, the scale-diseased person must call out, "Unclean, unclean!" when approaching other persons (Lev. 13:45).

Healing from ṣāraᶜat can come only from God. A certified mĕṣōrāᶜ who has been healed is required to undergo an eight-day purification ritual (Lev. 14:1-20). On the first day, the priest officiating meets the mĕṣōrāᶜ outside the camp, makes the inspection, and ascertains that the individual has indeed been healed; now the mĕṣōrāᶜ is referred to as the miṭṭahēr, the purifying one. A bird is killed and its blood mixed with mayim ḥayyîm, spring water, in a clay vessel. Cedarwood, crimson cloth,

---

16 Ibid., 210.

hyssop, and a live bird are dipped into this mixture. The priest sprinkles the mixture on the miṭṭahēr seven times and the live bird is freed. The miṭṭahēr must bathe, shave all personal hair, and launder his or her clothes. After this, the miṭṭahēr may enter the city but must remain outside of the house for seven days.

Since it must be assumed that the rite has eliminated some impurity, it is possible that the miṭṭahēr can no longer contaminate the profane by overhang.[17] However, the miṭṭahēr might still defile sacrificial food found in private homes by entering the house and so must stay outside.[18] Support for this claim is found in recent discoveries from Qumran:

> [The scale-diseased person shall dwell outside his tent seven d]ays. But now [i.e., outside Qumran] because their impurity is [still] with them [scale-diseased persons are entering] into the house con[taining] the purity of sacred [food] (4QMMT 66-68).[19]

It is presumed that if the miṭṭahēr touches clean persons during this week, they become unclean and must bathe and launder their clothes. If the miṭṭahēr touches any object, it must be washed; if it is earthenware, it must be broken (See Fig. 2).[20]

On the seventh day, the miṭṭahēr must again bathe, launder, and shave and then may go home. The possibility of defilement by

---

17 Ibid., 213. Wright, following the Rabbis (m. Neg. 14:2), suggests that all overhang potency is cancelled on the first day of purification. However, Qumran documents suggest that only contamination by overhang to the profane has been cancelled.

18 Milgrom, *Leviticus*, I, 993, "The reason cannot be that he contaminates the profane sphere by direct contact (cf. m. Neg. 14:2).... Note that the zāb contaminates all that he touches (Lev. 15:4-12, 25-27), yet is allowed to stay at home." Rather, the fear is that the mĕṣōraʿ will contaminate sacred food in the house by overhang. According to Milgrom, it is an axiom of the system that "each purification stage reduces impurity by one degree, but the sacred is more vulnerable to pollution than the common by one degree," 992-93. He exemplifies this with a chart, "Table of Purification Procedures and Effects;" Part 1 is reproduced above in the Introduction, Figure 2.

19 Tr. Milgrom in *Leviticus*, I, 843.

20 Cf. Wright, *Disposal*, 212; m. Kel. 1:4; m. Neg. 13:3, 7, 8, 11; Ant. 3:261-64; Ag.Ap. 1:279-81.

overhang has been totally eliminated; the miṭṭahēr will not contaminate by contact with the profane (Lev. 14:9) but must avoid contact with sancta. (The miṭṭahēr does not enter the sanctuary until the eighth day.)

The miṭṭahēr brings three lambs, flour mixed with oil, and a separate quarter-log of oil to the sanctuary on the eighth day for the various sacrifices necessary to conclude the required purification: whole, cereal, purification, and reparation offerings. The priest daubs the right ear, hand, and foot of the miṭṭahēr with the blood of the reparation offering and then repeats the daubing with oil.

Although the miṭṭahēr can substitute turtle-doves for the lambs in the whole and purification offerings, a lamb must be offered for the reparation offering. With these rites, the afflicted person regains a layman's access to the sanctuary as a totally clean individual.

Thus, the seventh day ritual restores the person to the community, the eighth day to the sanctuary and thus to God.[21] Each part of the ritual has reduced the impurity of the mĕṣōrāᶜ by one degree.

J. Milgrom has outlined the meaning of each part of the rite. The purification offering purges the sanctuary; the whole and cereal offerings expiate the sin that might have caused the affliction. The reparation offering atones in case the mĕṣōrāᶜ had unconsciously come into contact with sancta (e.g., sacrificial food; cf. Uzziah: 2 Chr. 26:16-21; Lev. 5:17-19).[22] The daubings of blood and oil give the mĕṣōrāᶜ renewed access to the sanctuary and sancta.

In the Ancient Near East, the vulnerable parts of the body, those on the outer extremities, as well as the corners of structures were smeared to effect purification. This was a magical rite thought to ward off demons who were considered the cause of

---

21 "Leprosy" in *EJ*, XI, 36.

22 Cf. the ʾāšam of the mĕṣōraᶜ and the ʾāšam talûy of the Rabbis, Milgrom, *Leviticus*, I, 363-364.

disease.[23] In Israel all associations with magic or demons are neutralized. For a cogent analysis of the meaning of scale disease in Israelite society and its connection with death, see J. Milgrom, *Leviticus*, I, on Chapters 13 and 14.

The Bible records several cases of negaʿ ṣāraʿat. The ṣāraʿat of Naaman, referred to above, was transferred to Elisha's covetous servant, Gehazi (2 Ki. 5:27). Four mĕṣōrāʿîm brought the news of the vanished Syrians to the city of Samaria (2 Ki. 7:3). The Book of Lamentations, too, refers to those who cry out, "Unclean! Turn away; turn away! Don't touch!" (4:15). This is based on the mĕṣōrāʿ's call (Lev. 13:45). Also Isaiah says God will bring a scab on the heads of the daughters of Zion (Isa. 3:17).

Further examples illustrate the fact that Israel, like her neighbors, considered various skin diseases to result from a divine curse.[24] In explaining the laws regarding the house affected with ṣāraʿat, God says to Moses and Aaron, "When you come into the Land of Canaan, which I give you for a possession, and *I put* a leprous disease in a house in the land of your possession..." (Lev. 14:34). Thus, God attributes the incidence of the affection to himself. Miriam is punished with ṣāraʿat for slandering Moses and trying to usurp his authority (Num. 12:9-11). Deuteronomy threatens, "The LORD will smite you with Egyptian boils...and with scabs and itches from which you shall never recover" (28:27; cf. also Lev. 26:21). Likewise, David vows, "May the house of Joab never be without someone suffering from discharge or ṣāraʿat" (2 Sam. 3:29). King Uzziah, although not a priest, presumed to burn incense before the LORD, and for this

---

23 Ibid., 35

24 Cf. M. L. Davies, "Levitical Leprosy: Uncleanness and the Psyche," *ExT* 99 (1988) 136-139, who recognizes that ṣāraʿat is a divine curse but tries to explain the phenomenon medically: "Gehazi's LL [Levitical Leprosy] was a neurodermatitis brought on by guilt," 136-139. Not only does this reduce the divine element in the curse, so important to the writer, but it does not seem textually possible since the text explicitly states that Gehazi went out from Elisha's presence "mĕṣōraʿ kaššeleg." Sawyer tries to prove the nonexistence of the divine curse element in this disease by etymological means, 241-42. Nevertheless, it is the clear understanding of the Bible and of the Rabbis, Lev. 14:34; b. Ber. 5b.

sacrilege, God smote him with ṣāraʿat (2 Chr. 26:23).[25] Job's skin disease was interpreted by his friends as a curse from God (Jb. 22:5; cf. 11:6)[26]

If God consents to forgive and heal the mĕṣōrāʿ, sacrifices will expiate whatever sin has been committed. The lack of purification rites in the narratives about ṣāraʿat does not mean that they did not take place but only that they were not of concern to the writer.

Unlike her neighbors in the ancient world, Israel did not consider her priests able to cure disease. They possessed no magical secrets which could help them exorcise the sources of disease. Only God could heal. A prime example of this principle is the occasion of Miriam's punishment. Aaron, although he is the high priest, is powerless to help Miriam and pleads with Moses to pray for her (Num. 12:11-12).[27] Nevertheless, the priest occupies an important position as the one who pronounces the disease and verifies its cure. Evidently the priest, on account of his role, is immune to the contamination power of the mĕṣōrāʿ; there is no evidence of priests undergoing purification after contact with mĕṣōrāʿîm in the line of duty.[28]

---

25 J. Milgrom, *Cult and Conscience*, 80-82; J. Morgenstern, "Amos Studies II: the Sin of Uzziah," *HUCA* (1937-38) 12-13. It is strange that although Uzziah is quarantined, he is allowed to remain in the city. Wright suggests that this was a concession on account of Uzziah's royalty. Nevertheless, he had to defer the throne to his son Jotham, *Disposal*, 176-77.

26 Recent evidence from Qumran supports this notion, cf. E. Qimron, "Notes in the 4Q Zadokite Fragments on Skin Disease," *JJS* 42/2 (1991) 258-259 for further discussion; cf. also J. Baumgarten, "The 4Q Zadokite Fragment on Skin Disease," *JJS* 41 (1990) 153-165, who creates a composite text from the Fragments 4Q266, 268 and 272 which demonstrates that an evil spirit has caused the disease, 159, cf. discussion on 162; also cf. 1QH 1:32. The Rabbis certainly understand scale disease to be the result of sin, t. Neg. 6:7; b. Arakh. 16a; Lev. R. 17:3; 18:4.

27 Numbers 12; cf. Milgrom *Leviticus*, I, 887-89.

28 Cf. the immunity of the high priest on the Day of Atonement after touching the goat, Milgrom, *Leviticus*, I, 1048.

Having set forth the biblical data on ṣāraʿat I will now turn to the primary focus of this chapter: How do the Rabbis interpret this material? What do they emphasize? What do they add? Why?

J. Neusner says that the Rabbis add nothing principally new to Scripture; their information represents only logical refinements:

> All we have is a reprise and logical expansion of biblical rules...its (Tractate Negaim's) structure is defined by theme and not by problematic.[29]

To a large degree Neusner is correct. Where Scripture says that a bright spot is a sign of ṣāraʿat, the Rabbis want to know how bright. Where Scripture says hair in the bright spot confirms it as unclean, the Rabbis want to know how much hair.

Neusner concedes to only one principally new item in the rabbinic view of ṣāraʿat, the distinction of the uncleanness of negaʿ from that of ṣāraʿat:

> What is new in Negaim is therefore solely the recognition of negaʿ as separate and distinct from ṣaraʿat. So far as the Mishnaic system is concerned, the inclusion of negaʿ as a separate source of uncleanness from ṣaraʿat is important chiefly as an expression of the notion that the sage plays a part in the system. But, it must be observed the role of the sage in the determination of the uncleanness of ṣaraʿat is not to be gainsaid.[30]

Neusner claims that, according to the Rabbis, negaʿ and ṣāraʿat represent separate diseases and that this is the result of the rabbinic effort to extend the power of the priest in the pronouncement of the mĕṣōrāʿ to the Sage. He points to R. Aqiba's insistence that an expert in the laws of nĕgāʿîm perform the examination (m. Neg. 3:1; 4:7-10; 7:2; Sifra Taz. Neg. 1:9). Although the lay examiner cannot make the pronouncement, he can instruct the priest who might not know the laws. Hence, the

---

29 Neusner, *Purities*, XXII, 277.

30 Ibid., 153, 186.

Sage is really the powerful determinator, and the priest pronounces merely what he is told to pronounce.[31]

Neusner sees the destruction of the Temple as a factor in the promulgation of these ideas:

> With the broadening of the realm of the sacred to encompass the community therefore comes the extension of the sanctity of the priesthood to all who qualify themselves to function as did priests...What I think Aqiva contributes in the cited rulings is recognition of the difference between the age in which the Temple stood and the present age, in which it lies in ruins.[32]

While I agree that the Sages were concerned that the priest pronouncing the disease be instructed by the Sage if he were not knowledgeable, there is no evidence that they understood the terms ṣāraᶜat and negaᶜ to refer to two separate diseases, each under the primary jurisdiction of priest and Sage, respectively.[33] Furthermore, the notion that the priest must be instructed before pronouncing his decree is accepted already at Qumran (CD 13:5-6, cf. Chapter 2 above).

I will examine the clearest of Neusner's proof texts below:

> For negaᶜîm come only because of gossip, and ṣaraᶜat comes only to those who are arrogant (t. Neg. 6:7, tr. Neusner).

> "And behold, he is healed" (Lev. 14:3) - for his negaᶜ has left him. "The negaᶜ" (Lev. 14:3) - for lo, the white hair has departed. "The ṣaraᶜat" (Lev. 14:3) - for lo, the quick flesh has departed (Sifra Mes. Neg. par. 1:6-8, tr. Neusner).

---

31 That the priest was regarded as the authority for the certification of ṣāraᶜat in the Second Temple period is clear from the story of a mĕṣōraᶜ whom Jesus healed. After healing the man, Jesus sent him to the priest for certification (Mt. 8:4; Mk. 1:44; Lk. 5:14).

32 Neusner, *Purities*, XXII, 155.

33 But cf. Qumran where there is evidence that negaᶜ and ṣāraᶜat represented separate categories. The Temple Scroll refers to מנוגעים בצרעות ובנגע (11QT 48:15). It is not clear how the sectarians defined the terms בצרעות ובנגע but the text does represent a division of the two terms predating R. Aqiba.

"A reddish white negaʿ" (Lev. 13:42) teaches that it [the bald spot] is rendered unclean with a variegation. "Ṣaraʿat" (Lev. 13:42) teaches that it is rendered unclean with raw flesh. And is the opposite proposition not logical? If the boil and the burning, which are unclean because of white hair, are not unclean because of raw flesh, a bald spot on the forehead, and a bald spot on the scalp, which are not made unclean with white hair, logically should not be made unclean with raw flesh, Scripture says, "ṣaraʿat" - teaching that it is made unclean with raw flesh (Sifra Taz. Neg. 11:1, tr. Neusner).

"[And] the meṣoraʿ" (Lev. 13:45). [The verse describes the deportment of the meṣoraʿ.]...I know it only in this instance (Neusner: re meṣoraʿim). How do I know that I should include others who are afflicted with negaʿim? Scripture says, "Unclean, unclean will he call out" (Lev. 13:45) (Sifra Taz. Neg. 12:7, tr. Neusner).

At first glance it might appear that the Rabbis thought of ṣāraʿat and negaʿ as two different diseases each with its own cause (arrogance or gossip) and symptom (white hair or raw flesh). However, this does not prove to be the case when examining the rest of the literature. I would agree with the scholars who regard ṣāraʿat as a more specific designation of the general term negaʿ.[34] Ṣāraʿat refers to the specific affections of Leviticus 13, whereas negaʿ is a general term meaning "affection" or "plague."

With regard to the first proof text, Tosefta Negaim 6:7, passages from the Sifra demonstrate that there is no reason to distinguish separate causes for nĕgāʿîm and ṣāraʿat because both result from gossip and arrogance. For gossip I quote the Sifra on Deuteronomy 24:80:

Take heed of negaʿ ṣāraʿat to keep [the laws] very much and to do them; remember what the Lord God did to Miriam (Sifra Mes. Neg. par. 5:7).

Both terms, negaʿ and ṣāraʿat, are used here. Contrary to Neusner's assumption from the Tosefta, the Sifra does not distinguish separate diseases here. Neither does it relegate

---

34 B. A. Levine, *Leviticus*, Jewish Publication Society, 76 n. 2 on Negaʿ; Milgrom, *Leviticus*, I, 776; Elliger on Lev. 13:2.

arrogance to the term ṣāraʿat but uses the more inclusive term, negaʿ:

> R. Simeon b. Eleazar says, "Also because of arrogance do negaʿim come, for so do we find concerning Uzziah" (Sifra Mes. Neg. par. 5:9, tr. Neusner).[35]

Proof texts #2 and #3 seem to separate negaʿ and ṣāraʿat, making each responsible for different symptoms. I suggest that the division of negaʿ and ṣāraʿat here is stylistic. First of all, the designation of negaʿ in each passage is different: in the first it is referred to white hair and in the second to a variegated spot.

Secondly, to assume that the Rabbis really meant to assign the two terms to separate symptoms is to ignore the many passages of Scripture in which one of the terms is used for a symptom the Rabbis have supposedly relegated to the other term. According to Lev. 13:25, white hair, supposedly a sign of negaʿ, is said to be an indication of ṣāraʿat. Also, the neteq, scall, contains no raw flesh, the supposed sign of ṣāraʿat, but Scripture refers to it as a type of ṣāraʿat (Lev. 13:30).

Furthermore, fabrics and houses, too, are described as affected by nĕgāʿîm (Lev. 13:47; 14:37). In these cases, nĕgāʿîm are greenish-reddish. Hence, it is impossible to define negaʿ by the contribution of white hair alone.

In the final proof text above, Sifra Taz. Neg. 12:7-8, Neusner has misunderstood the Sifra. Its aim is not to compare ṣāraʿat with negaʿ. A look at the Scriptural passage behind the Sifra reveals that two verses describing the deportment of the mĕṣōrāʿ (Lev. 13:45-46) appear after the discussion of the one who has ṣāraʿat in addition to baldness. The Sifra clarifies that those affected by all types of ṣāraʿat, not just that which appears on a bald head, will follow the deportment rules of verses 45-46.

---

35 An examination of the Scriptural basis for these Sifra texts reveals that both the text in Deuteronomy (24:80) and that in 2 Chronicles (26:20) include both roots, negaʿ and ṣāraʿat, in describing the affection; there is certainly no segregation of the two to separate affections in Scripture.

Although negaʿ and ṣāraʿat do not represent different diseases, I agree with Neusner that they are not synonymous. "Nĕgāʿîm" appears to be a general term meaning "plagues" or "affections," and "ṣāraʿat" refers to the particular types described in Leviticus 13. When the terms are used together as negaʿ ṣāraʿat, the meaning is: "an affection of scale disease."

Philologically, this is evident in the joining of the two in the construct state. There is no intervening wāw adding one term to the next, rather the second term restricts the first.[36] Furthermore, negaʿ is used in several places in Scripture to denote not only plagues of ṣāraʿat but other types as well, even those brought through Moses upon Egypt (Ex. 11:1; 1 Ki. 8:37-38; Ps. 91:10; cf. Gen. 12:17; Ps. 73:5, 14).

Nevertheless, both words can refer to the same situation either generally, "affection/plague," or specifically, "scale disease." As scholars have noted, although etymologically difficult to analyze, ṣāraʿat does follow the same morphological structure as other diseases, e.g., qāraḥat, dalleqet.[37] The root of negaʿ, on the other hand, means "touched," possibly a reference to a divine curse (see above).

Neusner marvels that there are no separate data describing separate purification rites for negaʿ or for ṣāraʿat. However, this fact merely provides further proof that both terms refer in Lev. 13 and 14 to the same set of ailments.[38]

Because of his insistence that the Rabbis understand ṣāraʿat and negaʿ to refer to separate diseases, Neusner reads into Leviticus 13 and into the Sifra subtleties which do not exist. For example, since the Sifra states that ṣāraʿat is to be the size of a split bean (Sifra Taz. Neg. 1:6-7), Neusner says the definition of the negaʿ is taken from that of ṣāraʿat: the negaʿ is to be the size of a split bean.

---

36 But cf. 11QT 48:15 where there is an intervening wāw: מנוגעים בצרעות ובנגע ובנתק.

37 Sawyer, 245.

38 Neusner, *Purities*, VIII, 240.

Also, since the term ṣāraʿat is used when the Sifra defines the four shades of the disease, Neusner makes a comparison: ṣāraʿat is unclean in four specific shades; negaʿ, by contrast, is not so defined. His proof text is Sifra Taz. Neg. 15:10. Nĕgāʿîm in fabric need only fade in any degree to become clean. Negaʿ is not defined in four shades. As I stated, this argument is based on a shaky presupposition: that negaʿ is a contrastive ailment to ṣāraʿat. If one sees the two terms working in unison to describe a single type of affection, Neusner's distinctions become superfluous.

Let us return to Neusner's categorical statement that "all we have [in Negaim] is a reprise and logical expansion of biblical rules." Aside from the above insistence on the Sage's prominence, Neusner sees no other agenda in Tractate Negaim except the clarification of ambiguous matters in Scripture.

While it is the main thrust of this dissertation to prove the biblical foundations of the rabbinic impurity system, it must be acknowledged that even one who is only defining and clarifying details is an interpreter. The way in which the gaps are filled represents an interpretation. It is fortunate that other early Jewish writings exist with which to compare the rabbinic interpretation for they remind the reader that the Rabbis' approach is not nearly as self-evident as they wish to convey.

I would suggest that the Rabbis have a clear agenda and that it is as follows: The Rabbis wish to reduce the incidence of ṣāraʿat as much as possible, hence their definition of the disease is very narrow. By the rules of the Mishna it would be difficult to be designated a mĕṣōrāʿ.[39] Nevertheless, one who truly is a mĕṣōrāʿ must be banished from the community entirely in accordance with Scripture. Thus, the Rabbis regard the contamination of ṣāraʿat as a serious matter indeed but alleviate the difficulties it presents by limiting the incidence of the disease through a narrow definition.

This agenda, nevertheless, is not extrinsic to the Torah but is developed out of a serious regard for its authority. As discussed

---

39 "Leprosy" in *EJ*, XI, 38: the disease appears to be limited to baheret. According to its symptoms it may be defined as vitiligo, or leuce, a very rare skin disease.

in the preceding chapter, the Torah levies heavy sanctions on those who do not observe its purity code.

I will examine the sources in two areas: 1) the pronouncement of the disease, and 2) the contamination power of the disease. In the first a restrictive interpretation of Scripture is evident; in the second there is an expansive interpretation.

The laws regarding the pronouncement of the disease reveal an effort to limit the incidence of the disease. First of all, gentiles are unaffected by ṣāraʿat (m. Neg. 3:1; 7:1; 11:1; 12:1; Sifra Mes. Neg. par. 5:1-6; b. Git. 82a). Scripture is clear that the gēr tošab, i.e., the resident alien, is affected by the laws of impurity (Lev. 17:15; cf. 17:8, 10, 13; 20:2; Num. 15:27-29), but the Rabbis refer to Lev. 14:3-4 in which God says, "And I shall put a disease of ṣāraʿat in a house in the land of *your* possession," and thus limit pronouncement of the disease to Israel (Sifra Mes. Neg. par. 5:1-6).[40]

Certain places, too, are excluded from susceptibility. Jerusalem is not made unclean by affections of ṣāraʿat, however, Galilee is susceptible (t. Neg. 6:1). The Talmud states that ṣāraʿat does not exist in Babylonia (b. Ket. 77b). Again, there is no Scriptural basis for excluding Jerusalem or Babylonia from this malady.

When the suspected mĕṣōrāʿ comes to the priest, a variety of conditions in addition to those set forth in Scripture must be met in order for him to be certified. The priest must be able to see all of the affected area at one glance (t. Neg. 2:12), the suspected person must assume a certain position for the examination (m. Neg. 2:4), and only certain body places are susceptible (m. Neg. 6:8). The affected area must be at least the size of a split bean (m. Neg. 7:4; t. Neg. 3:4; Sifra Taz. Neg. 1:6), and affections of different varieties cannot be combined to meet the requisite size.

---

40 Milgrom suggests that the gēr tošab, resident alien, was probably considered subject to the laws of impurity in the Holiness Code but not in the Priestly Code and that these laws were certainly inclusive of the gēr tošab by 70 C.E., *Leviticus*, I, 772. However, the Rabbis interpret gēr as "proselyte," and hence limit the purity laws to the nation of Israel (m. Neg. 3:1). Cf. also Neusner, *Purities*, VIII, 122, 181.

For example, scalp baldness and forehead baldness cannot be combined to meet the prescribed size for baldness (m. Neg. 10:9-10; Sifra Taz. Neg. par. 5:2-3).

Color is important as well. The white spot of the baheret must be as white as snow; lesser whites are determined for the other affections. Only the four specified shades will cause spreading (Sifra Taz. Neg. 2:17; par. 2:4).[41]

Since only living (raw) flesh is mentioned as possibly recurring (Lev. 13:14), the Rabbis assume that white hair, even if it does recur, will not contaminate (t. Neg. 3:9; Sifra Taz. Neg. 5:4). Considering the usual homogenization technique which the Rabbis use to fill in Scripture's gaps, it is surprising that they do not make the analogy that white hair is to follow the given rule concerning raw flesh.

Affections are to be examined only at certain times:

> They do not examine the affections at dawn or at sunset, and not inside the house, and not on a cloudy day, because the dim appears bright, and not at noon, because the bright appears dim...R. Judah says, "At four, five, six, eight, and nine" (Sifra Taz. Neg. 2:3; m. Neg. 2:2).

This further inhibits the pronouncement of scale disease.

The rules for the house affected with ṣāraʿat reveal similar limitations on pronouncement. First of all, a house is only affected if it is made of stones, wood, and soil since these are the materials mentioned in Lev. 14:45. In addition, only the original stones or wood can be affected (Sifra Mes. Neg. 5:3).

A clear effort toward limitation of the affection is the Mishna's statement that the upper room of a house is not to be considered part of the house if it contains affected stones or wood. Thus, if the affection appears in the beams of the house, one assigns them to the upper room separately as if the beams were separated from the house. If the affection appears in the

---

41 Lev. 13:38-39 explains that certain white spots, i.e., dull white spots, do not contaminate. They are called bōhaq, often translated "tetter."

upper room but not in its beams, one assigns the beams to the house (m. Neg. 13:3; Sifra Mes. Neg. 5:3).

There must be two spots in the affected house, each the size of a split bean, in order for it to become unclean. This is because Scripture speaks of the houses' walls in the plural (Lev. 14:37, 39). Hence, there must be at least two affections, each on a separate wall (b. San. 87b).

One should not break open vents in a windowless house when inspecting it:

> As to a dark house, they do not break open windows in it to examine its affection (m. Neg. 2:3; t. Neg. 1:8; Sifra Mes. Neg. 7:6).

Again, the desire not to pronounce the decree of ṣāraʿat is evident.

Evidently, the incidence of a house actually pronounced with ṣāraʿat was rare if ever. The Tosefta describes a quarantined ruin at Gaza and a place of infected stones in Galilee but then states that such a house has never happened and never will! (t. Neg. 6:1)

Ṣāraʿat in garments, too, is narrowly defined. Wool and flax are affected only if they are in their original states and only if the item really forms a garment. Scripture teaches that the affection takes on a greenish-reddish color in garments. Hence, the Rabbis state that only the greenest of greens and the reddest of reds define the disease (t. Neg. 1:5; Sifra Taz. Neg. 14:2). Because of this color consideration, some Sages insist the garment must have been white to begin with (m. Neg. 11:3; t. Neg. 5:2-3). This view automatically excludes all naturally colored or dyed fabrics.

The rabbinic handling of the issue of quarantine is interesting. Scripture clearly designates two weeks for shutting up the suspected person or house. At the end of each week the person or house is examined for fading signs. However, if there is no improvement after the second week, the person/house is certified with the disease. The Rabbis institute an additional week for inspection. It is clear that this third week applies for houses and less certainly for persons (m. Neg. 3:8; t. Neg. 1:15; 4:7-8;

Sifra Taz. Neg. 4:6).[42] The effect of the additional week is obvious: it gives the suspected item one more chance for improvement before the priest pronounces his verdict.

Finally, all doubts in the matter of pronouncement of ṣāraʿat are decided on the side of leniency (m. Neg. 5:1; t. Neg. 2:7; Sifra Taz. Neg. par. 4:8). In light of the above restrictions on pronouncement, this is not surprising.

I will turn now to the matter of contamination. Here one finds stringency. It is imperative that a certified mĕṣōrāʿ not come in contact with those who are pure. Contact is understood by the Rabbis in a more comprehensive manner than is evidenced by a simple reading of Scripture.

The mĕṣōrāʿ must be placed within the larger rabbinic system of impurities. In many places the Rabbis emphasize that the mĕṣōrāʿ is like the dead (m. Neg. 13:12; t. Neg. 7:6; b. San. 47a; b. Hul. 7b; b. Ned. 64b; b. AZ 5a). Only the corpse and the mĕṣōrāʿ are excluded from walled cities; only these two contaminate by overhang. Ṣāraʿat is even defined in terms of a squared handbreadth, the same measurement used to define corpse contamination. The mĕṣōrāʿ is sent out of all three camps (the Divine, the Levitical, and the Israelite), an exclusion demanded only of the corpse and the mĕṣōrāʿ (m. Kel. 1:7; b. Zeb. 117a; b. Pes. 66b-67a). Indeed, the connection of the corpse and ṣāraʿat is biblical (Num. 12:12; Jb. 18:13).[43] However, the Rabbis clarify exactly what that means in terms of contamination.

Looking at the chart below (Fig. 3) one can see what the picture of ṣāraʿat contamination was in the minds of the Rabbis. Mĕṣōrāʿîm, since they are ʾabôt ṭumʾâ, contaminate persons and susceptible objects in the first degree. This can be accomplished by a variety of means. A clean person who merely walks into a room

---

42 Neusner, *Purities*, XXII, 221, ascribes this third week of quarantine to the Ushan period despite the claim of the Sifra that this week is Yavnean or Scriptural.

43 Thus, the notion that the mĕṣōraʿ is like the dead does not begin at Usha (opp. Neusner, XXII, 218). Milgrom compares the purification rites between the corpse-contaminated person and the mĕṣōraʿ and makes further connections between the two, see *Leviticus*, I, 816-20.

FIG. 3 THE CONTAMINATION OF THE MĔṢŌRĀʿ IN THE RABBINIC SYSTEM

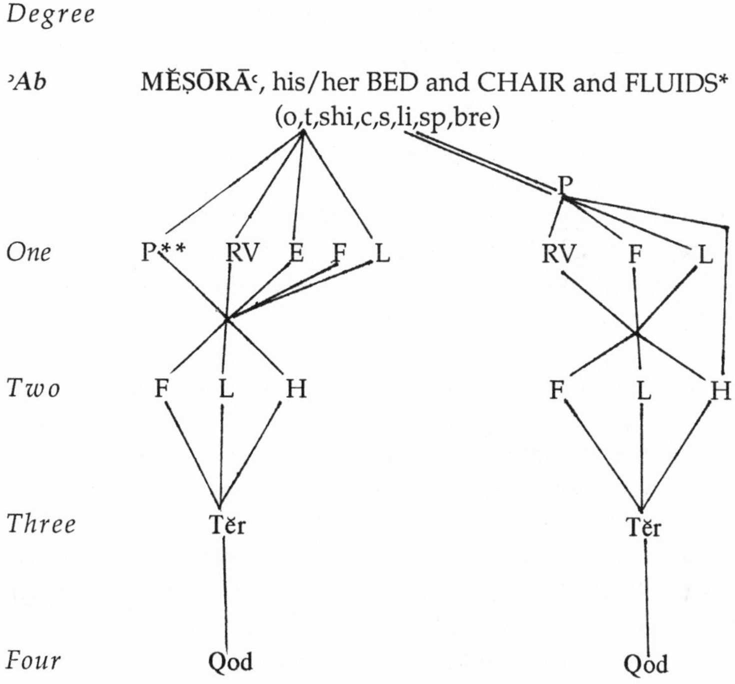

References:
Branch 1: m. Zab. 5:1, 6, 10; m. Neg. 13:9; 14:2; Sifra Mes. Neg. 5:5-8; Sifra Mes. Neg. par. 1:4; par. 2:6; Sifra Taz. Neg. 12:7; b. Nid. 28b, 34b.
Branch 2: m. Zab. 5:1, 6, 10.

* Rashi states that fluids of the mĕṣōrāʿ are ʾabôt ṭumʾâ; Maimonides states that these fluids are only in the first degree like other liquids the mĕṣōrāʿ touches, Rashi on b. Nid. 28b; *Code*, X, Couch 5:5; b. Nid. 34b.

** Persons must bathe and launder only if they have been subject to ṣāraʿat by overhang long enough to eat or lie down under it. Otherwise, only bathing is necessary (m. Neg. 13:9; Sifra Mes. Neg. 5:5-8).

in which the mĕṣōrāʿ is present becomes impure. Since the text does mention lying or eating in a house affected with ṣāraʿat (Lev. 14:47), the Rabbis stipulate that a person must have been in the room long enough to eat a piece of bread or lie down, otherwise, only bathing not laundering is necessary (m. Neg. 13:9; Sifra Mes. Neg. 5:5-8).

The Rabbis extend the notion of contamination by overhang beyond the simple meaning of Scripture. Typically, they test the limits of biblical principles. In this case, having recognized that the power of the tent to convey impurity lies in its overhang, they explore the possibilities of other overhangs to contaminate. The Rabbis suggest that the overhang of many things, e.g., a tree, an awning or even another person can convey impurity (m. Neg. 13:7).

It is true that the Scrolls extant, as well as Josephus, only refer to impurity by overhang in the context of residences. However, one should not conclude too quickly that the sectarians did not make such extensions; there is simply no evidence of it at present.

Other means by which the mĕṣōrāʿ will transfer impurity to a clean person are: by touching, shifting or carrying without contact, spitting, or breathing (m. Zab. 5:6; see below for saliva and breath). The saliva of the mĕṣōrāʿ is defiling because the saliva of the zāb, who bears less impurity, is defiling. The zāb's lesser impurity is evidenced by the lesser restriction and fewer purification rites required of him (See Chapter 6, below). Also, Scripture states that mĕṣōrāʿîm must cover their mouths (Lev. 13:45). This was done probably as the Arabs and Babylonian Jewish mourners of the rabbinic era who lowered a mantle over their heads covering their mouths (b. MQ 24a; Sifra Neg. Taz. 12:7; Tg. Onq. and Tg. Ps.-Jon. on Lev. 13:45).[44]

Although Scripture never ascribes impurity to breath, the Rabbis are afraid that even the breath of the mĕṣōrāʿ will defile, probably because the mouth of the mĕṣōrāʿ must be covered. This is clear from the discussion of two Rabbis on how many cubits

44 Milgrom, *Leviticus*, I, 803.

away from the mĕṣōrāʿ one should walk. The discussion ends when one Rabbi decides that when the wind is blowing a person should keep a greater distance away from the mĕṣōrāʿ (y. BB 3:9; Lev. R. 16:3). The concern over breath is reinforced by Maimonides who says that the mĕṣōrāʿ may study the Torah but only with closed lips.[45]

In addition, the Rabbis homogenize the laws of genital discharges (Lev. 15) with the laws of ṣāraʿat. Thus, the special mode of contamination of bed and chair applicable to the zāb is applied as well to the mĕṣōrāʿ (m. Zab. 5:6; b. Zeb. 15b, Munich ms.). This is done on the basis of the position of the mĕṣōrāʿ in the system as a more potent impurity bearer than any of those mentioned in Leviticus 15. The Talmud states categorically that all fluids of the mĕṣōrāʿ are unclean from the analogy of the zāb (b. Nid. 34b).[46]

One who comes in contact with the mĕṣōrāʿ via any of these means must bathe and launder and remain impure until the following evening. Susceptible objects which come into contact with the mĕṣōrāʿ by any of these means, too, must be washed and remain unused until sunset. Earthenware cannot be purified by water but must be broken. Food and liquids are contaminated by any such contact as well. Hands are made unclean, too, but only in the second degree (m. Zab. 5:1).

Below are some passages from Mishna Tractate Zabim which discuss the contamination potency of the mĕṣōrāʿ:

> ...A general rule did R. Joshua state: Whoever imparts uncleanness to clothes, when he is in contact imparts uncleanness to food and drink, putting [them] into the first remove. But he does not impart uncleanness either to man or to clay utensils. After he separates from the things which make him unclean, he imparts uncleanness to liquid, putting [it] into the first remove, and to food and the hands, putting [them] into the second remove. And he does not impart uncleanness to clothes (m. Zab. 5:1).

---

45 *Code*, X, 10:6; cf. b. MQ 15a.

46 Rashi states that the fluids of a mĕṣōraʿ are ʾabôt ṭumʿâ (Rashi on b. Nid. 28b). Maimonides claims that these fluids are like the liquids the mĕṣōraʿ touches and hence in the first remove (*Code*, X, couch 5:5).

> ...He who touches the Zab, the Zabah, and the menstruating woman and the woman after childbirth and the meṣoraᶜ, a bed or chair [that any of these have lain or sat upon] imparts uncleanness at two removes and renders [heave offering] unfit at one further remove. [If] he separated, he imparts uncleanness at one remove and renders unfit at one further remove (m. Zab. 5:6).

The latter text also explains that touching, shifting, and carriage are treated as the same mode of conveyance as to stringency. A further passage states:

> He who touches...the meṣoraᶜ during the period of his counting [clean days, preparatory to the purification rite]...imparts uncleanness at one remove and renders unfit at one remove. This is the general rule: Whatever touches any one of all the Fathers of Uncleanness which are listed in the Torah imparts uncleanness at one remove and renders unfit at one remove, except for man. [If] one separated, he imparts uncleanness at one remove and renders unfit at one remove (m. Zab. 5:10).

Thus, all susceptible items become impure in the first degree. They in turn will contaminate any food or liquids with which they come in contact, however, this contact must be by touch, not overhang, spitting, etc.[47] Only food and liquids will become unclean by those items in the first degree of uncleanness. Liquids will always be contaminated in the first degree and will contaminate other food or liquids. Unclean food or liquids can contaminate tĕrûmâ, and impure tĕrûmâ in the third degree of uncleanness can defile qodōšîm in the fourth degree (See Introduction for further explanation of the system).

Persons still in contact with the mĕṣōrāᶜ will contaminate other susceptible items they touch (excluding other persons and earthenware) up to two degrees, tĕrûmâ at a third degree, and qodōšîm at a fourth (m. Zab. 5:6).

Houses, garments, and skins affected with ṣāraᶜat are contaminating by overhang and by touch. If an affected garment is in a room with a clean person, even if there is no contact, the clean person is made unclean (Sifra Taz. Neg. 16:12). An affected

---

47 See b. Yoma 6b, ed. I. Epstein, for explanation.

house will contaminate all who enter it or touch it on any side (m. Neg. 13:4).

Even quarantined houses or persons contaminate to a certain degree. A quarantined house renders those who enter it unclean, but it is unclean on the inside only; those who touch its outside are not affected (Sifra Mes. Neg. par. 7:13). The musgār, a quarantined person suspected of ṣāraʿat, is considered unclean until the diseased spot either breaks out over the whole body or fades to the size of less than a split bean (m. Neg. 7:4; Sifra Taz. Neg. 2:10). The musgār contaminates by touch but not by overhang (t. Meg. 1:12; b. Meg. 8b; b. Yeb. 74b; Bertinoro on m. Meg. 1:7). This can be deduced from the Talmud's equation of a musgār and a corpse-contaminated person; the latter cannot contaminate by overhang.

The purifying mĕṣōrāʿ who is counting the required week before re-entering his or her house contaminates as well but only by direct contact, i.e., not by carriage, overhang, etc. (m. Neg. 14:2; m. Zab. 5:10; m. Kel. 1:1; Sifra Mes. Neg. par. 1:4). The chart below (Fig. 4) illustrates the potency of the purifying mĕṣōrāʿ during the purificatory period. As Scripture states, the mĕṣōrāʿ must observe certain purification rites at set stages in the reinstatement process including bathing, laundering, shaving, etc. (see above). Each stage removes a certain amount of impurity. The chart below shows at the left the stage of the ṣāraʿat impurity, in the center its effect on profane, susceptible items, and on the right its effect on sancta. The sigla show the types of contact by which the purifying mĕṣōrāʿ conveys impurity. Brackets show assumptions based on the referenced information.

Thus, the difference in the perspective of the early priests and that of the Rabbis is that the latter have added new modes of contamination, including, shifting and breathing. Also, the mĕṣōrāʿ can contaminate via bed or chair. The Rabbis retain the system which the Bible presents and seem to be merely clarifying details. However, they, in fact, expand the stringency of the contamination of ṣāraʿat in ways which Scripture does not demand. Scripture says nothing about the breath of the mĕṣōrāʿ

FIG. 4 THE CONTAMINATION OF THE MIṬṬĀHĒR IN THE RABBINIC SYSTEM

Stage	*Contam. to Profane*	*Contam. to Sancta*
Mĕṣōrāʿ	o,t,shi,carr, sp,bre,s,li	airborne
Miṭṭahēr: Day 1	t	[o,t,shi,carr, sp,bre,s,l]
Miṭṭahēr: Day 7	none	t
Miṭṭahēr: Day 8	none	none

References: m. Kel. 1:1; m. Neg. 14:2; m. Zab. 5:10; Sifra Mes. Neg. par. 1:4; b. BB 9b; b. Meg. 8b being contaminating. Neither does it demand that the bed or chair of the mĕṣōrāʿ be a pollutant. Nor does it suggest that overhangs such as trees and awnings can convey contamination.

The restrictions levied on certified mĕṣōrāʿîm enforce the Rabbis' concern to exclude them and the possibility of contamination by them from the community. It is impossible to know, of course, how much they are responding to current situations involving mĕṣōrāʿîm and how much they are proposing for the era of the new Temple. I think that their concern would apply in either case because 1) at present there is no possibility of purification from ṣāraʿat without the officiating priest, the bird rites and concluding sacrifices; such a hopeless person should not be allowed to mingle within the community and 2) when the new Temple is built, Scripture's mandates will be in effect, and responsibility for keeping sancta from any impurity will again be a primary concern with a penalty of excision from the community in the event of contamination.

What are the restrictions on the mĕṣōrāʿ? As Scripture demands, mĕṣōrāʿîm must rend their clothes and call out, "Unclean, unclean!" in order to warn others of their presence.[48] The Gospels record stories of first century mĕṣōrāʿîm who plead with Jesus to heal them (Mt. 8:2-4; Mk. 1:40-45; Lk. 5:12-14; 17:11-19). In one case, the writer says they stood at a distance (Lk. 17:12), apparently to avoid contaminating him in any way.

I noted above that the mĕṣōrāʿ is not allowed within walled cities. The penalty for entry, according to the Babylonian Talmud, is 40 lashes (b. Pes. 67a). The mĕṣōrāʿ must keep away from all other types of impurity bearers since Scripture says, "He shall dwell alone (Lev. 13:46)" (Sifra Taz. Neg. 12:12-13; b. Arakh. 16b; cf. also b. Pes. 67a).[49] It is noteworthy that the ten mĕṣōrāʿîm who

---

48 Women are excluded from the commandment to rend clothes, Sifra Taz. Neg. 12:1; b. Ker. 8b.

49 These passages confirm that the notion did exist among the Rabbis (along with a more moderate view, cf. Sif. Zut. on Num. 5:2) that impurity bearers should reside apart from each other and that this was not just the view of sectarians, cf. Milgrom, *Leviticus*, I, 805. Also

approach Jesus do so as he is entering the city (Lk. 17:12). Evidently, they live outside the city as the Torah prescribes.

The mĕṣōrāʿ may have sexual intercourse except during the purification week (m. Neg. 14:2). The Babylonian Talmud explains that Scripture's "tent," in the command to stay out of one's tent for seven days, refers to one's wife.[50] According to the Mishna, a partition was made in the synagogue to segregate the mĕṣōrāʿ from the other congregants. The mĕṣōrāʿ entered first and left last so as to have no contact whatever with those who were clean (m. Neg. 13:12; t. Neg. 7:11).

Even in late sources there are still ostracizing attitudes toward the mĕṣōrāʿ. Resh Laqish cast stones at mĕṣōrāʿîm. Other Rabbis hid from them. R. Meir refused to eat eggs from a district of mĕṣōrāʿîm; R. Ammi and R.Assi refused to enter such an area (Lev. R. 16:3). Restrictions recorded in the Talmud include the following: Mĕṣōrāʿîm may not cut their hair, wash their clothes, or greet other persons (b. MQ 15a).[51]

Rabbinic sources also describe the purification of the mĕṣōrāʿ. According to the Babylonian Talmud, bird rites were performed in accordance with Scripture. The Rabbis state that even the blood of these offerings defile, requiring those who have contact with it to bathe and launder their clothes (b. Yoma 61b). In the Second Temple there existed the Cell of the Mĕṣōrāʿîm in the northwest corner of the Court of the Women. This is where the mĕṣōrāʿ came on the eighth day to immerse before offering the concluding sacrifice (b. Yoma 16a; 30b.) Then, the priest daubed his or her right ear, thumb, and big toe with blood and oil at the Nicanor Gate. The mĕṣōrāʿ was not allowed to enter the sacred

---

Josephus thinks the mĕṣōraʿ should be secluded from other impurity bearers, Ant. 3:264.

50 b. Hul. 141a, but this command was not incumbent on female mĕṣōraʿîm.

51 The Munich manuscript adds a requirement on those with scale disease to overturn their couches (b. MQ15b). This is probably due to the contamination conveyed by the bed or seat of the scale-diseased person, as discussed above.

area so merely held out the ear, thumb, or toe for the priest to daub (b. Yoma 30b-31a).

I cannot leave the subject of rabbinic intensification of the contamination of and restrictions on a mĕṣōrāʿ without pointing out that a slight difference in attitude does exist among the rabbinic sources. The Sifra reveals a slightly less stringent attitude than the Mishna.[52]

The Sifra states that even if only part of the white hair or raw flesh is gone, the mĕṣōrāʿ is healed because Lev. 14:3 reads, "...*of* the ṣāraʿat" (Sifra Mes. Zab. par. 1:7). As noted above, the Sifra goes so far as to say that only the original stones or wood can even be affected by ṣāraʿat (Sifra Mes. Zab. 5:3). Neither of these provisions exist in the Mishna.

Also the Babylonian Talmud, edited in the sixth century, tends to be more lenient than the Mishna, edited at the end of the second century. The Rabbis of the Talmud state that one is only contaminated in a house affected by ṣāraʿat if entering it in the customary manner (b. Shebu. 17b). In another place the Talmud bases its more lenient attitude on an illustration from Scripture. It states that mĕṣōrāʿîm were allowed in the camp when the Israelites were traveling. Only when they stopped and set up the tabernacle were mĕṣōrāʿîm excluded (b. Taan. 21b), i.e., without the existence of sancta the presence of mĕṣōrāʿîm posed no threat. Perhaps this sheds some light on the Rabbis' view of their own situation in which no sanctuary existed. Most lenient perhaps is the Talmud's statement that ṣāraʿat does not exist in Babylonia (b. Ket. 77b).

Some Rabbis resist the strictness of the majority opinion of the Sages on ṣāraʿat, but they are overruled. For instance, some state that the mĕṣōrāʿ should not have to shave all body hair (b. Sot. 16a). R. Eliezer and R. Simeon struggle with the difficulty of purifying a mĕṣōrāʿ who has no right big toe, thumb, or ear. They

52 However, I disagree with Neusner who claims that the Sifra, in opposition to m. Neg. 13:7, suggests the mĕṣōraʿ can only contaminate in his or her own house, VII, 106. Rather, the Sifra supports the notion that even the overhang of trees will convey the impurity of the mĕṣōraʿ, Sifra Taz. Neg. 12:14.

suggest, in opposition to the rest of the Sages, that such a person could still be purified by other means (b. San. 88a). R. Judah, editor of the Mishna, suggested that the mĕṣōrāᶜ only contaminates in another person's house if entering it by permission of the owner (t. Neg. 7:11), but this idea is not the majority opinion.

What can be concluded from the foregoing data? I think several conclusions are warranted: 1) The Rabbis exhibit a great hesitance to confirm anybody a mĕṣōrāᶜ. They do not wish to create this difficult (and after 70 C.E. irremediable without sacrifices) circumstance, if at all possible. 2) On the other hand, one who is a certified mĕṣōrāᶜ represents a dynamic force, the parameters of which are not to be underestimated. The Rabbis restrict mĕṣōrāᶜîm severely and apply more impurity to them than what seems to be demanded by the pĕšāṭ of the text. 3) It is the sacred regard for the authority of the Torah which guides the concern of the Rabbis and gives rise to the preceding conclusions. One can see that the Rabbis would not have extended the impurity of the mĕṣōrāᶜ to equal that of the zāb if they had not thought it was demanded by the biblical system. For them there had to be a logical whole, not just lack of contradiction, but an interrelated system of impurity dynamics resting on biblical principles. More importantly, the Torah's sanctions on impure persons had to be avoided at all costs.

A final comment grows out of the notice that earlier rabbinic sources seem more stringent than later ones. Against those who suggest that the destruction of the Temple had little or no effect on the development of the laws, I would say that those living during the time of the Temple or in the years directly after its destruction were of a much different mindset than the later Rabbis of the Talmud. The earlier Sages were stringent because they either remembered or heard others tell of Temple practice, or they were eagerly awaiting the rebuilding of the new Temple in which correct purification procedures requiring the cult would be reinstituted. The later Sages are more interested in alleviating the contamination of ṣāraᶜat because they do not wish to condemn anyone to a hopeless situation in which purification is impossible without sacrifices. They want to alleviate the difficulty of observing the Torah without the cult.

CHAPTER 6

THE IMPURITY OF BODILY DISCHARGES

Certain bodily discharges are considered by the Rabbis to defile persons and objects in various ways. These are limited to flows from the male and female genital organs. In this chapter I am interested to explain the contamination produced by these flows in the rabbinic system in an effort to reveal its absolute dependence on Scripture. Contrary to the view of some that the Rabbis wanted to extend the effects of this impurity even to creating new modes of contamination, I suggest that the opposite is true. The Rabbis prefer to limit the effects of the impurity of discharges but are circumscribed by the authority of Scripture. The biblical text must be interpreted in accordance with inherent principles and cannot be blatantly overruled.

I will proceed in three ways: First, I will examine the contamination of impure flows according to the Bible. The Priestly Code constitutes a system and this material was understood as a system by the Rabbis. Second, I will set forth the system of the Rabbis on impure flows, demonstrating how the rabbinic system is based on the priestly one with an effort to limit contamination if possible. The rabbinic material is complex and varies sometimes between sources, but a system is discernible. Finally, I will focus on certain key principles which have been labelled by scholars "rabbinic extensions," e. g., midrās, contamination via pressure without direct contact, and show that they are in fact explicit or implicit in Scripture. To state my conclusion in advance, the Rabbis did wish to limit the contamination of this impurity but could only do so 1) when they were not crossing explicit biblical rules and 2) if they were operating by principles which could be supported by Scripture.

In order to understand the extent of the connection between the Rabbis and Scripture one must realize that the Rabbis are not inventing a system of uncleanness on bodily discharges but are inheriting and interpreting a system. In other words, Scripture's rules on bodily discharges form a system. This system has been thoroughly diagrammed by D. Wright based on the implications of the meager explicit data available in Leviticus 12 and 15 (Figs. 1-5). It is important to realize, that although these charts are different than those of the Rabbis due to rabbinic interpretation, the idea of a purity system is not new with the Rabbis. Many elements thought to be new in the rabbinic system are already present in the Bible.

Let us examine the biblical system carefully. The impurity list of Leviticus 11-15 emphasizes the impurity of various discharges from the genital organs. The persons who emit these discharges are: the yôledet, the woman who has just given birth and is bleeding, the zāb, the man with an abnormal sexual emission outside of sexual intercourse, probably gonorrhea; the zābâ, the woman who emits vaginal blood outside of the regular course of her menstrual cycle; the man who has a seminal emission, whether due to sexual intercourse, šikbat-zeraᶜ, or not, baᶜal qerî; and the niddâ, the menstruant.

First, a note about terms. The word zāb derives from the root zûb meaning to "ooze" or "flow" (cf. Isa. 48:21; Lev. 20:24). This flow lasts "many days" (Lev. 15:25). The Rabbis logically concretize the term "many" to indicate at least three (m. Zab. 1:3). The Rabbis clarify that flux is not semen; the latter is the result of

FIG. 1 THE CONTAMINATION OF THE ZĀBÂ IN THE BIBLICAL SYSTEM

(Copied from D. P. Wright, *The Disposal of Impurity,* 194)

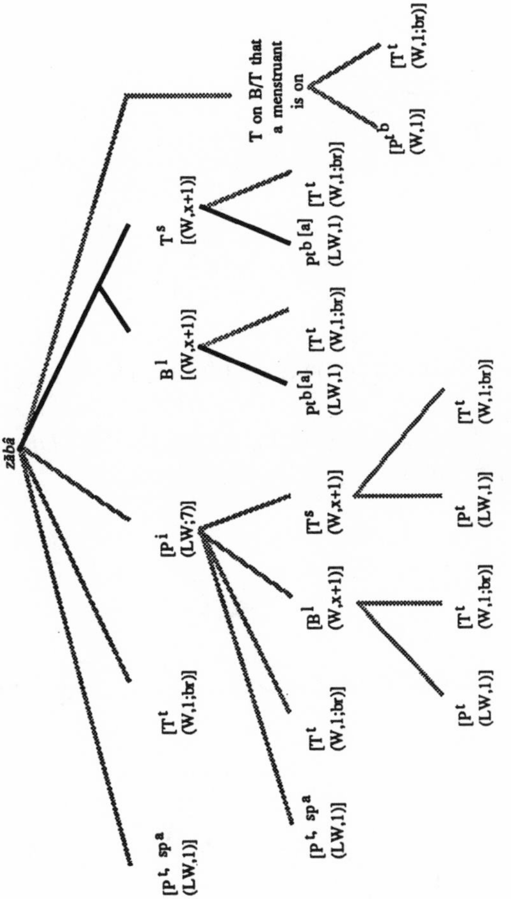

FIG. 2 THE CONTAMINATION OF THE ZĀB IN THE BIBLICAL SYSTEM

(Copied from D. P. Wright, *The Disposal of Impurity*, 182)

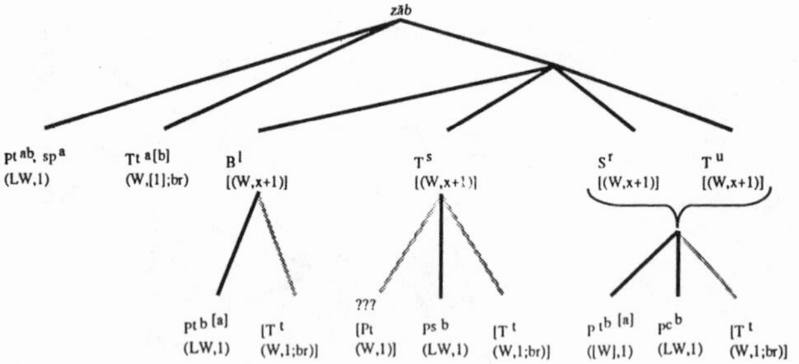

FIG. 3 REVISED THIRD BRANCH OF FIG. 2

(Copied from D. P. Wright, *The Disposal of Impurity*, 188)

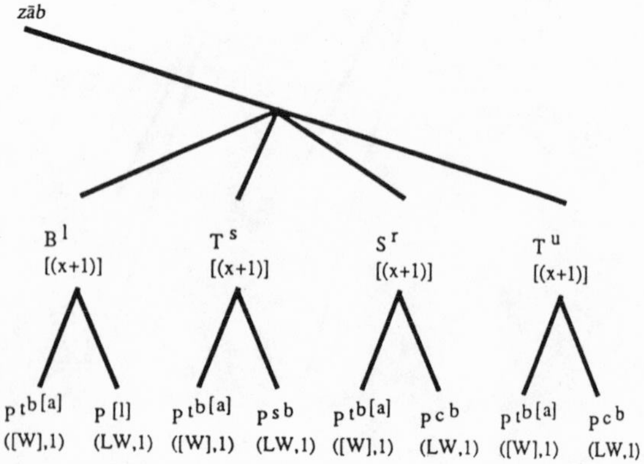

FIG. 4 THE CONTAMINATION OF THE MENSTRUANT IN THE BIBLICAL SYSTEM

(Copied from D. P. Wright, *The Disposal of Impurity*, 190)

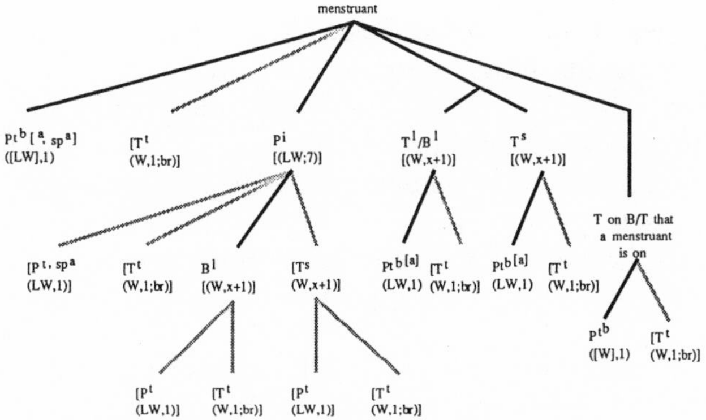

FIG. 5 THE CONTAMINATION OF SEMEN IN THE BIBLICAL SYSTEM

(Copied from D. P. Wright, *The Disposal of Impurity*, 196)

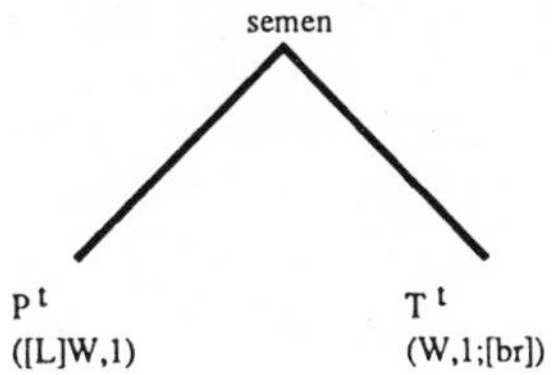

an erection, the former is not (t. Zab. 2:4). Flux is usually equated with gonorrhea but can refer to any abnormal, urethral secretion.[1]

The word **niddâ** means "discharge" and derives from the root **ndd** which, in its **hiphʿil** and **piʿel** constructions, means "to chase away." J. Milgrom gives the etymological background of the term in his commentary on Leviticus, comparing biblical usages of this root with Ugaritic and Akkadian parallels which have the meaning, "to drive out, throw, or cast down." Milgrom concludes that **niddâ**, a nominal construction of **ndd** means literally "expulsion" or "elimination" with clear reference to the vaginal blood eliminated from the menstruant's body. He further states that the term came to refer as well to the menstruant herself who was not only discharging blood, but was herself "discharged" or excluded from society:

> ...niddâ came to refer not just to the menstrual discharge but to the menstruant herself, for she too was "discharged" and "excluded" from her society not by being kept at arm's length from others but, in many communities, by being banished to and quarantined in separate quarters.[2]

What is the relationship between the five impurity bearers listed above? Which is most seriously contaminated? In answering these questions, it can be assumed that a rule applying to a less potent impurity bearer will apply to a more potent impurity bearer. There is a certain "pecking" order between the five types; they are not all equally defiling.

Before attempting to discern the degree of potency among these impurity bearers, one must be aware of the greater impurity of vaginal blood over discharges from the male organ. It seems paradoxical that blood is such a severe pollutant since it is the only detergent for the altar, however, human blood is never

---

1 Ibid., 907. Milgrom cites, among others, J. Preuss, *Biblisch-talmudische Medizin*, 410.

2 Milgrom, *Leviticus*, I, 745. For comparative material on the expulsion of the menstruant in various cultures cf. 948-953.

appropriate for the altar. Also, the blood of a living person is never ritually contaminating unless it flows from the vagina.

Contamination and purification requirements of those in contact with vaginal blood reveal its greater potency over male sexual flows. Touching the chair of the menstruant requires laundering and washing (Lev. 15:22), whereas touching the zāb's chair requires washing only (15:10). Contact with vaginal blood through sexual intercourse renders a man impure for seven days (15:24). Contact with semen by sexual intercourse renders both parties unclean only until the next evening (15:18).

Looking further at contamination and purification requirements I conclude that either the yôledet or the zābâ is the most impure of the five impurity bearers. The yôledet is unclean as a menstruant for seven days after the child's birth if it is a boy and 14 days if it is a girl. She remains impure to a lesser degree for an additional 33 (boy) or 66 (girl) days. She must also bring a sacrifice (Lev. 12:6). Scripture provides no rules about her contamination potential to others. Nevertheless, she would probably affect them like the menstruant during the first stage of her impurity, since Scripture compares her impurity to that of the niddâ: "...She [the parturient] shall be impure for seven days; she shall be impure as during the period of her menstrual infirmity" (Lev. 12:2, tr. Milgrom). Thus, like the menstruant, the yôledet is contaminating to the profane world during the first stage of her impurity. After this initial one or two week period, the parturient can convey impurity only to sacred personnel/objects (Lev. 12:4).

Although the yôledet must observe a longer period of purification than the zābâ, the latter probably bears the more severe impurity. Like the parturient, the zābâ must bring a sacrifice at the close of her purification. However, the nature of her situation is different. Unlike the blessing of procreation, the zābâ's condition is the result of a divine curse. David curses Joab for his treacherous murder of Abner: "...may the house of Joab never be without a zāb, or a mĕṣōrāʿ..." (2 Sam. 3:29). Additionally, zābîm cannot be purified unless they are first healed from the affliction. The Gospels record an example of a zābâ who had been afflicted for 12 years; she was trying to reach Jesus in order to be healed (Mk. 5:25-34). Thus, the zābâ's abnormal condition may place her at the top of the impurity charts of those with flows.

The zābâ is certainly in a more serious condition, as to ritual defilement, than the niddâ. The zābâ remains unclean for seven days after her cure; the niddâ is only unclean for a seven-day period, *in toto*. Also, the zābâ is required to bring a sacrifice to the sanctuary on the eighth day; for the niddâ, bathing and laundering suffices (cf. Lev. 15:21).

As stated above, the zābâ's condition is probably more serious due to its abnormality. The menstruant's loss of blood is a regular occurrence and is a normal part of her life. The zābâ's condition is unexpected and reflects an unpredictable loss of blood. D. Kraemer points out that the Torah considers menstruation a "natural bodily function" exemplified even in the order of the text of Leviticus 15. Kraemer says:

> The Torah's account of these laws uses the common chiastic structure (A-B-B-A, where A = unnatural flow and B = natural flows). Menstruation, here equated with seminal emission, is clearly the less severe of the potential flows which a woman might experience.[3]

The zāb must be considered a major impurity bearer, more potent than the menstruant but less potent than the zābâ. Like the latter he must bring a sacrifice, not required of the menstruant, but since his flow is less potent than vaginal blood, he would be considered somewhat less impure than the zābâ.

The man who emits semen, in or out of sexual intercourse, must be considered the least impure of all five of these impurity bearers. Scripture teaches that he conveys impurity only to the woman with whom he has intercourse (Lev. 15:18). Unlike the zāb he is not required to launder his clothes (Lev. 15:18; Dt. 23:1). Nevertheless, if other persons or objects (e.g., his bed or clothes) come into direct contact with his semen, they must be washed

---

3 D. C. Kraemer, "A Developmental Perspective on the Laws of Niddah" in *Conservative Judaism* 38/3 (1986) 27.

(Lev. 15:17). If contact is made only with the man who emitted the semen, apparently, no contamination follows.

With the foregoing comments on the relationship of these impurity bearers to each other, several *a fortiori* conclusions regarding the contamination they convey can be made. For example, the zābâ, since she bears greater impurity, can be assumed to convey at least as much impurity as the zāb and the niddâ.

The zābâ conveys contamination in several ways. First of all, because of the seriousness of her impurity, the zābâ pollutes the sanctuary even though she does not approach it. The fact that she must offer a sacrifice after the seven-day period of impurity indicates that she has indeed polluted the sanctuary. This is not the case with those on normal menstrual cycles. The Rabbis, too, notice the danger of zābîm to the sanctuary and point out that it is only after the building of the tabernacle that they are banished from the camp.[4]

The zābâ contaminates like the menstruant. The pericope devoted to the zābâ (Lev. 15:25-30) appears to be an abridgement of the preceding pericopes on the zāb and the menstruant. Lev. 15:25 makes it clear that the zābâ is unclean "as in the days of her (menstrual) impurity." The Bible is clear that an Israelite is contaminated for seven days if he has intercourse with a menstruant (Lev. 15:24); *a fortiori* with a zābâ.

The more common means of contracting impurity from the menstruant are repeated for the case of the zābâ. For example, touching her bed and chair causes impurity; the writer is concerned that this may happen accidentally.

The impurity transmitted by actual contact between a clean person and a zābâ can be assumed. This is supported by verses 7 and 19 in which those touching a zāb or a menstruant are unclean and must wash their clothes and bathe. Although the text is silent on the impurity resulting from the menstruant's touch, the zāb conveys no impurity if he washes his hands before touching a

---

4 Num. R. 7:1; Lev. R. 18:4; J. Neusner, *The Idea of Purity in Ancient Judaism*, 97.

clean person. Earthenware vessels which the **zāb** has touched, presumably without washing his hands, must be broken and wooden vessels must be rinsed with water (15:12). Perhaps these rules regarding the zāb's touch may be assumed for the **zābâ** and the menstruant as well, but one cannot be sure.

As stated above, the one who emits semen only contaminates the woman who had intercourse with him (Lev. 15:18); persons who touch him are unaffected. However, objects which come into direct contact with semen must be immersed (Lev. 15:17).

The unique contamination quality of the bed and seat of those with genital flows is most likely due to their possible contact with the discharge. A greater contamination applies in the case of the menstruant and the zābâ confirming the evaluation that blood was considered a more potent source of impurity. Touching the zāb's seat or anything else under him (except the bed) only requires bathing; touching the menstruant's or zābâ's seat requires the person to launder as well.

The chart below (Fig. 6) illustrates the contamination power of those with genital discharges. All references are to Leviticus 15; bracketed numbers give the verse which supports the particular information. Data in parentheses are not directly stated in the passage but are implied.

I have included the **yôledet** since, as stated above, she can be assumed to convey at least as much impurity as the **niddâ**. On the other hand, the man who emits semen is not included since he transmits uncleanness only to the woman who had sexual contact with him.

Thus, one can see that in almost every form of contact with these four impure types, clean persons must bathe and launder their clothes. The only two exceptions are: 1) contact with all items under the zāb other than the bed and 2) contact with the niddâ. With regard to the former, the zāb's bed clearly has been singled out as conveying greater impurity, probably since it has been exposed to more intensive or longer contact with him. With respect to the niddâ, verse 19 is clear that contact with her only imparts uncleanness "until the evening," a phrase which implies

FIG. 6 PURIFICATION RULES FOR CONTACT WITH THOSE WITH FLOWS

Action of Clean Person	**zāb**	**niddâ**	**zābâ/yôledet**
Touch bed of	b,l [5]	b,l [21]	b,l [27]
Touch anything under	b [10]	b,l [22]	b,l [27]
Lie on bed of	(b,l)	(b,l)	(b,l)
Sit in chair	b,l [6]	(b,l)	(b,l)
Carry anything under	b,l [10]	(b,l)	(b,l)
Touch the unclean person	b,l [7]	b [19]	(b,l)
Be spat upon by	b,l [8]		(b,l)

only a requirement to bathe not to launder (See Chapter 3). This leniency might be due to the normalcy of her situation and the impracticality of requiring those near her to launder their clothes every time they brush up against her. Those who touch her bed or chair, however, since they could be in direct contact with her flow, are required to bathe and launder.

Sitting or carrying suggests more intensive or longer contact, and hence the impurity is greater than that resulting from touching alone. The sitting of the menstruant on her bed or chair is intense enough to cause something else on the bed orchair to transmit impurity to yet a third party. Verse 23 reveals this tertiary transmission of impurity. There have been several interpretations of this verse based on different renderings of hûʾ and its antecedent here. The Septuagint reads hîʾ rather than hûʾ: "And if she is on the bed or on the object upon which she may sit when he touches her, he shall be unclean until evening. However, that the bed has potency without her continued presence on it is clear already from verse 21:

> Anyone who touches her bedding shall launder his clothes, bathe in water, and remain impure until evening.

The bed cannot be less potent when the menstruant is on it.

The Samaritan text has a similar meaning, "If she is on the bed or on the object she sits on when he touches it (the bed) he shall be unclean." Again, the question is: why is laundering assumed when one touches the bed, but not assumed if the menstruant is still on it.[5]

Now, from the participle yōšebet it is clear that both parties must be on the bed at the same time for the transmission of impurity to take place. However, this does not agree with verse 5: just touching the bed without the menstruant's pressure contaminates sufficiently so as to require a person to bathe and launder. Hence, what is the point of yōšebet here?

---

5 Ibid.; Wright, *Disposal*, 192-93 n 46.

The interpretation produced by Milgrom that the antecedent of the first hûʾ in verse 23 is kol kĕlî, any object, may be correct. Accordingly, if the menstruant yōšebet, is sitting, on the bed, then any object which is on the bed becomes unclean and anyone who touches that object must bathe but does not need to launder. This interpretation provides a reason for why the menstruant must remain on the bed for the said transmission of impurity to take place. Grammatically, the participle yōšebet, not found elsewhere in Chapter 15, denotes simultaneous sitting of the menstruant on the bed while a clean person is touching the kĕlî that is on the bed. Hence, a person touching a garment on a bed at the same time the menstruant is sitting on that bed becomes impure (15:22-23). This mode of transmission of impurity can be assumed for the yôledet and the zābâ as well.

The apparent concern of the writer of Leviticus 15 for contamination to the Israelite by zābîm renders suspect the observance of the rule of Numbers 5 which requires them to be banished. What contact could there be with the bed or chair of a zāb who lives outside of the camp? Also, the provision that zābîm may touch others if they first wash their hands leads one to think there were people around them. Perhaps, as with persons contaminated by a corpse, two traditions are present. Milgrom suggests that this is an example of minimalist and maximalist interpretations of purity inherent in Scripture itself. The more lenient tradition, or minimalist interpretation, is the view of the Priestly Code, the Pentateuchal strand comprised of cultic material contained primarily in Leviticus and sparingly in Exodus and Numbers. The late editors of the Pentateuch, who wrote the Holiness Code and incorporated it into the final edition of the Torah, excluded the zāb from the camp apparently reviving a more ancient law.[6]

---

6 J. Milgrom, "The Scriptural Foundations and Deviations in the Laws of Purity of the Temple Scroll" in *Archaeology and History in the Dead Sea Scrolls*, ed. L. H. Schiffman, 85-86; cf. I. Knohl, lecture at University of California, Berkeley, fall, 1989; Milgrom, Leviticus, I, 986-1000. Other scholars regard Num. 5:1-4 as either utopian (S. Cohen, "Menstruants and the Sacred in Judaism and Christianity" in *Women's*

How does one purify from the impurities resulting from genital discharges? A parturient most likely immerses after a week (boy) or after two weeks (girl). Although Scripture does not state the necessity of immersion for the parturient, I assume that this was necessary in order to diminish her impurity from affecting the sacred and profane realms to affecting sancta only. (See Chapter 3 above for full explanation of the nature and power of immersion.) Certainly, the Rabbis understood Scripture to require the parturient to immerse (m. Nid. 4:3). After her second stage of impurity (at the end of 33 or 66 days, see above), the parturient's cleansing concludes by her sacrifice of a bird and a lamb or of two birds, if she is poor (Lev. 12:6-8). Her extensive purification process reflects the seriousness of her impurity.

Zābîm, too, must undergo a complex purification ritual. They first must experience seven days without a flow of blood or sexual emission in order to confirm that they are truly healed. After this week they must bathe in spring water, mayim ḥayyîm, and launder their clothes. Spring water is specified only for the purification of the corpse-contaminated, the mĕṣōrāʿ, and the zāb, but may have been implicitly required for all those with impure flows. On the eighth day they are to bring two birds for whole and purification offerings to the sanctuary. Zābîm who intentionally do not purify themselves, like all other impurity bearers, are subject to death by divine agency (Lev. 15:31).

A menstruant must bathe and launder her clothes seven days after her impurity began and then she will be clean at sunset. Although Scripture never states so directly, one can infer from the text that the menstruant must bathe at the end of her period of impurity. The phrase, "be unclean until evening," assumes the necessity to bathe (See Chapter 3, above). While it is true that this phrase is not mentioned with regard to the purification of the

---

History and Ancient History, 275) or as only applicable to the Israelite Camp in the wilderness before settlement in Canaan (Wright, *Disposal*, 172-73). Cohen suggests that the category of zāb in Num. 5:2 stands for all those with sexual discharges and hence regards the passage as utopian. Wright interprets the passage literally but says it only describes the wilderness experience.

menstruant herself, it is present in the description of those who touch her (Lev. 15:19) or touch items on which she sits or lies (Lev. 15:21-22). Thus, I conclude from an *a fortiori* argument that if those who touch the menstruant must bathe, so must she. The Rabbis hold that the menstruant must bathe as evident from the Mishna (m. Miq. 8:1, 5; see Chapter 3, above).

A man with a seminal emission need only bathe and wait for sunset (Lev. 15:16; 22:4-7). Only his clothes or other items which came into direct contact with semen need to be washed (see above).

The Bible gives a few examples of persons who were considered impure due to genital discharges. Josephus logically assumes that it was due to a seminal emission (**mikrēh laylâ**) that David was thought to be impure and therefore absent from Saul's table (1 Sam. 20:26; Ant. 6:235). On another occasion the priest Ahimelech agreed to give David and his men the holy bread of presence because they had abstained from intercourse and so were undefiled.

> And the priest answered David, "I have no common bread at hand, but there is holy bread; if only the young men have kept themselves from women" (I Sam. 22:4).

The writer of 2 Samuel states that Bathsheba was purifying herself from her uncleanness when David noticed her (2 Sam. 11:2, 4). Included in the curses David pronounces on the house of Joab is the eternal presence of a family member suffering from an abnormal genital discharge (2 Sam. 3:29).

I will now try to ascertain the contamination of bodily discharges in the Rabbinic system. This is a more complex matter than ascertaining the rabbinic view of, for example, corpse impurity. The issue is complicated by the fact that not only persons with impure flows function as **ʾabôt ṭumʾâ**, but also their pressure on certain objects makes the latter function as **ʾabôt ṭumʾâ**. In addition, there is not always total agreement between the sources on every issue and this will be obvious below.

First of all, the Rabbis define the terms **zāb** and **zābâ**: 1) The **zāb** is a man who has had three abnormal genital discharges in a time frame of three consecutive days (m. Zab. 1:3). As noted above, the Rabbis clarify that flux is not semen because it is not the result of an erection but rather a secretion (t. Zab. 2:4). 2) The **zābâ** is a woman who has a flow of menstrual blood outside of the monthly menstruation period. The flow must be on each of three consecutive days beyond the seven allotted for menstrual impurity (Sifra Mes. Zab. par. 5:9; cf. Lev. 15:25).

In the rabbinic view, the **yôledet** (in her first stage of impurity), **zābâ**, **zāb**, and **niddâ** transmit, with one exception, the same degree of impurity. Following the biblical system, the man who emits semen does not defile persons who touch him or whom he touches. Thus, he is in a different category of impurity, and I will discuss him separately.

To facilitate matters I will refer to the **yôledet**, **zābâ**, **zāb**, and **niddâ** collectively as "one with a flow." To be sure, the Rabbis did understand there to be a hierarchy of impurity between the four types (m. Kel. 1:1-4); that is clear from the different purification requirements of Scripture. However, their *contamination potential* in the rabbinic system is for the most part the same (m. Zab. 5:1, 6, 10). When there is a distinction I will note it.

The contamination of one with a flow can be analyzed in three categories: 1) effect on persons, 2) effect on objects, and 3) the effect of **midrās**-uncleanness. Persons are affected by touching, carrying, shifting, or having intercourse with the one with a flow. (I will treat the contamination of persons by the pressure of the one with a flow separately in the discussion on **midrās**.) A person who is touching the one with a flow functions as an **ʾab ṭumʾâ** as long as the two are still in contact. While touching one with a flow an individual can contaminate rinsable vessels (including clothes, but excluding earthenware), food, and liquid in the first degree, and hands in the second degree but will not contaminate other persons (m. Zab. 5:1). (See Introduction for full discussion of "degree" in the rabbinic impurity system.) However, once separated from one with a flow, the individual is considered impure in the first degree and thus only contaminates liquid in the first degree and food and hands in the second degree. The whole matter is explained in m. Zab. 5:1:

> He who is touching the zāb, or whom the zāb is touching, he who is shifting the zāb, or whom the zāb is shifting imparts uncleanness to food and drink and rinsable utensils while in contact with them but not while carrying them (without contact). A general rule did R. Joshua state: Whoever imparts uncleanness to clothes while in contact imparts uncleanness to food and drink, putting them into the first degree and to the hands, putting them into the second degree. But he does not impart uncleanness either to persons or to clay utensils. After he separates from the things which make him unclean, he imparts uncleanness to liquid, putting it into the first degree, and to food and the hands putting them into the second degree. And he does not impart uncleanness to clothes (translation mine).

It is clear from this passage that an individual who is still in contact with one with a flow contaminates to a greater degree than after separation.

Mishna Zab. 5:10 discusses the same issue:

> ...This is the general rule: Whatever is touching any one of all the Fathers of Uncleanness which are listed in the Torah imparts uncleanness at one degree and renders unfit at one degree, except for persons. Anyone who separated (from any of these uncleannesses), imparts uncleanness at one degree and renders unfit at one further degree (translation mine).

This passage reveals that all items susceptible to first degree uncleanness (e.g., vessels, clothes, food) contaminate at one further degree and make tĕrûmâ unfit at a second. People are excluded because while in contact they contaminate non-priestly items at two degrees and make tĕrûma unfit at a third (m. Zab. 5:1). Separated, both persons and objects contaminate equivalently.

Also, shifting or being shifted by one with a flow without direct contact is equally contaminating as touch (b. Git. 61b). Mishna Zab. 5:6 corroborates this principle already found in 5:1:

> Anyone who is touching the zāb, the zābâ, the niddâ, the woman unclean after childbirth, and the mĕṣōrāʿ, or a bed or chair on which

> any of these have lain or sat, imparts uncleanness at two degrees and renders unfit at one further degree. If he separated, he imparts uncleanness at one degree and renders unfit at one further degree. All the same is the one who touches and the one who shifts, and all the same is the one who carries and the one who is carried (translation mine).

This passage states that contact with one with a flow either directly or by shifting causes one to contaminate other items to two degrees if still in contact and to one degree if separated. Of course, tĕrûmâ is always contaminated even at a third degree and qodōšîm to a fourth (See Introduction).

Carriage is another means of contamination by one with a flow. An individual who carries or is carried by the unclean person becomes unclean as an ʾab ṭumʾâ if still in contact and in the first degree if separated. Mishna Zab. 5:2 reads:

> And further—another general rule did they state: Whatever is carried above the Zab is unclean. And whatever the Zab is carried upon (without contact) is clean, except for something which is suitable for sitting and lying, and [except for] man. How so? [If] the finger of the Zab is under the course of stones, and the clean person is above them, he imparts uncleanness at two removes and renders [heave offering] unfit at one [still further remove]. [When] he separates, he imparts uncleanness at one remove and renders teruma unfit at one [still further remove]. [If] the unclean person is above them and the clean person is below them, he imparts uncleanness at two removes and renders unfit at one still further remove. [When] he separates, he imparts uncleanness at one remove and renders unfit at one [still further remove]. [If] food and drink, bed and chair, and maddaf [articles not used for sitting and lying] are above [the course of stones, and the Zab's finger was below], they impart uncleanness at two removes [or: one remove] and render unfit at one. [When] they separate, they impart uncleanness at one remove and render unfit at one remove. [And if] the bed and chair are below them, [and the Zab's finger was above,] they impart uncleanness at two removes and render unfit at one. [When] they separate, they impart uncleanness at two removes and render unfit at one. [If] food and drink and maddaf are below them [and the Zab's finger was above the course of stones], they remain clean. (cf. b. Erub. 27a)

This passage reveals that a person still carrying or being carried by the zāb contaminates at two degrees and makes tĕrûmâ unfit at a third. Since this is the same as one touching or shifting a niddâ, I assume the susceptible items are the same: rinsable vessels, food, and liquids in the first degree; food, liquids, and hands in the second degree; tĕrûmâ and qodōšîm, as per usual, in the third and fourth degrees, respectively.

The Sifra (Mes. Zab. par. 2:2) explains that the person under (and so carrying) the zāb does not contaminate persons and clothes, but this is a discussion distinguishing the difference between the bed under the zāb, which does impart uncleanness to persons and clothes, and the person under the zāb which does not impart uncleanness to persons and clothes, i.e., the individual cannot impart midrās impurity. However, the person carrying the one with a flow does make clothes (Lev. 15:10) as well as other rinsable vessels unclean while still carrying the impure person (m. Zab. 5:2). After separation, the individual contaminates as a person with first degree uncleanness (m. Zab. 5:2).

A fourth means of contamination is by intercourse. If a man has intercourse with a yôledet, zābâ, or niddâ, he will contaminate as an ʾab ṭumʾâ (Sifra Mes. Zab. 7:3; b. Nid. 33a). It is not surprising that he will contaminate other persons and vessels in the first degree, making food and hands unclean in the second, because he is an ʾab ṭumʾâ. It is noteworthy that a woman having intercourse with a zāb, however, is not affected by intercourse with him (Sifra Mes. Zab. 8:8). This represents the only difference in the contamination conveyed by the zāb from that of the yôledet, zābâ, and niddâ.

The Talmud emphasizes the fact that the man who has intercourse with a woman with a flow contaminates to a greater degree than one touching her. The Rabbis point to Lev. 15:24 which states that "her (the niddâ's) impurity is upon him (the one who had intercourse with her)":

> As it might have been presumed that he imparts no uncleanness to man or earthenware, it was explicitly stated, "And her impurity be upon him," as she imparts uncleanness to man and to earthenware, so does he impart uncleanness to man and earthenware (b. Nid. 33a).

However, the Talmud points out that since Scripture says the bed he lies on is just "unclean," it is referring to a lighter uncleanness and not one which will transmit uncleanness to persons and clothes (b. Nid. 33a).

The Sifra (Mes. Zab. 7:3) gives the same argument. Neusner has translated the conclusion of the argument as follows: "The purpose of Scripture in so stating matters is to remove him from a form of uncleanness that is most severe [namely, that effected by the menstruating woman], and to apply to him a form of uncleanness that is less severe [with the consequences as specified]. Specifically, he will impart uncleanness only to food and to drink.

However, Neusner has misunderstood what it is that the Rabbis insist must be considered impure. I would translate the same passage as follows:

> The Scripture's only purpose in stating this [that the bed will be unclean] is to remove it [the bed] from a severe form of impurity and apply to it a light form of impurity, so that it will not contaminate anything but food and drink.

It is not the man who has intercourse with the **niddâ** who should be removed from a severe form of uncleanness, for the Talmud passage quoted affirms that he imparts uncleanness even to other persons and earthenware (b. Nid. 33a), *a fortiori*, to food and liquid. Rather, it is the bed of the man who has had intercourse with the **niddâ** which, unlike the bed of the **niddâ**, is not able to transmit impurity to persons and vessels and should be considered to be in a lesser degree of uncleanness. This is what the Talmud and the Sifra wish to clarify. In other words, although the man who has intercourse with the **niddâ** conveys impurity like the **niddâ** in many ways, this similarity has a limit with respect to his bed, a much less impure item than the **niddâ**'s bed.[7]

The Rabbis follow the biblical purification requirements on persons in contact with those with flows in any of these ways.

---

7 Cf. Soncino translation of Nid. 33a.

However, whereas according to the Torah (Fig. 6 above) all persons in such contact must bathe and launder their clothes except the one who touches a niddâ or the item other than a bed or seat under a zāb, the Rabbis interpret Scripture slightly differently. Regarding the niddâ, the Rabbis note no difference between the niddâ touching a clean person or a clean person touching the niddâ. As is the case of all persons with a flow, contact, no matter who initiated it, requires bathing and laundering.

On the other hand, the Rabbis totally eliminate from the category of susceptible items objects other than beds or seats under the one with a flow. To be susceptible to impurity, the item must be an object for sitting or lying. In their view, kōl ʾašer yihyeh taḥtāyw does not refer to items under the zāb but to items which the zāb is under (b. Nid. 33a). These items, as I will explain below, contaminate only food and liquid. It is clear that the Rabbis wish to limit the contamination of those with flows especially with regard to persons.

The rabbinic reasoning regarding the niddâ is that if the bed or chair of the niddâ contaminates persons and clothes (Lev. 15:21-22), *a fortiori*, the niddâ does so. Hence, one who touches the niddâ must bathe and launder (Sifra Mes. Zab. par. 4:9). The phrase, "yiṭmaʾ ʿad hāʿāreb" is applied to items touched by the individual who had direct contact with the niddâ. Since this person is in first degree impurity, the items he or she could contaminate could only include rinsable vessels and food, but not persons or earthenware, in the second degree.

A final note on purification of persons. Individuals are purified in stages. The first day cleansing of the zāb, for example, takes away his power to contaminate earthenware by carrying it (Sifra Mes. Zab. 5:11).

Susceptible objects (see Introduction) are contaminated in the first degree by touching, carrying, shifting, or being above the one with a flow. For contamination by touch let us look at m. Zab. 5:10 again (quoted above). The passage states that anyone who is touching [kol-hannōgēaʿ] a father of impurity imparts uncleanness at one degree and renders tĕrûmâ unfit. Thus, the item is in the first degree of uncleanness. The Mishna then states, "Except for man." This exclusion makes it clear that objects and man are meant by the summary statement and that **kol-hannōgēaᶜ** should be translated "whatever" instead of "whoever." With this translation objects contaminate to the same degree whether they are still in contact with one with a flow or whether they have been separated; unlike persons they are in the first degree of uncleanness in either situation. I assume that like the person who has separated from contact with one with a flow, these objects can only contaminate liquid in the first degree, food and hands in the second, and invalidate **tĕrûmâ** and **qodōšîm** (cf. m. Zab. 5:1). The Talmud mentions the example of the curtain which the zāb has touched; it is unclean in the first degree (b. Men. 24b).

Objects can also be contaminated by shifting or being shifted by one with a flow. The Tosefta reads:

> [If a Zab knocked against] the chest, box, or cupboard, even though they hold [requisite] volume [are large and hold two **kors** of liquid measure (m. Kel. 15:1) and are not susceptible to uncleanness on their own], they [utensils which are in them] are unclean. R. Nehemiah and R. Simeon declare clean. [They agree, however: And if they [utensils inside of the insusceptible chest, etc.] were shifted they are unclean. This is the principle: Whatever is [shifted] through the force of tremor is clean, through the force of shaking is unclean (t. Zab. 4:6; cf. m. Zab. 4:3).

Mishna Zabim 3:1 gives further examples of items shifted by one with a flow, including the situation of a zāb and a clean person on a shaky tree or ladder. The clean person is made unclean because he or she is subject to the zāb's shifting. From the rule that persons can be contaminated whether they shift the zāb or the zāb shifts them (m. Zab. 5:1), I assume the same is true for the susceptible object.

If an object is supported or carried by one with a flow even without contact it is made unclean in the same degree as by touch or shifting. The Mishna (Zab. 5:2) teaches that objects carried above the **niddâ** become unclean in the first degree, contaminate food in the second, and make **tĕrûmâ** unfit at a third. These objects are specified as food, liquid, the bed and chair of the zāb, and maddāp (see below). After they separate from being carried, their contamination remains the same: first degree. This reading reflects the early manuscripts, Kaufmann and Parma, and the Geniza fragments; these sources state that these objects contaminate at one degree making tĕrûmâ unfit at one more degree.[8]

Neusner explains this dilemma as due to a combination of two issues: 1) the bed and chair above the zāb are more potent items, hence they can impart uncleanness at two degrees (so the later mss.), and 2) food and liquid can only impart uncleanness at one degree (so the early mss.). However, the Sifra states that the bed and chair are clean above the zāb (Mes. Zab. par. 3:5-6). I think the solution is to read the Mishna according to the early manuscripts which state that food, liquid, the bed and chair of the zāb, and maddāp "impart uncleanness at one degree" whether still above the zāb or not. The Sifra's more lenient attitude that the bed and chair above the zāb are clean is not surprising since it takes a more lenient stance than the Mishna on more than one occasion (cf. Chapter 4 above).

What is maddāp? Since the Mishna (Zab. 5:2) lists the items which contaminate above the zāb as food, liquid, bed and chair, and maddāp, one can assume that maddāp is something other than food, liquid, beds, or chairs. The Talmud supports this interpretation as we will see below.

Maddāp is usually used by Mishna-Tosefta to denote a light impurity status in which the impure item contaminates only food and liquid. It is not necessarily an impurity related to discharges (m. Par. 10:1-2; m. Toh. 8:2). In some passages maddāp refers to a lighter impurity status of items located above the zāb in comparison to the bed and chair below the zāb :

> For the zāb makes a bed and chair under him render man unclean and render unclean garments and imparts to what is above him maddāp-uncleanness (so that) it makes food and drink unclean,

---

8 *Ginze Mishnah*, ed. A. I. Katsch, 318-319; *A Collection of Mishnaic Geniza Fragments with Babylonian Vocalization* (Hebrew), ed. I. Yeivin, 56.

> (modes of transfer of uncleanness by) which the corpse does not impart uncleanness (t. Zab. 3:3, translation mine; cf. m. Zab. 4:6).

It is not clear from Mishna-Tosefta what these maddāp items are. Some have suggested the bed and chair, but these are listed separately.

The Babylonian Talmud is less ambiguous. It limits the definition of maddāp to 1) a light status of any type of impurity (first degree) or 2) the bed covering of the niddâ (b. Nid. 33a). Tractate Nidda states that maddāp is a bed covering and derives the whole notion from Scripture:

> Whence is the law concerning the cover above a zab deduced? From the Scriptural text, "And whosoever toucheth any thing that was under him shall be unclean." For what could be the meaning of "under him"? If it be suggested: Under the zab [it could be objected: This] is derived from, "And whosoever toucheth his bed." Consequently it must mean: "Whosoever toucheth any thing under which the zab was"; and this is the cover above the zab; Scripture segregated it from a grave uncleanness and transferred it to a lighter uncleanness in order to tell you that it imparts uncleanness to foods and drinks only (b. Nid. 33a).

In any case, an item labelled maddāp is contaminated above the one with a flow in the first degree just like something touched, carried, or shifted by the unclean person.

The principle of maddāp has been an attempt of the Rabbis to decrease the contamination potential of those with flows. Lev. 15:10 states clearly that anyone who touches anything under the zāb becomes unclean. The Rabbis reverse the syntax to read, "anything which the zāb is under is unclean." This helps to limit the impurity of items under the one with a flow to only that which can be used as a bed or a chair on which the impure individual has put pressure and to the person who touches, carries, or presses upon that object. (The conveyance of impurity by pressure is explained below in the discussion of midrās.)

The Rabbis know very well that they have introduced the concept of maddāp, and so they do not consider it very seriously. The redactor of Talmud Tractate Nidda comments, "Hence we are dealing with a rabbinical uncleanness. A deduction (from the wording) also supports this view, for the expression used is 'middaf' which is analogous to the Scriptural phrase, 'a driven [niddaf] leaf'" (b. Nid. 4b). The diagram below (Fig. 7) illustrates the contamination power of those with flows in the rabbinic system.

Finally, the unique feature of the impurity of bodily discharges is contamination via pressure: midrās-uncleanness. The term midrās immediately connotes in the minds of most scholars a rabbinic principle. H. Danby defines it as follows:

> Lit. "place of treading." It denotes the degree of uncleanness suffered by an object which any of those enumerated in Lev. 12:2; 15:2, 25, sits, lies, or rides upon or leans against. Any object which is fit to sit, lie or ride upon, and which is usually sat, lain, or ridden upon (without affecting that object's proper function if it is not primarily a seat, couch, or saddle) is deemed to be "susceptible to midras-uncleanness."[9]

J. Neusner refers to midrās simply as:

> ...the mode of transfer of uncleanness through the pressure of the zab and his fellows [e.g. the zaba, parturient and menstruant] upon beds and chairs.[10]

Hence, midrās is a technical term for a distinct mode of contamination from impure flows: that transmitted by pressure. In addition, the term often refers to the degree of contamination: an object suffering midrās impurity can make susceptible items, including persons, unclean in the first degree.

The bed, chair, or anything else which one with a flow used for sitting, lying, leaning, or treading (forms of pressure) without affecting its normal use [hereinafter referred to as bed/chair] contaminates persons who lie on, sit on, stand on, hang from, lean on, touch, or carry them (m. Zab. 2:4). How does the bed or chair acquire this status? The Sages are clear that the greater weight of a person with a flow must have been applied to a bed or chair in some way: the impure individual must have stood on,

---

9 *The Mishnah*, ed. H. Danby, 795.

10 Neusner, *Purities*, XXII, 52.

FIG. 7 THE CONTAMINATION OF THOSE WITH FLOWS IN THE RABBINIC SYSTEM

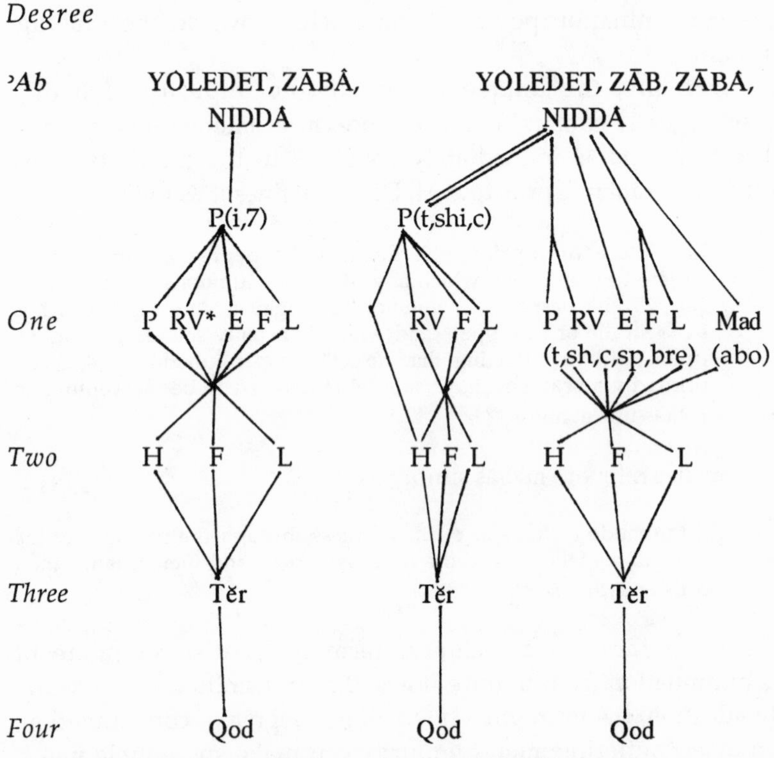

* The bed and chair of the man who has intercourse with any woman with a flow can be contaminated merely by sitting or lying on them without direct contact (m. Zab. 5:11).

References:

Branch 1: m. Zab. 5:11; Sifra Mes. Zab. 7:3; 8:8; b. Nid. 33a
Branch 2: m. Zab. 5:1-2, 6, 10; Sifra Mes. Zab. par. 2:10-11; par. 4:10
Branch 3: m. Zab. 5:1, 6; Sifra Mes. Zab. par. 2:11; b. Men. 24b; b. Git. 61b
Branch 4: m. Zab. 3:1; 4:6; 5:1-2, 10; t. Zab. 4:6; b. Men. 24b; b. Git. 61b
Branch 5: Sifra Mes. Zab. par. 3:1-2; b. Git. 61b
Branch 6: m. Zab. 5:2

leaned on, hanged from, lain on, or sat on these objects (m. Zab. 5:5; 2:4). Only then will they transmit uncleanness at two degrees and make tĕrûma unfit at a third.

This principle is illustrated in Tosefta Zabim 4:8:

> [If] the Zab is on one side of the scale and a bed or chair is opposite him, if the Zab goes down, it imparts uncleanness at one remove and renders [heave-offering] unfit at one. And if it outweighed the Zab, it imparts uncleanness at two removes and renders [heave-offering] unfit at one remove. In the case of a man, whether he outweighs the Zab or whether the Zab outweighs him, he imparts uncleanness at one remove and renders [heave-offering] unfit at one remove.

When the zāb is heavier than the bed or chair, it is made unclean because it has been subject to the zāb's pressure, but only in the first degree. However, if the bed or chair is heavier, its weight lifts up the zāb and hence is subject to the zāb's greater weight and is made unclean as an ʾab ṭumʾâ.

Another example is found in m. Zab. 4:4:

> A Zab who was lying on five benches, or on five bags—[If they are set] lengthwise, they are unclean. [If they are set] breadthwise, they are clean (tr. mine). [Cf. Maimonides (*Code* X, couch 7:4): Since the greater part of his body was not supported by each of them.]

If a zāb lies on many chairs at the same time, none can transmit uncleanness as an ʾab ṭumʾâ, since none bears his greater weight: in this regard they are clean. However, they are still unclean in the first degree for having been touched by the zāb. Also, if the midrās-contaminated bed or chair changes its function it can no longer contaminate as an ʾab ṭumʾâ but as an object unclean in the first degree (cf. m. Kel. 28:5).

How does a person become unclean by the bed or chair? M. Zab. 2:4 explains:

> The Zab [also: menstruant, meṣoraʿ, and woman after childbirth] imparts uncleanness [even not in direct contact] to the bed [and chair and saddle] in five ways so that it imparts uncleanness to man and imparts uncleanness to garments [touched while in contact with the unclean bed]: (1) standing, (2) sitting, (3) lying on it, (4) suspended [against its weight], and (5) leaning on it. And the

> bed imparts uncleanness to man in seven ways so that he imparts uncleanness to clothing: (1) standing, (2) sitting, (3) lying, (4) suspended, (5) leaning, (6) through contact, and (7) through carrying (bracketed comments mine; cf. m. Zab. 5:3).

Thus, touching any part of the bed or chair defiles (m. Zab. 5:6; Lev. 15:21).

Interestingly, the person who is still touching, pressing, or carrying the bed/chair renders rinsable vessels, food, and liquid unclean in the first degree. However, if separated, the individual becomes impure in the first degree and makes only liquid unclean in the first degree and food and hands impure in the second (Sifra Mes. Zab. par. 2:10-11; m. Zab. 2:4; 5:3).

The Sages distinguish the saddle from other types of seats. This view is based on Lev. 15:9 which regards riding on the saddle of the zāb as a less impure activity than sitting on his chair (v. 6). The Rabbis insist that even one who is still in contact with the zāb's saddle must be actually carrying it in order to render other items impure in the first degree. Mere touching the saddle will not make a person function as an ʾab ṭumʾâ (Sifra Mes. Zab. 3:12; 4:1-2; par. 4:15).

Objects are made unclean by the bed/chair only by direct contact; carriage without contact effects no impurity (m. Zab. 5:3). The example of m. Zab. 5:5 concerns tĕrûmâ which is on a piece of paper on the bed of the zāb; the tĕrûmâ is clean because it has not experienced the weight or contact of the zāb or his bed/chair. If the objects are touching the bed/chair they take on first degree uncleanness and will impart uncleanness to the usually susceptible items in the other degrees (Sifra Mes. Zab. par. 2:1).

Below are some examples. Picture a zāb and a clean person sitting on a boat (m. Zab. 3:1). If the latter is heavier and the boat drops on one side, the zāb will be suspended to some degree by the clean person. Because the latter is bearing the greater weight of the zāb, his or her clothing (an item used for sitting or lying) will become impure with midrās-uncleanness and thus contaminate as an ʾab ṭumʾâ. If the zāb is heavier, the clean individual is to some degree carried by him, but there is no requirement to launder since no midrās impurity is incurred. The individual becomes impure in the first degree.[11]

Again, when two people ride on an animal and the lighter of the two has a flow, the clothes of the person become unclean with midrās since they are subject to the weight of the one with the flow (m. Zab. 3:1). Danby describes the action clearly:

> The clean person by his weight causes the boat, raft or beast to sink to one side and rise at the other; thereby the zab is indirectly lifted up or suspended by him.[12]

R. Joshua wanted to extend the effect of midrās even further than his colleagues. He explains that a menstruant sitting on a boat with a clean woman will contaminate even the cap on the latter's head because, even though not at present, the cap could be used for lying or sitting. The Sages disagree with R. Joshua because the cap, unlike the menstruant's clothes, is not subject at present to her pressure.[13]

It is important to remember that midrās uncleanness can be imparted only to items used for sitting or lying. The Mishna presents a case where a zāb and a clean person open and close a door from opposite sides at the same time producing simultaneous contrary action. The clean person is rendered unclean although no contact between the two has been made. Neusner considers this a case of midrās impurity, but that is impossible. Only objects used for sitting or lying are susceptible to midrās even as he states himself. The door is not such an object. This situation only involves indirect shifting one of the other; no midrās impurity is incurred.

---

11 S. N. Lehrman, *Zabim*, tr. into English with notes by I. Epstein, *The Babylonian Talmud, Seder Tohorot,* 510 n 2; P. Blackman, *Mishnayoth*, VI, 706; H. Danby, 769.

12 Danby, 769.

13 R. Joshua brings proof for his argument by suggesting a case where a zāb is carrying a tub of clothes on a boat (m. Zab. 4:1). Although he does not touch the clothes and although they are not fulfilling their normal function, his pressure on them makes them unclean.

An instructive paradox summarizing this discussion is found in Mishna Ohalot 1:5:

> Man and clothing are made unclean by the Zab. More strict [is the rule concerning] man than [that concerning] clothing, and [more strict is] that concerning clothing than that concerning man. For the man who touches the Zab renders clothing unclean, but clothing which touches the Zab does not render clothing unclean. More strict [is the rule concerning] clothing, *for the clothing which bears the [weight of the] Zab* renders man unclean, but the man who bears the [weight of the] Zab does not render man unclean

Thus, clothes which are not only in contact with but bear the full weight of one with a discharge defile persons because they are functioning as ʾabôt ṭumʾâ. The diagram below (Fig. 8) illustrates the contamination power of midrās.

The foregoing discussion centered on the contamination effect of those with flows, the yôledet, zābâ, zāb, and niddâ, but what is the extent of contamination conveyed by one who emits semen? I have excluded the latter from the category of those with flows since his impurity is not a flow but a one-time discharge, and thus in the rabbinic system, as in the Bible, he is less contaminating to other persons and objects than persons with flows.

As the chart (Fig. 9) indicates, the man who emits semen is not an ʾab ṭumʾâ, but is unclean in the first degree. Semen, on the other hand, is an ʾab ṭumʾâ. The Mishna includes semen in a list of ʾabôt ṭumʾâ and describes the contamination it conveys:

> The one who is touching a [dead] unclean reptile, or semen, or one that is unclean with corpse impurity...renders unclean at one degree and invalidates at one [further] degree. This is the general rule: whatever is touching one of all the Fathers of Uncleanness that are stated in the Torah imparts uncleanness at one degree and renders unfit at one degree, except for persons. Anyone who has separated [from any of these impurities] imparts uncleanness at one degree and renders unfit at one [further] degree (m. Zab. 5:10, translation mine).

As discussed above with reference to persons touching one with a flow, persons still in contact with an ʾab ṭumʾâ render

FIG. 8 THE CONTAMINATION OF MIDRĀS IN THE RABBINIC SYSTEM

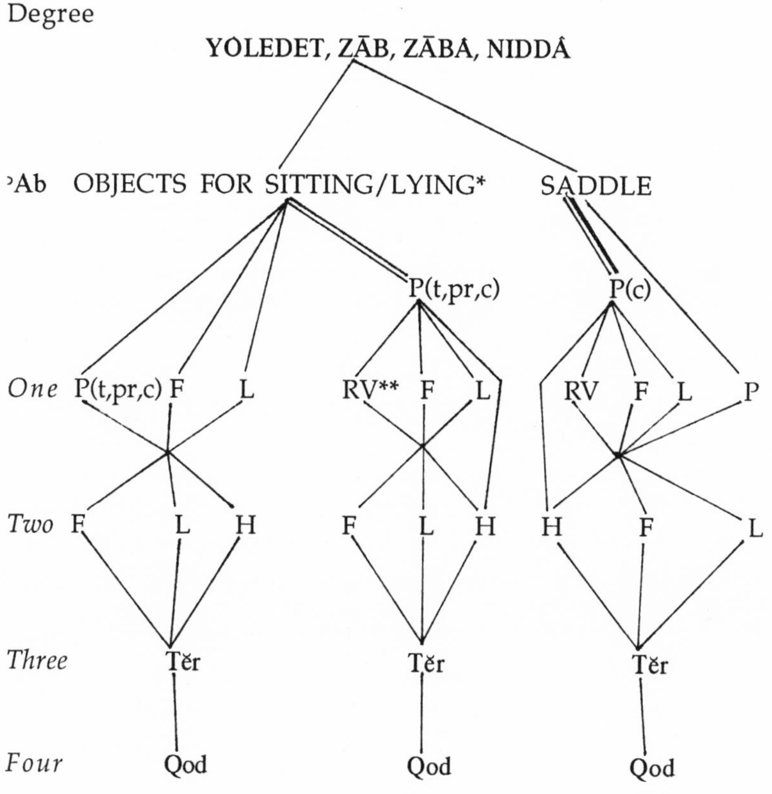

* The greater weight of any of the four must have been applied to the object for sitting/lying.

** Earthenware is not subject to midrās (b. Shab. 84b).

References:

Branch 1: m. Zab. 2:4; 3:1; 5:2-3; Sifra Mes. Zab. par. 2:1; par. 2:10; par. 4:1.

Branch 2: Sifra Mes. Zab. 3:12; 4:1-2; par. 4:15

FIG. 9 THE CONTAMINATION OF SEMEN IN THE RABBINIC SYSTEM

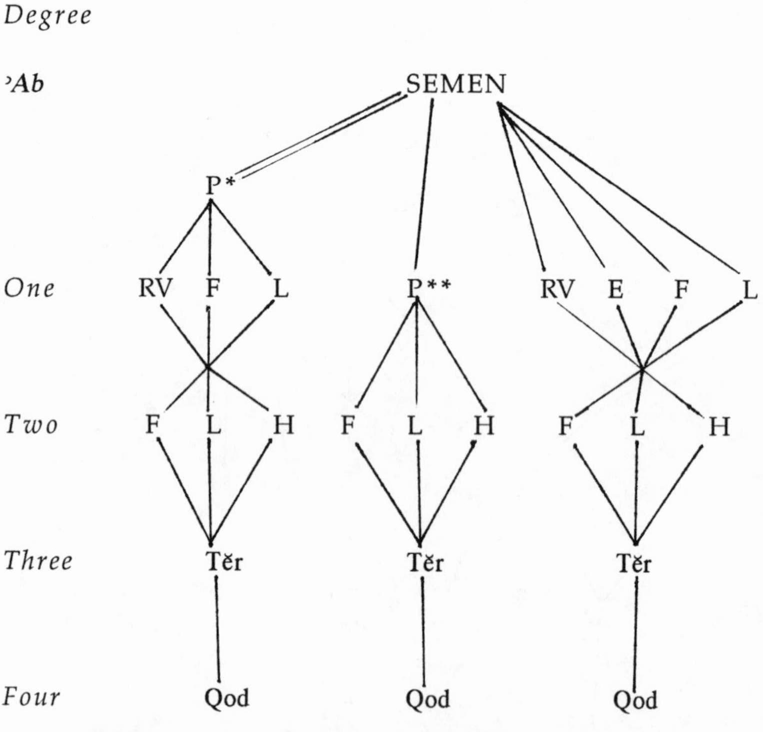

* Includes a man or woman still in contact with semen

** Includes a man or woman who had direct contact with semen but are no longer in contact

References:

Branch 1: m. Zab. 5:10; Sifra Mes. Zab. 6:4; Lev. 15:18-19

Branch 2: m. Zab. 5:10-11; b. BB 9b; b. Naz. 66a; m. Yad. 3:1

Branch 3: Lev. 15:18-19; 22:4ff.

ordinary susceptible items unclean at two degrees, tĕrûmâ at a third degree, and qodōšîm at a fourth. Susceptible objects (e.g., vessels, food, and liquid), which are in contact with an ʾab ṭumʾâ, in this case semen, render other ordinary items unclean only at one degree, tĕrûma and qodōšîm at further degrees. The person who has separated from contact with semen is unclean in the first degree and renders ordinary susceptible items unclean in the second degree, tĕrûma in the third, and qodōšîm in the fourth.

The sources are clear that semen is defiling to persons only if they come into direct contact with it; if they carry an object with semen on it but make no contact with the semen itself, they are not made impure (b. Naz. 66a; cf. m. Zab. 5:11). Thus, the notion of midrās does not apply to contamination by semen (Sifra Mes. Zab. 2:8). Probably earthenware, too, would be contaminated by semen only through direct contact via its interior. If persons who are touching the zāb cannot contaminate earthenware by touch, *a fortiori*, those who are in contact with semen (m. Zab. 5:1).

As the Bible prescribes, the woman with whom a man has intercourse is made unclean (Lev. 15:18). As Wright has noted, bathing as well as laundering is required for both of these individuals. The laundering requirement is simply relegated to and expanded in a verse of its own (v. 17). For the Rabbis, the laundering requirement demands the washing of any rinsable vessels with which the semen is in contact, not just clothing (see below). The Rabbis point out, however, that after a man has had a seminal emission, he only contaminates like the person who touches a dead reptile (m. Zab. 5:11); both need only to bathe and wait for sunset (cf. Lev. 11:31; 15:18; 22:4-7; Sifra Mes. Zab. 2:8; b. Naz. 66a). Neither impurity bearer conveys uncleanness to persons or vessels, only to food, drink, and hands.

In comparing the biblical and rabbinic systems it is easy to see where the Rabbis got the notion that touching or carrying those with bodily flows and having intercourse with any woman with a flow defiles. Also, the bed and chair of those with flows are clearly contaminating according to Scripture and thus one would expect them to be so for the Rabbis.

However, there are some principles in the rabbinic system which are not as easily discerned in the Bible and scholars have labeled them rabbinic innovations. These include: 1) midrās, 2) the notion that continued contact with unclean persons or their seats creates more contamination than after separation, and 3) the system of degrees of uncleanness. First, midrās. The issue here is whether or not the Rabbis developed the notion of midrās uncleanness by extracting certain interesting details from Leviticus 15 and then expanding them by a process of logic divorced from Scripture, or if they were merely interpreting the text carefully with an eye toward limiting contamination whenever possible. My view is the latter.

I will examine the first view. Although Neusner repeatedly claims that the concept of midrās is part of the legal heritage of the first-century Sages and is based on Scripture, he seems to suggest that the Sages already hold to certain views about the subject and so focus only on certain details of Leviticus 15 from which they make inferences to fit their own agenda. In a section entitled, "Midras and Maddaf," Neusner explains:

> The notion that under some circumstances, what is made unclean imparts uncleanness to still another object or substance [a fundamental premise of midras impurity]...is assuredly to be discerned in the verses before us. Whether or not the person who wrote the verses meant to emphasize that matter, of course, we do not know. Someone who wanted information on the topic, however, will readily have found it in Scripture. The eisegetical act is to deem the detail, perhaps stated tangentially and without intended significance by the original author, to be portentous, and to draw consequences from it.[14]

Thus, Neusner is saying that the Sages for some reason focused on the laws of contamination of Leviticus 15 and isolated certain ones because they were already interested in the subject. Through a process of logical reasoning they unraveled their implications without further recourse to Scripture.

---

14 Neusner, *Purities*,.XVIII, 176. Further argument against this line of reasoning is presented above in the Introduction above.

Neusner then describes the process by which the Rabbis have developed their concept of midrās. This development takes place by logic alone, one principle giving birth to another. The concept is in full bloom during the first century because the Houses take it for granted.[15]

According to Neusner, the process does not evolve along the lines presented in the Sifra. The Sifra formally links the concept of midrās to Scripture but does not describe the actual development of the laws. Neusner presents his understanding of how the laws evolved and explains:

> In this exercise [the steps of logic from Scripture to Mishna] we do not follow the path of Sifra and its greatest exegetes...who tell us the principles of formal exegesis by which laws are derived...My interest is not in the technology of exegesis, but rather in the hypothetical logic by which a rule produces a principle, and by which the principle generates further developments, only at the end inviting formal-exegetical linkage to Scripture.

Thus, according to Neusner, a group of Sages in the first century or prior to it isolated certain details of Leviticus 15 and began thinking about their implications. One idea led to another, one principle grew out of the next, and by 70 C.E. the concept was taken for granted by everyone. Centuries after its origin the concept was linked to Scripture, in ways in which it did not in fact develop, in the form of the Sifra.

Neusner seems to complicate the issue and evoke unnecessary questions, for example: What was it about these particular verses that illicited so much attention from the group studying them? What prevents the Sifra from being a valid representation of the way in which the laws developed? Also, if the laws are based on Scripture but not in the manner of the Sifra, what purpose does the Sifra serve? Certainly people would recognize the contrived nature of the Sifra. I am not suggesting that the Rabbis were not using logic when they made their conclusions from Leviticus 15, but I am claiming that they recognized the logic inherent in the text itself rather than at some

15 Ibid., XXII, 52-53.

point imposing their own logical system onto Scripture and later linking the two artificially in the form of the Sifra.

I see no reason to regard the Sifra as an artificial process centuries after the notion of midrās was established. It seems clear to me even from the Mishna that the Rabbis are just unpacking the implications of Scripture. The only agenda I detect is a desire to limit the power of impurity whenever possible.

I think Neusner has weakened the link between the Rabbis and Scripture when he should have strengthened it. The careful reader of Leviticus 15 will find the source of the rabbinic discussion on midrās. There is no reason to consider the idea to have evolved from Scripture by logical means and then later to have been pasted to it in a way in which it did not develop. Rather, the transfer of impurity by pressure is a valid understanding of Leviticus 15, and the Rabbis merely spell out the implications of that principle.

The fact that the Rabbis expound on the conveyance of impurity by pressure more than they discuss the matter of touch is because the latter is more obvious in Leviticus 15 and the implications clearer. However, although Scripture acknowledges contamination via modes of pressure, it does not clarify the issue. The Rabbis interpret the text in such a way as to limit this type of contamination just to objects suitable for sitting or lying.

In what follows I will present the way in which the Rabbis derive the principle of midrās from Scripture. The Sages understand Leviticus 15 to imply a network of laws in which the pressure of all those with flows contaminates all objects which can be used for sitting or lying to the degree that they affect all items like clothes. Since Scripture is clear that clothes on one in contact with the bed/chair are unclean, all objects like clothes, i.e., rinsable vessels, are also unclean.

Several relevant verses from Leviticus 15 must be cited:

> Verses 5-6: And the man who touches his bed must launder his clothes, wash in water, and be unclean until the evening. And whoever sits on anything the zāb has sat upon must launder his clothes, wash in water, and be unclean until the evening.

> Verse 10: And whoever touches anything that was under him shall be unclean until the evening. And whoever carries such a thing shall wash his clothes and bathe himself in water and be unclean until the evening.
>
> Verse 22: And everyone who touches any thing on which she sits shall launder his clothes and bathe in water and be unclean until the evening.
>
> Verse 23: And if [the thing] is on the bed or on anything upon which she is sitting when he touches it, he will be unclean until the evening.

Verse 5 clearly states that one who touches the zāb's bed must bathe and launder. This implies that 1) the bed or chair is functioning as an ʾab ṭumʾâ since like the niddâ and zāb it imparts uncleanness to persons and clothes, and 2) that all susceptible objects are affected by the bed or chair since clothes (in the category of rinsable vessels) are affected (Sifra Mes. Zab. par. 2:10-11).

Verse 6 adds that one who sits on anything which the zāb has sat on must bathe and launder. The clear meaning of these verses is that one who touches the bed or anything else under the zāb is unclean.

The Sages notice that it is via modes of pressure that the zāb has contaminated the bed/chair, either by lying (bed) or sitting (chair), to the extent that they can contaminate persons without the zāb's continued pressure. Thus, they have grounds for their emphasis on contamination by pressure as well as touch and carriage.

Once it is agreed that pressure is the key, then all forms of pressure can be assumed (Sifra Mes. Zab. 2:7). However, Scripture points out the bed and seat in particular (Lev. 15:4-6, 9, 21-23, 26). Thus the Sages have evidence for limiting this type of contamination to only objects which can be used for sitting or lying without losing their normal function (Sifra Mes. Zab. 2:1-4; b. Shab. 59a). The notion that *anything* which the zāb sits on is susceptible is dropped (cf. b. Nid. 49b).

Nevertheless, verse 10 teaches that *anything* which was under the zāb contaminates the bearer. As demonstrated above, the Talmud reinterprets this verse completely adding the notion of maddāp.

One might argue that the bed and chair are not contaminated by pressure but by contact with the flow of the impure person. However, even if one rejects the contamination of the bed/chair by pressure, verse 10 is clear that carrying the zāb's bed, another form of being subject to the pressure of the zāb, contaminates the bearer to a greater degree than touching it; touching the bed requires bathing but carrying it requires laundering as well as bathing. Hence, pressure is a more severe mode of contamination than touch.

In verses 22-23 one finds more transfer of uncleanness by pressure without direct contact. The Rabbis do not read verse 23 as Milgrom, who interprets a tertiary transmission: niddâ to bed to object on bed to person touching object. They do not solve the problem of why the niddâ's continued presence of the bed is necessary since the bed can contaminate one who touches it without the niddâ still on it (v. 5).

They are rather interested in the fact that the woman's greater weight began this transmission of impurity because she was sitting on the bed. From this, the Sages deduce that mere indirect contact without pressure from either the clean on the unclean or vice versa will not convey contamination to persons (Sifra Mes. Zab. par. 4:14).

The Sifra is also concerned about explaining the difference between the saddle and the bed and consequently uses verse 23 to explain the lesser impurity conveyed by the saddle than the bed. "Hakkĕlî ʾašer hî yōšebet ʿālāyw" must refer to the saddle since the consequence of sitting on it is only bathing ("yiṭmaʾ ʿad-hāʿāreb"), whereas merely touching the bed requires bathing and laundering (cf. vv. 5, 6, 22)[16]

[16] Sifra Mes. Zab. par. 4:15; Rashi and Rashbam on Lev. 15:23, *Miqraʿot Gedolot,* III, 44b, 45a.

The Talmud makes an effort to limit the contamination of midrās impurity. Midrās does not affect earthen vessels for fear of breaking them (b. Bekh. 38a; b. Shab. 84a). Clothing must be at least three handbreadths square to be susceptible to midrās (b. Men. 103b and b. RSh 13a), and leather must be at least five handbreadths square (b. Hul. 123b). A young girl who experiences her first flow of blood does not convey midrās uncleanness yet since she has not been established as a menstruant (b. Nid. 10b). New converts who have been circumcised but not yet immersed do not yet convey impurity by this means (b. AZ 57ab). The Rabbis are concerned that only items which can be cleansed in a miqveh be considered appropriate beds or chairs (b. Shab. 84b). The Sifra quotes R. Simeon as saying that the bed must be under the zāb's control to contact midrās uncleanness; in other words, it must be his bed (Sifra Mes. Zab. par. 2:7; cf. Lev. 15:5).

Thus, although the Rabbis understand the mode of contamination by pressure to be a biblical ordinance which contaminates even persons and vessels, they strive to limit its effects in various ways. Doubts concerning midrās in a public place are declared clean (m. Toh. 5:7). In addition to the random laws of the preceding paragraph, the Rabbis have limited Lev. 15:10 to only those items which can be used for sitting or lying by the invention of the principle of maddāp.

Like midrās, the notion that an item still in contact with impurity is more impure than after separation from that impurity seems to be a rabbinic invention. However, I will demonstrate below that this principle is firmly rooted in Scripture. Since this issue is discussed in connection with the contamination of impure flows, I will treat it here.

The principle of the lesser potency of a person/object which has separated from the impurity source as opposed to one which is still in contact with it is discussed many times in the Mishna. Tractate Zabim, especially, spells out the difference in contamination if one is still in contact with the impurity or has separated from it:

> ...A general rule did R. Joshua state: Whoever imparts uncleanness to clothes, when he is in contact, imparts uncleanness to food and drink, putting [them] into the first remove, and to the hands, putting [them] into the second remove. But he does not impart uncleanness either to man or clay utensils. After he separates from the things which make him unclean, he imparts uncleanness to liquid, putting [it] in the first remove, and to food and the hands, putting [them] into the second remove. And he does not impart uncleanness to clothes (m. Zab. 5:1).

> He who touches (1) the **Zab** and (2) the **Zabah** and (3) the menstruating woman and (4) the woman after childbirth and (5) the meṣoraᶜ: [He who touches] (1) a bed or (2) a chair [on which any of these have lain or sat, imparts uncleanness at two degrees and renders unfit at one further degree. Separated, he imparts uncleanness at one degree and renders unfit at one further degree. All the same is the one who touches and the one who shifts, and all the same is the one who carries and the one who is carried (m. Zab. 5:6; cf. also Sifra Mes. Zab. par. 2:11).

The Rabbis, on more than one occasion, distinguish between the greater impurity of the person still in contact with the source of uncleanness and the one who is no longer attached or subject to it. The former is in a status somewhere between a father of impurity and an offspring in the first degree and the latter is in the first degree.

This notion could never have been accepted by the Rabbis unless it was based in some way on Scripture. Even the contrived concept of maddāp had to be linked to Scripture. Looking carefully at the verses describing the contamination effects of persons with flows on clean persons, one notices that the verbs for "touch," nōgēaᶜ, "carry," nôśēʾ, and "sit," yōšeb, are usually participles. In other words, the clean person is, e.g., still touching or carrying the zāb when the contamination described takes effect. I list the relevant passages below underlining the participles:

> verse 6: wĕhayyōšēb ᶜal-hakkĕlî ʾašer-yēšēb ᶜālāyw hazzāb
> verse 7: wĕhannōgēaᶜ bibĕśar hazzāb
> verse 10a: wĕkol-hannōgēaᶜ bĕkōl ʾašer yihyeh taḥtāyw
> verse 10b: wĕhannôśēʾ ʾotām
> verse 19: wĕkol-hannōgēaᶜ bāh
> verse 21: wĕkol-hannōgēaᶜ bĕmiškābâ

verse 22: wĕkol-hannōgēaʿ bĕkol-kĕlî ašer-tēšēb ʿālāyw
verse 23: wĕʾim ʿal-hamiškāb hûʾ ʾô ʿal-hakkĕlî ʾašer-hî yōšebet ʾālāyw

Thus, the general principle developed by the Rabbis which distinguishes an individual still in contact with impurity from one who has separated from it is based on Scripture.

The question arises, why does Scripture use participles? What difference does it make whether or not a person is still in contact with the impurity bearer since his or her clothes are polluted at the moment of contact, and so it makes no difference to their status (they must be washed in any case) whether the individual remains in contact or not? This question is valid in a discussion about clothes, but when the Rabbis read Scripture's requirement to launder one's clothes, they understood the regulation to apply to all rinsable vessels. They do not single out clothes for a special category. Only earthenware is a special case and must be broken, not rinsed, if polluted. The rabbinic attitude here is based entirely on Scripture which lists clothes in a list of rinsable vessels and treats earthenware separately. Compare the two verses below:

> And anything upon which any of them falls when they are dead shall be unclean, whether it is an article of wood or a garment or a skin or a sack, any vessel that is used for any purpose; it must be put into water, and it shall be unclean until the evening; then it shall be clean. And if any of them falls into any earthen vessel, all that is in it shall be unclean, and you shall break it (Lev. 11:32-33).

Thus, it is very important for the Rabbis to point out the distinction of whether a person is still in contact with impurity or has separated from it. If still in contact, all rinsable vessels the individual touches will become unclean. However, if already separated from the impurity, the person is not potent enough to contaminate rinsable vessels.

Now, the question arises, how can the Rabbis treat all vessels collectively when Scripture clearly speaks only of washing *clothes* in so many instances? When people come into contact with, for example, a zāb or eat a carcass, their clothes are on them. Clothing is affected by a person's contact with a Father of

Impurity because it is immediately in contact, albeit secondarily and indirectly, as well. Scripture requires such persons to wash their clothes, i.e., not the clothes they touch but those they are wearing. Thus, the Rabbis consider the Torah's requirement to launder clothes to be due to the fact that they are in contact, however indirectly, with an ʾab ṭumâ. The likelihood of touching, e.g., the zāb with a pot or a sack in one's hand is much more remote. However, if other rinsable vessels do come into such indirect contact with a source of impurity, they, too, will have to be washed.

Finally, we must examine the biblical roots of the principle that the farther away from the impurity source the contact is made, the lesser the impurity. Neusner insists that this concept is foreign to the Bible and begins after 70 C.E. at Yavneh. He says the notion of degrees is

> part of the larger Yavnean inquiry into the greater susceptibility to receive uncleanness of heave offering and Holy Things than of ordinary food, on the other. The removes of uncleanness are integral to the development of that theme.[17]

Neusner says that Tractate Zabim commences the development of degrees and that it is not found in Scripture but in the group before the turn of the first century which chose to take Scripture on the zāb seriously. Again, he says:

> The system before 70 is not incomplete in its failure to make distinctions among removes of uncleanness or levels of sanctification...except for the Zab's effect on clothing I am unable to think of a single part of the system before 70 which either by analogy or by contrast stands behind the issue formulated in rich and diverse ways thereafter.[18]

Neusner supports his claim by declaring that the Bible makes no distinction between uncleanness transmitted to tĕrûmâ, and that transmitted to unconsecrated food: "We thereby exclude (from the biblical verses) any consideration of the effects of

---

17 Neusner, *Purities*, XXII, 92.

18 Ibid., 189-190.

various sorts of uncleanness and modes of transfer of uncleanness upon heave offering and unconsecrated food." I would simply disagree with this statement. Numbers 18:29-32 states that tĕrûmâ is holy and is not to be polluted:

> Out of all the gifts to you [the Levites], you shall present every offering due to Yahweh, from all the best of them, giving the *hallowed* part from them...When you have offered from it the best of it, then the rest shall be reckoned to the Levites as produce of the threshing floor...And you shall bear no sin by reason of it, when you have offered the best of it. And you shall not profane the *holy* things of the people of Israel, lest you die.

Thus, the tĕrûmôt, or contributions, given to the priest are holy. In fact, all priestly prebends are invalidated if made impure:

> The person [priest] who touches any such [impurity bearer] shall be unclean until the evening and shall not eat of the holy things unless he has bathed his body in water. When the sun is down he shall be clean; and afterward he may eat of the holy things, because such are his food (Lev. 22:6-7).

With the easement of purity laws on the laity found in Deuteronomy, it becomes permissible for laypersons to eat while unclean (Dt. 12:15). Those who present food for the Levites, tithes, by contrast, must swear that it has not been subject to impurity (Dt. 26:14).

Now, back to degrees. Leviticus 15 clearly distinguishes between the impurity transmitted directly by the impurity source and that received by a secondary transmission. For example, someone who touched the object on the bed which the menstruant was lying on but who did not touch the bed would be made impure to a lesser degree than one who had actually touched the bed. This becomes clear by using Milgrom's interpretation above of verse 23. Touching the bed requires bathing and laundering; touching the object on the bed requires only bathing. Thus, if someone was in contact with something which had been contaminated by an impurity source, he would be less unclean than if he had contacted that source directly. Although the Rabbis did not interpret the text of Lev. 15:23 in this manner, it may very well reflect the true intention of the priestly writer.

Other verses support the notion of degrees. Verse 10 explains that touching the seat under the zāb requires bathing only, however, carrying the seat, implying more extended contact, requires the bearer to launder as well. Thus, the impurity is transmitted from its source (the zāb) to the bed/chair to the person to the clothes, several degrees.

Another example is the case of the man who has had sexual intercourse with the menstruant (v. 24). Contact of this nature is so intimate that the man takes on the seven-day impurity of the menstruant herself and will transmit his contamination a further degree to any bed on which he lies. The text says "her impurity is on him." Thus, he must contaminate even persons and objects which touch him. However, his bed is not as potent as the bed of the menstruant. Again, several steps of impurity transmission are involved. The diagrams of the contamination of the zāb, zābâ, and the menstruant drawn by Wright (Figs. 1-4 above) indicate the greater contamination of persons and objects in direct contact with persons with impure flows as opposed to those subject to secondary or tertiary transmissions.

Moving outside of Leviticus 15 for a moment, we see the notion of degrees present in the contamination power of the corpse as well. A person contaminated by contact with or the overhang of a corpse is impure seven days (19:11, 14). However, anyone who touches the corpse-contaminated individual is impure only until evening (19:22). Thus, Scripture clearly recognizes degrees of uncleanness dependent on direct or indirect transmission of uncleanness from the impurity source. It is totally unnecessary to claim with Neusner that Scripture can be made to reveal pertinent information on degrees of cleanness "once one asks the question of removes of uncleanness and introduces it into the reading of Scripture."[19]

In conclusion, upon comparison of the biblical and rabbinic systems of impurity on bodily discharges I submit that key

---

19 Ibid., 144.

principles thought to be new concepts instituted by the Rabbis are often rooted in Scripture. Among these principles I include: 1) midrās, 2) continued contact with impurity vs. separation from it, and 3) the notion of degrees of uncleanness. The Rabbis read Scripture as a system and hence weighed seriously implicit as well as explicit data. They determined what was more seriously defiling by looking at contamination effects and purification requirements. They used analogic reasoning to determine affected items (e.g., clothes = all rinsable vessels).

It seems at first glance that the Rabbis have extended the contamination power of bodily discharges. However, looking closely, one can see that the only items affected by second, third, or fourth degrees are food, liquid, and hands. These items are especially important and must be addressed since many of the Sages did try to eat common food in purity and certainly priestly food had to be kept pure (See Appendix A).

G. Alon states that throughout all of the rabbinic period there were expansionist and restrictionist interpretations of Scripture with regard to purity. Indeed this is the case in Scripture itself. However, while differences do exist in the rabbinic sources, it is important to bear in mind that it is the halakha represented in the Mishna, not just an isolated opinion, which is concerned to maintain the purity of secular as well as sacred food. This is clear with regard to those with flows since they contaminate at two degrees to *ordinary* susceptible items and then to further degrees for tĕrûma and qodōšîm. To be sure, Maimonides in the 12th century says that only the sacred realm is of concern in matters of purity, but in the Tannaitic era, even ordinary food was protected by the halakha.

On the other hand, one can detect a desire to limit impurity in the Mishna whenever possible. As in the foregoing chapters, I note that the Mishna regards only certain items as susceptible to impurity. Additionally, only items used for sitting or lying are impure under the one with the flow. In the Talmud one finds even greater efforts to limit impurity, such as, the immunity of earthenware to midrās, the requisite sizes of clothing and leather for susceptibility, and the concern that only items which can be purified be considered susceptible to impurity.

Finally, in comparing the rabbinic understanding of impurity of discharges with that of the sectarians at Qumran, I find a much less stringent interpretation of Scripture among the Rabbis. In Part One it was noted that the sectarians of Qumran exclude all women (not just menstruants) from Jerusalem, regard even excrement as defiling, and declare a three-day impurity period for those with seminal emissions. Hence, the Rabbis, viewed in contrast to their own contemporaries, were not seeking to intensify the Bible's purity rules but were trying to make them operable within a Gentile society. The sectarians, by contrast, are found, partly due to their strict, unbendable interpretation of Scripture, in the Judean desert, isolated from the world.

CONCLUSION

The primary goal of this research has been to uncover the impurity systems of the Qumran sectaries and the Rabbis and to discover upon what basis their theories and interpretation rest. To achieve this goal I examined the topic in two parts. Part One set forth the exegetical principles of the Qumran sectarians (Chapter 1) as well as the particulars of each impurity's dynamics according to their system (Chapter 2). In Part Two I analyzed the rabbinic system focusing on the immersion required for all impurity bearers (Chapter 3) and on the dynamics of each category of impurity (Chapters 4-6).

The results of this study yield a more complete understanding of the concept of purity in sectarian as well as in rabbinic literature. What is certain is that in both cases the interpretation is based squarely on Scripture. The Qumran community and the Rabbis of the Mishna and Talmuds were diligent students of the Torah. Their careful interpretation of each word in the Torah grows out of their sacred regard for Scripture as divine revelation. To violate its laws is to cross the will of the Almighty who will not be slack in punishing offenders.

Even concepts which normally strike the student of this literature as characteristically sectarian or rabbinic have been demonstrated to be an outgrowth of Scripture. At Qumran, peculiar trademarks, such as, eating all food in a state of purity and elevating the status of the Temple City requiring three-day purifications before entering it, do not result from a separate agenda divorced from Scripture but from a particular reading of Leviticus 11 and Exodus 19, respectively (Cf. Appendix B).

Among the Rabbis one finds even more concepts which have been labeled invention which stand directly on Scriptural premises. With regard to immersion, the category of ṭĕbûl yôm, the prescriptions of the miqveh, and the notion that only water from its source purifies, all depend on Scripture. With regard to corpse impurity, the special potency of corpse-contaminated metal vessels, the notion that corpse impurity can travel, the special force of human intention, the necessity to examine the ground where a corpse has been found, the peculiar transmission of corpse impurity by overhang, and the sanctity of the red cow, all derive from Scripture. With regard to ṣāraᶜat, the extreme contamination of the mĕṣōrāᶜ even to the potency of saliva results from reading Scripture's laws as a system in which the mĕṣōrāᶜ ranks second only to the corpse. The mĕṣōrāᶜ must contaminate at least as much as those which bear less impurity. Also the limited definition of mĕṣōrāᶜîm is derived from Scripture. In the area of bodily discharges, I can find no reason to develop the notion of midrās unless it is based on Leviticus 15 as demonstrated above. Additionally, the impurity of one who remains in contact with a source of impurity being greater than one who has subsequently separated from that source must be based as well on Leviticus 15. The notion of degrees of impurity is a result of a close analysis of certain Scriptural passages, chiefly Leviticus 15 and Numbers 19.

This sacred regard for Scripture does not mean the sectarians and the Rabbis always reached the same conclusions, indeed, they did not. As discussed above (especially Chapter 3) the Torah, like all texts, is often gapped or ambiguous and thus lends itself to multivalent interpretation.

In comparing the interpretations of Scripture's impurity laws by the two groups in question, the sectarians appear more stringent than the Rabbis on almost every issue. The sectarians levy a fast on all impure persons until after they have immersed; the Rabbis do not attribute any ill consequence to eating ordinary food in impurity.

The sectarians insist that impurity bearers can increase their impurity by touching any other impurity bearer and require the former to bathe and launder before eating any food. The Rabbis do not endorse such a concept. According to the Sages impurity bearers can only contract additional impurity if they come into contact with greater impurity, i.e., impurity which requires more purification than what they are already obligated to perform.

With regard to corpse impurity, the sectarians regard everything in the house including locks and lintels impure; the Rabbis regard only certain items susceptible to impurity. The mĕṣōrāʿ cannot be considered pure until the evening of the eighth day according to the sectarians; the Rabbis consider him pure after the offering of sacrifices on the morning of the eighth day.

Those with flows contaminate any object by touch enabling it to contaminate others according to the sectarians. The Rabbis grant certain items this potency only if a person with a flow has placed his greater weight on them. The sectarians forbid women to live in the Temple City or for men to engage in sexual intercourse there. In the rabbinic system, women are not excluded from any city.

According to the sectarians, all parts of a carcass contaminate by touch and must not be brought into the Temple City. The Rabbis do not consider hides, hooves, and horns of carcasses contaminating. The sectarians forbid any profane slaughtering for a radius the distance of a three-day journey from the Temple City. The Rabbis place no restriction on place of slaughtering and only some of them ate all food in a state of purity.

Other examples of the sectarians' more stringent interperetation include the following: They insist that defecation may not take place within the Temple City nor on the Sabbath; the Sages do not consider excrement impure. Also, the sectarians bathe after contact with outsiders or their property; the Rabbis are divided on the issue of gentile defilement.

Thus, it is my conclusion that the sectarians utilize Scripture's silences to increase contamination or purification rulings in order to safely avoid transgression of Scripture. Hence, if Scripture prescribes a three-day purification at Sinai, it may well be its intention to demand three-day purifications before approaching any sancta on any occasion. Since Scripture does require all Israel to wash and launder their clothes on several occasions, it may be the divine author's wish for the reader to infer the laundering requirement after every impurity. In colloquial terms, "Better to be safe than sorry."

The Rabbis, by contrast, take advantage of Scripture's ambivalence to ease the life of the community rather than to lay unnecessary burdens upon it. For example, since Scripture only mentions certain materials in its impurity laws, it is reasonable to assume that only these items are susceptible to impurity. Also, Scripture makes a special effort to distinguish earthenware from other types of vessels and notes a different transmission of impurity applicable to it (the creeper must fall into it rather than on it), the Rabbis restrict impure earthenware to only those which have been polluted via their interior. This regulation certainly does alleviate daily life in which many earthen pots would be used. Since earthenware must be broken if impure, it certainly helps if the impurity must enter its interior. Accidental contact with its exterior does not defile.

The difference in these two approaches is illustrated graphically by the fact that the sectarians, due in large part to their inflexible interpretation of Scripture, in the end are forced to withdraw from the collective of Jewish society in Judea and to set up their own isolated and insulated community in the wilderness near the Dead Sea. The ancestors of the Rabbis, by contrast, remain within society applying the Torah to life's situations while remaining true to it, realizing that in isolation they are ineffective and stagnant. History bears out that it is only the efforts of the latter which have secured the traditions of Judaism for posterity.

A final note about the similarities of the two approaches may prove even more instructive than a comparison of differences. The fact that certain practices and beliefs not mentioned in the Torah were in effect in Israel long before R. Judah edited the Mishna is evidenced by many impurity traditions of the sectarians. Both groups of texts regard the blood of a corpse defiling. Neither group allows burial of the dead within a walled city. Both are explicit that the mĕṣōrāʿ is a sinner. Both accept the notion that the priest should be instructed if necessary before pronouncing a person a mĕṣōrāʿ. Both evidence the notion that mĕṣōrāʿîm should live apart from other types of impurity bearers. Both contain references to the quarantine of impure women. Both recognize the power of immersion to reduce impurity. Both advocate the practice of eating ordinary food in a state of purity. Both contain views which regard gentiles impure.

In conclusion, it is my strong opinion that not only rabbinic scholars but all who wish to make conclusions about first century Jewish beliefs and practices benefit from a comparison of the purity laws of the sectaries of Qumran and the Rabbis. No correct conclusion can be made, however, without the recognition that both groups are interpreting Scripture which they regard as inviolable.

APPENDIX A

DID THE PHARISEES EAT ORDINARY FOOD IN A STATE OF RITUAL PURITY?

In the recent debates over the identification of the Pharisees and their major concerns, an important issue has been put up for question: were the Pharisees concerned only about the purity of priests' food or were they also trying to eat their own food in a state of purity?

G. Alon has stated that the Pharisees of the first century did eat ordinary food in a state of purity:

> There is nothing to prevent the assumption that in the day of the writer [i. e. Mark] (and also of Jesus) the Associates and many of the people were accustomed to eating their ordinary food in levitical purity.[1]

Also, J. Neusner has said:

---

1 G. Alon, *Jews, Judaism and the Classical World*, 219.

> But, the Pharisees held that even outside of the Temple, in one's own home, the laws of ritual purity were to be followed in the only circumstance in which they might apply, namely, at the table. Therefore, one must eat secular food (ordinary, everyday meals) in a state of ritual purity *as if one were a Temple priest.*[2]

Recently E. P. Sanders has challenged the above view in his book, *Jewish Law from Jesus to the Mishnah.* Sanders opposes the notion that Pharisees were trying to live like priests and extend their purity laws to themselves. Rather, he argues that the concern for purity of food was about ensuring the purity of holy food (second tithe, sacrifices, and heave offering) not about ordinary food.

A careful re-examination of the issue suggests that Sanders' challenge is not as decisive as it would first appear. Although there is some evidence for his view, the majority of the evidence supports the original view of Alon and Neusner. I will proceed in two ways. First, I will present the evidence of the Mishna and Tosefta to show that there was a strong concern for eating ordinary food in purity in addition to maintaining the purity of priestly food, and second, I will attempt to prove the first century date of this concern.

In reviewing the rabbinic material let us first see whether or not Sanders' claims from the text are valid. Perhaps his strongest argument is from m. Nidda 10:6-7:

> At first did they say, "She who is sitting out the blood of purifying did pour water out for washing the Passover offering." They reverted to rule, "Lo, she is like one who has touched one who is unclean by reason of corpse uncleanness, so far as Holy Things are concerned," in accord with the words of the House of Hillel. The House of Shammai say, "Also: she is like one who is unclean by reason of corpse uncleanness." And they agree that she eats tithe and sets apart dough offering and brings near [to the other dough the vessel in which she has put the portion set apart as dough offering] to designate it as dough offering, and if some of her spit and blood of purifying fell on a loaf of heave offering, that it is

---

2 J. Neusner, *From Politics to Piety: the Emergence of Pharisaic Judaism*, 83; cf. J. Neusner, "The Fellowship (חבורה) in the Second Jewish Commonwealth," *HTR* 53 (1960) 126-127.

> clean. The House of Shammai say, "She requires immersion at the end." And the House of Hillel say, "She does not require immersion at the end."

In this passage, a woman in the second stage of childbirth impurity (after the initial 7 or 14 days) is allowed to eat second tithe and set apart dough offering. Also, her saliva will not contaminate heave offering. Sanders argues that if a Pharisee would allow such an impure person to touch these holy things he could not regard as necessary eating ordinary food in purity.[3]

This argument supports Sanders' view well, but it is important to point out that the principle of ṭĕbûl yôm is in operation here. The concept of ṭĕbûl yôm allowed an unclean person who has immersed and is only waiting for the prescribed time period to expire to participate in religious life. The second stage parturient is precisely in this situation. The Talmud refers to her as ṭĕbûlat yōm ʾarōk, "immersed for a long day." Although her fluids will not defile heave offering, the ṭĕbûlat yōm may not touch priestly food after she has separated and designated it as such (m. TY 4:1-2).[4] Furthermore, it is only her immersion at the end of the first stage which mitigates her impurity and allows her to eat second tithe (m. Neg. 14:3; m. Nid. 4:3).

A lenient attitude in the case of the parturient is certainly desirable for practical reasons. The second stage of a parturient's impurity continued for 33 days when a male child was born and 66 days when the child was female. It stands to reason that a lenient ruling would be sought so that the woman not miss her household duties for an additional 1-2 months; she has already missed 1-2 weeks on account of her first stage of impurity.

Sanders also points to the many debates in the Mishna over when to handle priestly food in purity.[5] He argues that if Pharisees always handled their own food in purity, why would they debate as to when to handle priestly food in purity. If they were handling all food in purity, this question should not have

---

3 E. P. Sanders, *Jewish Law from Jesus to the Mishnah*, 197, 209.

4 Cf. H. Albeck, *Šiša Sidre Mišna*, VI, 406-07.

5 Sanders, 197.

arisen. The answer to this objection lies in the fact that the Sages did distinguish between their food and that of the priests. It is clear already from the Bible that there is no punishment for contaminating ordinary food, only for priestly food. Leviticus 22:3 gives warning to the priests:

> If any one of all your descendants throughout your generations approaches the holy things, which the people of Israel dedicate to the LORD, while he has an uncleanness, that person shall be cut off from my presence: I am the LORD.

Therefore, although there was an effort to keep both types of food pure whenever possible, only in the case of priestly food were there serious consequences for defilement.

It has been observed that certain Sages are pointed out in the rabbinic sources as having eaten their ordinary food in a state of purity all the time, the implication being that most people did not do this. Sanders says the fact that these Sages are distinguished as being unusual implies that most people did not do this.[6]

Another argument Sanders poses has to do with the immersion necessary after sexual intercourse. Sanders says if a Pharisee had intercourse at night, he should have bathed before eating in the morning, but the Morning Bathers complain against the Pharisees for just this omission.[7] However, from the context their complaint is whether they bathe *every* morning before the morning prayer (t. Yad. 2:20). Pharisees would need to bathe only on those mornings on which they were unclean.

A final argument from Sanders' work has to do with the difficulty for laity to maintain purity for all meals when the women who prepared them were unclean for a quarter of each month. He points to the lack of comment in the Mishna on the apparent problem which he explains as due to the fact that there was no problem. The touch of the menstruant and even contact with her garments and furniture would have been defiling.

---

6 Ibid., 206; cf. Alon, 207.

7 Sanders, 231, 233.

Sanders says that Pharisees did not worry about the defiling touch of a menstruant and that they even slept together with their wives during this part of the month. He argues as follows,

> If Pharisees did not sleep with their wives while menstruating, we would have a collection of rules on separate furniture and its handling, or on the shelters where menstruants stayed. We do not have them, therefore they slept together.[8]

However, this argument is not so self-evident. The Mishna refers to houses for impure women in Tractate Nidda 7:4:

> All the bloodstains which are found anywhere are clean, except for those which are found in the rooms of or around **bêt haṭṭĕmēʾōt**, the house for impure women. The Samaritans' **bêt haṭṭĕmēʾōt**, imparts uncleanness by overshadowing, because they bury their abortions there (translation mine).

The best manuscripts (Kaufmann and Parma) support the reading as given, but some manuscripts read **bêt haṭṭumʾōt**, the house of impurities. However, even if the Mishna reads **bêt haṭṭumʾōt**, I do not alter my interpretation for the text would still be referring to a place which segregates impure persons, and the juxtaposition of the matter of Samaritan abortions clarifies that the reference is to impure women. The text is corroborated by the fact that Samaritans to this day seclude their women in separate chambers during menstruation.[9]

The Tosefta interprets **bêt haṭṭĕmēʾōt** or **bêt haṭṭumʾōt** as a miqveh (t. Nid. 6:15). However, this is difficult since it would be impossible to bury abortions in a **miqveh**. The Tosefta's misinterpretation may be due to the more prevalent existence of these houses in earlier times.

---

8 Ibid., 233.

9 A. Z. Aescoly, "Halacha and Customs among the Abyssinian Jews (the Falashas) in the Light of Rabbinic and Caraite Halacha," *Tarbiz*, 7/2, 124; cf. also ARN A 1, 2; Targ. Ps.-Jon. on Lev. 12:2, 5; 15:19. Further evidence for the practice of separating menstruants can be found in J. Milgrom, *Leviticus*, I, 763-65, 948-53.

The sectarians at Qumran certainly envisioned seclusion of menstruants in the end time in a special house; it is not known what their actual practice was. The following is from the Temple Scroll:

> And in every city you shall allot places...for women during their menstrual impurity and after giving birth, so that they may not defile in their midst with their menstrual impurity (11QT 48:14-17).

Additionally, Josephus refers to the seclusion of women during their menstruation (Ant. 3:261). Sanders agrees that priests would probably have lived in this manner; why is it so inconceivable for others? There are no rules for the separation of priests' wives while menstruating or their furniture any more than there are rules for Pharisees on this matter. Sanders concedes that Josephus' statement may refer to the upper class Pharisee like Josephus but not to the less wealthy.[10] It stands to reason that people observed these rules only as far as they were able, but that does not eliminate the rules.

Let us turn now to the evidence from the Mishna or Tosefta which supports the claim that the Sages did maintain a certain level of purity for eating ordinary food.

> 1) m. Hul. 2:5: He who slaughters a beast, a wild animal, or fowl, from which blood did not exude—they are valid. And they are eaten with dirty hands, because they have not been made susceptible to uncleanness by blood.

As Alon has noted, the text is clearly discussing ordinary food here because of the mention of the wild animal and fowl. The redactor assumes that it is necessary to state that under the special circumstances (the animal was not made susceptible to uncleanness) it is allowed to eat with unclean hands, because otherwise the reader would assume it to be forbidden.[11]

---

10 Sanders, 160.

11 Alon, 210.

> 2) m. Par. 11:5: Whoever requires immersion in water according to the rules of the scribes (1) renders the holy things unclean and (2) spoils the heave offering. "And he is permitted in respect to unconsecrated food and tithe," the words of R. Meir. And Sages prohibit in the case of tithe. After he has immersed, he is permitted for all of them.

Whether or not the Sages agree with R. Meir is inconsequential. The assumption of two levels of purity is what is noteworthy. The Sages assume that priestly food is most important, but a certain level of purity is important for secular food as well. It is clear that they recognize when an impurity is a ruling of the scribes and when it is biblical. R. Meir is very concerned not to defile holy food and even those who are unclean only by the scribes' standards are forbidden to touch it. However, it had to be stated that these are allowed to eat common food prepared in purity or else it would have been assumed that this was forbidden also.

> 3) t. AZ 3(6):10: And who is deemed an ʿam haʾareṣ? "Anyone who does not eat his unconsecrated food in conditions of cultic cleanness," the words of R. Meir.

Again, R. Meir, the teacher of Rabbi Judah, editor of the Mishna, emphasizes the importance of eating secular food in a state of purity.

> 4) m. Zab. 3:2: [After discussing many possible cases in which people might become unclean, the Mishna concludes:] And all of them are clean for members of the congregation and unclean [for those who eat] heave offering.

The words "members of the congregation" must refer to the food which the laity eats since the term is juxtaposed with heave offering.[12] Here again the Sages feel a necessity to point out that certain food is clean for lay Jews even though it is unclean for priests.

---

12 H. Albeck, VI, 445.

5) t. Miq. 6:7: All those who were declared (above to be unclean) are clean for ordinary food and unclean for heave offering, except a woman who discharges semen, who is unclean for common food, too (tr. Alon).

This text specifies a case where a person is unclean to eat common food prepared in purity. Certainly she would not be allowed to prepare food for those wishing to eat in purity.

6) m. Toh. 4:12: A matter of doubt concerning the unconsecrated food—this has to do with the cleanness of abstinence [pĕrišût].

This passage connects pĕrišût with concern over the purity of ordinary food. H. Albeck says the term pĕrišût is used with reference to the Pharisees because the Pharisees eat their ordinary food in purity.[13]

Additionally, all of the following three passages assume that eating secular food in purity is a requirement for the ḥabērîm, a special group of Jews who had taken it upon themselves to observe purity laws over and above the biblical requirements. Some have identified these with the Pharisees while others keep the two groups separate.[14] Certainly their concerns do overlap.

7) m. Dem. 2:3: He who undertakes to be a ḥabēr may not sell to an ʿam haʾareṣ wet or dry (foodstuff) or buy from him wet (food).... (translation mine)

8) t. Dem. 2:20-22: A ḥabēr may not say to an ʿam haʾareṣ: "Take this loaf and give it to ḥabēr So-and-so," because levitically clean food may not be sent by an ʿam haʾareṣ. If an ʿam haʾareṣ said to an ḥabēr: "Take this loaf and hand it to So-and-so, an ʿam haʾareṣ," he may not do so, for levitically clean food may not be delivered to an ʿam haʾares. If an ʿam haʾareṣ said to an ḥabēr, "Give me this loaf to eat," or "this wine to drink," he may not do so, because levitically prepared food may not be given to an ʿam haʾareṣ to eat (tr. Alon).

---

13 Ibid., 313.

14 E. Schurer-G. Vermes, *The History of the Jewish People in the Age of Jesus Christ*, II, 398: "In the language of the Mishnah and of ancient rabbinic literature in general this term [ḥabērîm] is synonymous with 'Pharisees.'" Cf. E. Rivkin, *A Hidden Revolution*, 141-142, identifies the Pharisees with the ḥākāmîm.

9) t. Dem. 2:2: He who gives the following four undertakings is accepted as a ḥabēr: That he will not give heave offerings and tithes to an ʿam haʾareṣ, that he will not prepare levitically pure food next to an ʿam haʾareṣ, and that he will eat secular food in purity (tr. Alon).

These passages reveal the requirement not only to eat secular food in purity but to keep the food itself from defilement of any sort. Such food can never be given to the ʿam haʾareṣ, and it may not be bought from him if it is wet. The concern here is not over tithed or untithed food, for the food the ḥabēr might give to him would already be tithed. Rather the concern is that the ʿam haʾareṣ will defile it. Sanders argues that these passages reflect the practice of the ḥabērîm in the time of the Mishna and that this concern cannot be retrojected back into the first century.[15] I will now turn to this issue.

The objection in full is that the passages discussed above from the Mishna and Tosefta reflect a situation current during the time of the writing of the Mishna and that arguments said to be between Hillelites and Shammaites are really only late arguments in early clothing. That is, they were instituted as late as the end of the second century but placed in the mouths of early prominent Sages to lend authority to a particular viewpoint.

I will counter this objection in three ways: 1) by examining the biblical material to see what can be assumed to have been the case in the first century since it is already instituted in the Bible; 2) by discussing the implications of the fact that the Temple existed in the first century but was lacking thereafter; and 3) by examining first century sources on our subject.

With regard to the biblical material, Sanders sometimes makes incorrect conclusions because he ignores the fact that there was a system to the impurity laws of Leviticus and Numbers. As discussed in detail above, in many cases rules of purification are not explicitly stated but they can well be assumed from the rest of the data. Thus, many Pharisaic food rules which Sanders calls

---

15 Sanders, 173.

"extensions" of purity should not be so classified for they are actually inherent in the Torah itself. The following examples have been discussed in the chapters above but are repeated here for their relevance to the food issue.

One such "extension" has to do with food protected by being in a closed container in a corpse-contaminated room. Sanders says: "It is post-biblical interpretation to say that the closed vessel protects what is in it so that the contents do not require sprinkling to remove corpse impurity...."[16] However, it is clear from Numbers 19:15 that the contents of such a vessel is protected. If "every open container without a lid fastened on it" is unclean, every closed container with a lid must be clean.

Moreover, the rule to immerse after contact with impurity is not of Pharisaic origin. Sanders acknowledges immersion as a biblical rule only after certain impurities, e.g., intercourse, but not for others, e.g., menstruation.[17] There is no need to take time here to re-examine the hierarchy of impurities in the Bible for this has been done in the chapters above. J. Milgrom and D. Wright have proven that certain impurities were more potent than others by carefully analyzing the contaminating effects of each one and the required purifications.[18] A menstrual flow requires a seven-day purification and contaminates the woman's clothing and furniture. Semen impurity does not have such potency and only a one-day impurity with required immersion is involved. If immersion was required for the latter it was certainly required for the former (cf. Bathsheba immersing herself at the time of her impurity, 2 Sam. 11:2, 4).[19] Thus, as I noted above, only the

---

16 Ibid., 190.

17 Ibid., 214.

18 Milgrom, *Leviticus*, I, 986-91; D. P. Wright, *The Disposal of Impurity*, 179-228.

19 J. Milgrom, by comparing the verses regarding carcass contamination (Lev. 11:40; 17:15; 22:5, et al.), has shown that the phrase yiṭmaʾ ʿad hāʿāreb implies immersion: 1) Lev. 11:24 implies that a carcass contaminates by touch, *a fortiori*, persons; 2) Lev. 11:40 implies ablutions

parturient in her second stage or the menstruant who had immersed would have been allowed to touch food to be eaten in purity.

Sanders misses important points because he does not recognize a biblical system on the matter of purity and so unless the Torah specifically says immersion or eating/handling food in a state of purity was required, he assumes it was not. However, there must have been a system to the laws for them to have been effective and meaningful. Certainly if the second tithe, which was eaten by ordinary Israelites, had to be separated in purity, holy food could not have been handled by impure persons.

On occasion it appears that Sanders has missed an explicit text. He states, for example, "There is no rite of purification in the Bible either for impure food or for the person who eats it."[20] Leviticus is clear that those who eat impure food must bathe and launder their clothes:

> Lev. 11:40: And he who eats of its (an animal's) carcass shall wash his clothes and be unclean until the evening; he also who carries the carcass shall wash his clothes and be unclean until the evening.

> Lev. 17:15: And every person that eats what dies of itself or what is torn by beasts...shall wash his clothes, and bathe himself in water, and be unclean until the evening; then he shall be clean.

Another such matter involves handling sacred food. Sanders considers the injunction to be pure when handling sacred food an innovation in Second Temple times.[21] This argument founders on logical grounds since if an impure person handled the food, it is automatically defiled and eating it in a state of purity will not change its status. In any case, the text of Leviticus is clear that sacred food cannot contact impurity:

(cf. 17:15; 22:5); 3) all who carry a carcass must launder, a fortiori, bathe (as in 15:5-7). For a full exposition of this argument, see Milgrom, *Leviticus*, I, 667.

20 Sanders, 24.

21 Ibid., 135.

> Lev. 7:19: Flesh that touches any unclean thing shall not be eaten; it shall be burned with fire.

> Lev. 22:3: Say to them, "If any one of all your descendants throughout your generations approaches the holy things, which the people of Israel dedicate to the LORD, while he has an uncleanness, that person shall be cut off from my presence."

These passages make it very clear that the sacrifice which contracts any impurity must be burned and that a person who willfully touches a sacrifice while impure is subject to kārēt: death by divine agency.[22] Thus, it is not, as Sanders suggests, an innovation in the time of the writer of Isaiah 66:20 or Judith 11:13 that impure people were forbidden to touch the priests' food.[23]

The Sages are emphatic about handling priestly food in purity not only because of the biblical command but because of the penalty attached to it. Defiling priestly food results in kārēt; defiling ordinary food results in no ill consequence.

Sanders on occasion contradicts his own argument by noting, "It is a transgression to bring any impurity into the presence of what is holy," and "Sometimes the only restriction with regard to impurity was that it should be kept apart from the holy."[24]

Thus, dating from biblical times, menstruants were already required to immerse after their impurity, those who ate impure ordinary food should immerse and be clean, and purity was already required for the handling of priestly food. However, by the first century the laws pertaining to eating holy food are extended to ordinary food as well.

In countering the argument that the many passages above which refer to eating secular food in purity refer only to the Sages of the end of the second century, one cannot overlook the important lack of the Temple at that time. Although some

---

22 D. J. Wold, "The Kareth Penalty in P: Rationale and Cases," *SBL Seminar Papers* 1 (1979) 24: "Nothing has been found in the biblical cases to suggest that kārēt was perceived as anything but a divine curse of extinction visited upon the sinner and his seed."

23 Sanders, 30.

24 Ibid., 146.

scholars have argued that the mishnaic Sages studied the rules about the Temple in order to make up for its loss, it seems just as logical that many of the laws which center around the Temple actually stem from Temple times when the matter would have been a daily concern.

The extension of the purity of priestly food to ordinary food is more meaningful if there really is pure priestly food, if there really is a cult around which religious life revolves. Alon makes a valid argument when he says:

> For one cannot explain what impelled the Sages to adopt a stringent attitude and to introduce new prohibitions in respect of levitical cleanness long after the Destruction, when these regulations were no longer related to the Temple and the sacred offerings. It is also far-fetched to suggest that the Sages of Usha promulgated many essential new Halakhot, that affected every Israelite and were a severe burden upon those who wished to observe them, without relying on earlier tradition.[25]

Even when one objects that all of the purity laws are not connected to the Temple, still it is God's presence among His people, most strongly represented by the Temple and its cult, which make purity rules necessary (Lev. 15:31).

An examination of texts from the first century reveals a consistent concern for impurity of food. No one questions the fact that the sectarians of Qumran bathed before eating (1QS 5:13; cf. 6:13-23).[26] Philo, although a diaspora Jew, insists that after intercourse the couple would immerse before touching anything (*De Specialibus Legibus* 3:631; cf. 205, 209). Even Sanders concedes that Josephus, a first century writer, may have been talking about his class who could afford it when he says that menstruants were secluded.[27]

Finally, the evidence of the synoptic Gospels, certainly first century sources, is perhaps the most compelling evidence that the

---

25 Alon, 214

26 L. H. Schiffman, *The Eschatological Community of the Dead Sea Scrolls*, 62.

27 Sanders, 160.

Pharisees did eat in a state of purity. Mark 7 is an account of the Pharisees reproaching Jesus' disciples for eating with unwashed hands. The story teaches that the Pharisees themselves actually immerse (*baptizo*) after coming from the marketplace (Mk. 7:4). Mark makes it clear that the concern to wash cups, pitchers, and kettles was prevalent among all the Jews. Even if one regards this statement as an exaggeration, the reference is clearly not to priestly food.

Sanders claims that Mark is describing the practice of Diaspora Jews who washed hands before prayer, and he cites many non-Palestinian texts which support that that was the custom.[28] However, Mark never mentions washing before prayer; he is talking about washing before eating.

The accusation as it appears in Luke is even stronger. A Pharisee wants to know why Jesus does not immerse (*baptizo*) before eating (Lk. 11:38). Jesus is clearly not a priest; it is the defilement of secular food which is the issue. Sanders does not refer to this passage.

Matthew's Jesus describes the Pharisees as washing the outside of cups and plates (23:25). He is obviously speaking of the importance of spiritual integrity over physical rituals of cleanness. If Jesus was not referring to a real life practice, the metaphor would have little strength.

Sanders would like to limit washing for ordinary food to the practice of just a few Pharisees and then only for Sabbath or festival meals.[29] This reduction is simply not warranted by the material I have presented. Nowhere do the first century writers restrict their comments on the issue to special meals. Of the many passages from the Mishna discussed above which refer to the distinction between purity for sacred and ordinary food none specifies that it is referring only to ordinary food at festival or Sabbath meals.

In summary, it is clear that although the Pharisees did not adopt the total regimen required for a priestly way of living, they

---

28 Ibid., 261-262.

29 Ibid., 39-40.

did think it important to eat like priests and to consider their own ordinary food as holy in some degree. There was never any confusion as to which ruling, the biblical or the scribal, was most important. What is evident is a conscious effort to make an extension of the laws for priestly food to the private home. This necessitated the separation of menstruating women whenever possible from preparing food. It also meant the refusal to eat food which may have contracted corpse impurity or any other biblical type of impurity. In no way do the Pharisees think of themselves as priests, but they do strive for a holiness above and beyond what the Torah prescribed for the lay Israelite.

APPENDIX B

A COMPARISON OF SECTARIAN AND RABBINIC INTERPRETATION OF THE BIBLICAL LAWS OF IMPURITY

Sectarian	**Rabbinic**	**Biblical**
No burial within walled cities; one burial ground for every 4 cities. 11QT 48:11-14	No burial within walled cities. m. Kel. 1:7	Num. 5:2, "Command the people of Israel that they put out of the camp every leper, and every one having a discharge, and every one that is unclean through contact wih the dead." Num. 31:19, "Encamp outside the camp seven days; whoever of you has killed any person, and whoever has touched any slain...."

Sectarian	Rabbinic	Biblical
The house of the dead is unclean incl. its walls, lintels, locks. All vessels incl. stone are unclean 7 days. The Torah states that the tent and all its contents must be sprinkled. 11QT 49:5-7; 11-16; CD 12:15-18	Only laypersons and certain items in the house of the dead are unclean. The house itself-if a building-is insusceptible. Stone, earth and dung are insusceptible to impurity. Other materials must form a usable receptacle to be susceptible. Locks and bolts are not susceptible. A tent, not a house, is susceptible because it is fabric. m. Kel. 2:l; 11:2; m. Oh. 5:5; Sif. Num. 126[162].	Num. 19:18, "Then a clean person shall take hyssop, and dip it in the water, and sprinkle it upon the tent, and upon all the furnishings, and upon the persons who were there..."; Lev. 11:32, "And anything upon which any of them [the 8 swarmers] falls when they are dead shall be unclean, whether it is an article of wood or a garment or a skin or a sack, any vessel that is used for any purpose..."; Num. 31:22, "Only the gold, the silver, the bronze, the iron, the tin and the lead, everything that can stand the fire, you shall pass through the fire, and it shall be clean...."
Corpse-contaminated persons bathe and launder on the first day, bathe, launder, an are sprinkled on Days 3 and 7. First day bathing and laundering may stem from Eze. 44:26 (Yadin). 11QT 49:13-17	There is no first day bathing or laundering requirement. Bathing, laundering, and sprinkling occur on Days 3 and 7 only. The mourner is forbidden to bathe. b. MQ 15b	Num. 31:19, "Whoever of you has killed any person, and whoever has touched any slain, purify yourselves and your captives on the third day and on the seventh day."

Sectarian	**Rabbinic**	**Biblical**
One is defiled if he or she touches the bone of a dead, not a living, person. All of these laws of the Torah center around the fact that it is the dead which defiles. 11QT 50:4-9	One is defiled if he or she touches the separated bone of a living or a dead person. Scripture refers to the dead man's bones in the expression "mēt" and to the separated bone of a living person in the expression "ʿeṣem ʾādām"; otherwise the two designations are redundant. Pal. Targ. Num. 19:16; cf. Sif. Num. 127[165], m. Eduy. 6:3; m. Kel. 1:5; t. Eduy. 2:10.	Num. 19:16, 18, "Whoever in the open field touches one who is slain with a sword, or a dead body, or a bone of a man, or a grave, shall be unclean seven days...then a clean person shall take hyssop, and dip it in the water, and sprinkle it upon the tent, and upon all the furnishings, and upon the persons who were there, and upon him who touched the bone, or the slain, or the dead, or the grave."
Touching the blood of a corpse is defiling. 11QT 50:4-9	Touching the blood of a corpse is defiling. Pal. Targ. (Num. 19:13) refers to touching a dead nepeš. The Torah equates nepeš and dam.	Lev. 17:14, "For the life, nepeš, of every creature is the blood, dam, of it"; Dt. 12:23, "for the blood, dam, is the life, nepeš...."
MĔṢŌRAʿ		
The mĕṣōrāʿ is considered a sinner. He must plead for mercy in order to be healed. 4QThrA1 1	The mĕṣōrāʿ is considered a sinner. b. Arak. 15b-16a; Lev. R. 17:3	Ṣāra'at is a curse from God, e.g., Miriam (Num. 12:9-10), Gehazi (2Ki. 5:27), Joab's progeny (2Sa. 3:29), cf. Lev. 26:21; Dt. 28:27.

Sectarian	Rabbinic	Biblical
Although the Guardian may instruct him, only a priest can pronounce a person a mĕṣōrāʿ CD 13:5-6	Only a priest can pronounce a person a mĕṣōrāʿ; if he is ignorant he may be instructed by a sage. m. Neg. 3:1; 4:7-10; Sifra, Mes. Neg. 1:1	Lev. 13:3, "And the priest shall examine the diseased spot ...when the priest has examined him he shall pronounce him unclean."
Separate places are allotted for mĕṣōrāʿîm outside of the Temple and ordinary cities. 11QT 46:16-18; 48:14-17; 4QThrA1 2	Mĕṣōrāʿîm are excluded from all walled cities. m. Kel. 1:7	Lev. 13:46, "He [the mĕṣōrāʿ] shall dwell alone in a habitation outside the camp"; cf. Num. 5:2.
Mĕṣōrāʿîm cannot enter the Temple City until the 8th day of purification.They are not pure until the evening of the 8th day. 4QMMT 71-72	The mĕṣōrāʿ can enter the city on the first day of purification after bathing and laundering. He is pure after offering sacrifices in the Temple on the 8th day. b. Yom. 16a, 30b	Lev. 14:8, "And he who is to be cleansed shall wash his clothes, and shave off all his hair, and bathe himself in water, and he shall be clean; and after that he shall come into the camp, but shall dwell outside his tent seven days." The mĕṣōrāʿ brings sacrifices to the sanctuary on the 8th day, 14:10-11.
Mĕṣōrāʿîm can increase another person's impurity by touch, interpreting the Torah's "Unclean, unclean" as "Unclean to the unclean." 4 QThrA1 3	Mĕṣōrāʿîm cry out "Unclean" to warn others of their approach; they must live apart from other types of impurity bearers. Sifra Taz. Neg. 12:12-13; b. Arak. 16b; b. Pes. 67a; cf. Ant. 3:264; Ag. Ap. 1:281	Lev. 13:45-46, "The mĕṣōrāʿ who has the disease shall wear torn clothes and let the hair of his head hang loose, and he shall cover his upper lip and cry, 'Unclean, unclean'.... He shall dwell alone in a habitation outside the camp."

Sectarian	**Rabbinic**	**Biblical**
Měṣōrā‘îm cannot eat after touching any other impurity bearer unless they have purified themselves. 4QThrA1 3; 4QOrdc 7-9	Purification is not necessary before eating common food - only before eating pure food (cf. Appendix A).	All Israelites eat only certain foods and are commanded to purify after contact with unclean carcasses There is no command, however, barring impure individuals from eating common food. Lev. 11:2.
FLOWS		
Allotted areas to the east of the Temple City and within ordinary cities for those with flows. 11QT 48:14-17	It is possible that there were quarantined areas for women with flows. m. Nid. 7:4; ARN A 2:3; Targ. Ps.-Jon. on Lev. 12:2; cf. Ant. 3:261	Num. 5:2, "Command the people of Israel that they put out of the camp every leper, and every one having a discharge, and every one that is unclean from contact with the dead."
Objects which the zāb has touched, lain on, or sat on will transmit impurity to persons. 4QThrA1 4-5	Only objects made for sitting/lying on which the zāb has applied his greater weight will transmit impurity to persons. m. Zab. 2:4; 5:6	Lev. 15:5-6, "And any one who touches his [the zāb's] bed shall wash his clothes, and bathe himself in water, and be unclean until the evening. And whoever sits on anything on which he who has the discharge has sat shall wash his clothes...." Lev. 15:10, "And whoever touches anything that was under him [the zāb] shall be unclean until the evening...."

Sectarian	Rabbinic	Biblical
No women allowed to live in the Temple City [based on 1) lack of installations for impurity bearers and 2) prohibition on sexual intercourse in the Temple City]. 11QT 45:7-10; CD 12: 1-2	Women are excluded only from the Court of the Israelites; there is a special court for women in the Temple complex. Women live in Jerusalem. m. Kel. 1:8; b. Yom. 16a	No prohibition for women to approach the sacrificial court (between the court entrance and the altar), cf. sacrifices of the parturient and zābâ, Lev. 12:6; 15:29.
SEMEN		
The one who emits semen cannot remain in the Temple City. 11QT 45:7-10	The one who emits semen does not convey impurity after his ablutions [=ṭĕbûl yôm] as long as he does not touch sancta until after sunset. Cf. m. TY 2:2-3; Sifra Shem. Sher. 8:9	Lev. 15:16, "And if a man has an emission of semen, he shall bathe his whole body in water, and be unclean until the evening," cf. also v. 18.
Those who emit semen are sequestered outside of the Temple City. 11QT 46:16-18	There is no indication that one who has emitted semen is sequestered. He is unclean in the first degree. Persons who touch him are not unclean, only those who touch the semen itself. b. Naz. 66a; cf. m. Zab. 5:10-11; Sifra Mes. Zab. 2:8	Lev. 15:17, "And every garment and every skin on which the semen comes shall be washed with water, and be unclean until the evening."

Sectarian	Rabbinic	Biblical
Those who have sexual intercourse must bathe and launder and must not enter the Temple City for three days. 11 QT 45:7-10; 4QOrdc 7-8; CD 12:1-2	Those who have sexual intercourse do not contaminate after ablutions [=ṭĕbûl yôm] as long as they do not touch sancta. m. TY 2:2-3; Sifra Shem. Sher. 8:9	Ex. 19:15, "And he (Moses at Sinai) said to the people, 'Be ready by the third day; do not go near a woman'"; Lev. 15:18, "If a man lies with a woman and has an emission of semen, both of them shall bathe themselves in water, and be unclean until the evening."
CARCASSES		
One who touches or carries any carcass (a dead animal not slaughtered ritually), including its skin, flesh, and claws must bathe and launder. 11QT 51:1-5	One who touches or carries the flesh of carcasses becomes unclean. Hides, horns, hooves, etc. do not convey uncleanness by touch. m. Hul. 9:1, 5; m. Toh. 1:4; m. Zab. 5:3	Lev. 11:39-40, "He who touches its [a clean animal's] carcass shall be unclean...he also who carries the carcass shall wash his clothes and be unclean...."
Food or drink cannot be brought into the Temple City in skins of non-ritually slaughtered animals; no such skins allowed in Temple City. 11QT 47:7-18	The hide of a nĕbēlâ does not convey uncleanness by touch. m. Toh. 1:4; m. Hul. 9:1	Lev. 17:3, "If any man...kills an ox or a lamb...and does not bring it to the door of the tent of meeting, to offer it as a gift to the LORD..., bloodguilt shall be imputed to that man...."

Sectarian	Rabbinic	Biblical
No profane slaughtering or eating of such is allowed in or around (distance of 3-day journey) the Temple City 11QT 47:7-18; 52:13-21	Only priests and some of the Sages ate all food in purity (e.g., those who were ḥaberîm, Pharisees). Cf. Appendix A	Lev. 17:15, "And every person that eats what dies of itself or what is torn by beasts, whether he is a native or a sojourner, shall wash his clothes, and bathe himself in water, and be unclean until the evening; then he shall be clean"; cf. Lev. 17:3 above and 11:40.
EXCREMENT		
"A place for a hand" may not be made in the Temple City, but rather at a place 3000 cubits northwest of it. 11QT 46:13-16	Latrines should be set up in every city. b. San. 17b	The Priestly Code is silent regarding the construction of latrines; Dt. 23:12-13, "You shall have a place outside the camp and you shall go out to it; and you shall have a stick with your weapons; and when you sit down outside, you shall dig a hole with it, and turn back and cover up your excrement."

Sectarian	Rabbinic	Biblical
Essenes do not defecate on the Sabbath. Wars 2:147-149	Excrement does not defile. Only urine of unclean persons can transfer impurity. m. TY 2:1; m. Makh. 6:7; t. Miq. 7:8; y. Pes. 7:11, 35b	The Priestly Code does not ascribe any impurity to excrement, but according to Dt. 23:14 defecation must take place outside the war camp "because the LORD your God walks in the midst of your camp...therefore your camp must be holy." Eze: 4:14, "Behold, I have never defiled myself!" [response to God's request that Ezekiel eat barley baked on excrement].
OUTSIDERS		
Essenes bathe after contact with outsiders or with their property. Wars 2:150; 1QM 9:8-9	Conflicting views exist with regard to contact with outsiders. Some Sages regard Gentiles unclean; others do not. m. Pes. 8:8; m. Toh. 5:8; 7:6; m. Nid. 7:3; t.Nid. 9:16; t. Zab. 2:1; Sifra Taz. Neg. par. 1:1; Mes. Zab. par. 1:1; b. Shab. 83a, 127b; b. Nid. 69b; cf. Acts 10:28; Ant. 12:145; 14:285; Wars 1:229	Lev. 18:24-28, "Do not defile yourselves...lest the land vomit you out when you defile it"; Jos. 22:19; "But now, if your land [the Transjordan] is unclean, pass over into the LORD's land where the LORD's tabernacle stands..."; All idolaters are metaphorically unclean. Isa. 52:1; 35:8; Jl. 3:17 (Eng.); Zech. 14:21

BIBLIOGRAPHY

Aescoly, A. Z. "Halacha and Customs among the Abyssinian Jews (the Falashas) in the Light of Rabbinic and Caraite Halacha" in *Tarbiz*, 7/2 (no date), pp. 121-134.

Albeck, H. *Šišâ Sidre Mišna*, 6 vols. Jerusalem and Tel Aviv: Bialik Institute and Devir, 3rd edition, 1967.

Allegro, J. *DJD V: Qumran Grotte 4*, I Oxford: Clarendon, 1968.

Alon, G. *Jews, Judaism and the Classical World: Studies in Jewish History in the Times of the Second Temple and Talmud*. Jerusalem: Magnes Press, 1977.

Alter, R. *The Art of Biblical Narrative*. New York: Basic Books, 1981.

Archaeology and History in the Dead Sea Scrolls, ed. L. H. Schiffman. Sheffield: JSOT Press, 1990.

Aristophanes. *The Thesmophoriazusae*. The Loeb Classical Library. Cambridge, MA: Harvard University Press, 1972.

Baentsch, B. *Exodus, Leviticus und Numeri*. Gottingen: Vandenhoeck und Ruprecht, 1903.

The Babylonian Talmud, ed. I. Epstein. 35 vols. London: Soncino Press, 1948.

Baillet, M. *DJD VII: Qumran Grotte 4*, III. Oxford: Clarendon, 1982.

Baumgarten, J. "The 4Q Zadokite Fragments on Skin Disease." *JJS* 41 (1990) 153-165.

__________. *Studies in Qumran Law*. Leiden: Brill, 1977.

de Beauvoir, Simone. *The Second Sex [Le Deuxieme Sexe*, 1949], tr. H. M. Parshley, 1953. New York: Bantam Books, 1970.

Bennett-Elder, L. "Female Ascetics in the Late Second Temple Period: Five Provisional Models." AAR National Convention, Kansas City, 1991.

Berlin, A. *Poetics and Interpretation of Biblical Narrative*. Sheffield: The Almond Press, 1983.

Blackman, P. *Mishnayoth*. 7 vols. New York: The Judaica Press, Inc., 1964.

Bokser, B. "Philo's Description of Jewish Practices." Protocol of the 30th Colloquy 5 June 1977. Berkeley, Center for Hermeneutical Studies, 1977.

Booth, R. P. *Jesus and the Laws of Purity: Tradition History and Legal History in Mark 7*. Sheffield: University of Sheffield, 1986.

Borg, M. Conflict, *Holiness and Politics in the Teachings of Jesus*. New York: E. Mellen Press, 1984.

Bowman, J. "Did the Qumran Sect Burn the Red Heifer?" *RQ* 1/1 (1958)73-84.

Boyarin, D. "Behold Israel according to the Flesh," I. Forthcoming.

__________. "Behold Israel according to the Flesh: Death, History and the Erotic Life of God and Israel," II. Forthcoming.

__________. *Intertextuality and the Reading of Midrash*. Bloomington: Indiana University Press, 1990.

Büchler, A. *Der galiläische ʿAm ha-ʾAreṣ des zweiten Jahrhunderts*. Vienna, 1966.

__________. *Studies in Sin and Atonement in the Rabbinic Literature of the First Century*. London: Oxford University Press, 1928.

Burton, J. W. "Some Nuer Notions of Purity and Danger." *Anthropos* 69 (1974) 517-36.

Callaway, P. R. "Extending Divine Revelation." In *Temple Scroll Studies,* ed. G. J. Brooke, 149-62. Sheffield: JSOT Press, 1989.

Cantarella, E. *Pandora's Daughters.* Baltimore, MD: John Hopkins University Press, 1981.

Cohen, S. *From the Maccabees to the Mishna.* Philadelphia, 1987.

__________. "Menstruants and the Sacred in Judaism and Christianity." In *Women's History and Ancient History,"* ed. S. B. Pomeroy. Chapel Hill, NC: University of North Carolina Press, 1991.

Cohen, Y. "The Attitude to the Gentile in the Halakhah and in Reality in the Tannaitic Period (Hebrew)." Dissertation at Hebrew University, 1975.

A Collection of Mishnaic Geniza Fragments with Babylonian Vocalization (Hebrew), ed. I. Yeivin. Jerusalem: Makor Publishing, Ltd., 1974.

Countryman, W. *Dirt, Greed, and Sex.* Philadelphia: Fortress, 1988.

Culpepper, A. "Zoroastrian Menstrual Taboos." In *Women and Religion,* ed. J. Plaskow, 199-210. Missoula, MT: Scholars Press, 1974.

Danby, H. *The Mishnah.* Oxford: Oxford University, 1933.

Davies, M. L. "Levitical Leprosy: Uncleanness and the Psyche." *ExT* 99 (1988) 136-139.

Davies, P. R. *The Damascus Covenant.* Sheffield: JSOT Press, 1983.

__________. "The Temple Scroll and the Damascus Covenant." In *Temple Scroll Studies,* ed. G. J. Brooke, 201-10. Sheffield: JSOT Press, 1989.

De Dea Syria, ed. H. W. Attridge and R. A. Oden. Missoula, MT: Scholars Press, 1976.

De Specialibus Legibus, tr. F. H. Colson. In Loeb Classical Library, ed. T. E. Page, et al., vol. 7. Harvard University Press, 1937.

Dillmann, A. and V. Ryssel, *Die Bu¨cher Exodus und Leviticus*. Leipzig: F. Hirzel, 1897.

Douglas, M. *Natural Symbols: Explorations in Cosmology*. New York: Vintage Books, 1973.

__________. *Purity and Danger: An Analysis of the Concepts of Pollution and Taboo*. London: Routledge and Kegan Paul, 1966.

Eilberg-Schwartz, H. *The Human Will in Judaism: the Mishnah's Philosoophy of Intention*. BJS 103. Atlanta: Scholars Press, 1986.

Elliger, K. *Leviticus*. HAT, 4. Tubingen: J. C. B. Mohr, 1966.

Encylopedia Judaica. Jerusalem: Ktav, 1972.

Enşiqlopedyah Talmudit, ed. S. Y. Zavin, VIII, IX, XIX, XX. Jerusalem: Talmudic Encyclopedia Publishing, Ltd., 1989.

Euripides. *Medea*. Loeb Classical Library. New York, 1919.

Feldman, E. *Biblical and Post-Biblical Defilement and Mourning: Law as Theology*. New York: Ktav and Yeshiva University, 1977.

Fiorenza, E. S. "Cultic Language in Qumran and in the New Testament." *CBQ* 38 (1976) 159-77.

Foley, H. *Reflections of Women in Antiquity*. New York: Gordon & Breach, 1981.

Frazer, J. *The Golden Bough: a Study in Magic and Religion*. 13 vols. New York: St. Martin's Press, 1955.

Friedman, T. "The Shifting Role of Women, From the Bible to Talmud," *Jud* 36 (1987) 479-87.

Gaster, M. *Samaritan Traditions and Law*. Search Publishing Co., 1932.

Ginze Mishnah, ed. A. I. Katsch. Jerusalem: Mossad ha-Rav Kuk, 1970.

"Goy." In ***Enşyqlopedyah Talmudit***, ed. S. Y. Zavin. VIII, 286-366. Jerusalem: Talmudic Encyclopedia Publishing, Ltd., 1989.

Gray, G. B. *Numbers*. ICC. New York: Charles Scribner's Sons, 1903.

Halevi, I. *Dorot ha-Rishonim*. 6 vols. Jerusalem, 1967.

"Heset." In ***Enşyqlopedyah Talmudit,*** ed. S. Y. Zavin. IX, 587-605. Jerusalem: Talmudic Encyclopedia Publishing, Ltd., 1989.

Hoffmann, D. Z. *Leviticus*. I. Jerusalem: Mossad Harav Kuk (Hebrew). Trans. of *Das Bu¨ch Leviticus,* I. Berlin: M. Poippelauer, 1905-6.

Hulse, E. V. "The Nature of Biblical Leprosy and the Use of Alternative Medical Terms in Modern Translations of the Bible." *PEQ* 107 (1975) 87-105.

Kalisch, M. M. *Leviticus*. 2 vols. London: Longmans, 1867-72.

Klinzing, G. *Die Undeutung des Kultus in der Qumrangemeinde und im Neuen Testament*. Gottingen, 1971.

Knohl, I. Lecture from dissertation given at the University of California, Berkeley, fall 1989. [Ph. D. dissertation, "The Conception of God and Cult in the Priestly Torah and in the Holiness School," Hebrew University, 1988.]

Kraemer, D. C. "A Developmental Perspective on the Laws of Niddah." In *Conservative Judaism*, 38/3 (1986) 26-33.

Kuhn, H. W. *Enderwartung und gegen wartiges Heil. Untersuchungen zu den Gemeindeliedern von Qumran (Studien und Untersuchungen zum Neuen Testament,* IV. Gottingen: Vandenhoeck & Ruprecht, 1966.

Lacey, W. K. *The Family in Classical Greece*. Ithaca, NY: 1969.

Leach, E. and D. A. Aycock. *Structuralist Interpretations of Biblical Myth*. Cambridge: Cambridge University Press, 1983.

Lehrman, S. N. **Zabim**. In *Babylonian Talmud Seder Tohorot*, ed. I. Epstein. London: Soncino Press, 1948.

"Leprosy." *EJ* 11 (1972) 33-39.

Levine, B. A. *Leviticus*. Philadelphia: Jewish Publication Society, 1989.

____________. "The Temple Scroll: Aspects of Its Historical Provenance and Literary Character," *BASOR* 232 (1978) 5-23.

____________. In *Archaeology and History in the Dead Sea Scrolls*, ed. L. H. Schiffman. Sheffield: JSOT Press, 1990.

Levine, L. "R. Simeon b. Yohai and the Purification of Tiberias: History and Tradition." *HUCA* 49 (1978)

Licht, J. *Megillat ha-Serakhim*. Jerusalem: Bialik Institute, 1965.

Lieberman, S. *Tosefta Kifshutah*. New York: Jewish Theological Seminary, 1973.

Maimonides. "The Book of Cleanness." *Code of Maimonides*, X. Tr. H. Danby. Yale Judaica Series, VIII. New Haven, CT: Yale University Press, 1954.

__________ . *Mišnah ʿim Peruš Mošeh ben Maimon*, vol. 6:2. Tr. Y. Kafah from Arabic. Jerusalem: Mossad Harav Kuk, 1963.

Malina, B. *The New Testament World: Insights from Cultural Anthropology*. Atlanta: John Knox Press, 1981.

McCready, W. O. "The Sectarian Status of Qumran: The Temple Scroll." *RQ* 11/2 (1983) 183-91.

Mekhilta de Rabbi Ishmael, ed. by H. S. Horowitz and Y. A. Rabin, second ed. Jerusalem: Bamberger and Ehrman, 1960.

Mekhilta de-Rabbi Ishmael, ed. by J. Z. Lauterbach. 3 vols. Philadelphia: Jewish Publication Society, 1933.

Meigs, S. "A Papuan Perspective on Pollution." *Man* 13 (1978) 304-318.

Menander. The Loeb Classical Library. New York, 1921.

Midrash Tanhuma, ed. S. Buber. Tr. J. T. Townsend. Hoboken, NJ: Ktav, 1989.

"Mikveh." *EJ* 11 (1972) 1534-44.

Milgrom, J. "4QThrA1: An Unpublished Qumran Text on Purities." In *Dead Sea Scrolls Studies* (tentative title), forthcoming.

__________. *Cult and Conscience: the ASHAM and the Priestly Doctrine of Repentance*. Leiden: Brill, 1976.

__________. "Further Studies in the Temple Scroll," I. *JQR* 81 (1980) 1-17.

__________. "Further Studies in the Temple Scroll," II. *JQR* 81 (1980) 89-106.

___________. "Israel's Sanctuary: the Priestly Picture of Dorian Gray." *RB* 83 (1976) 390-99.

___________. *The JPS Torah Commentary: Numbers*. Philadelphia: Jewish Publication Society, 1990.

___________. *Leviticus*, 2 vols. AB. Garden City, NY: Doubleday, 1991.

___________. "The Paradox of the Red Cow (Num. XIX)." *VT* 31 (1981) 62-72. [A Hebrew version appears in *Beth Mikra* 89-90 (1982) 155-163.]

___________. "The Qumran Cult: Its Exegetical Principles. In *Temple Scroll Studies*, ed. G. J. Brooke, 165-80. Sheffield: JSOT Press, 1989.

___________. "Sancta Contagion and Altar/City Asylum." *SVT* 32 (1981) 278-310.

___________. "The Scriptural Foundations and Deviations in the Laws of Purity of the Temple Scroll." In *Archaeology and History in the Dead Sea Scrolls*, ed. L. H. Schiffman, 83-100. Sheffield: JSOT Press, 1990.

___________. "Sin Offering or Purification Offering?" *VT* 21 (1971) 237-39.

___________. *Studies in Cultic Theology and Terminology*. Leiden: Brill, 1983.

___________. *Studies in Levitical Terminology*. Berkeley: University of California, 1970.

___________. "Studies in the Temple Scroll." *JBL* 97 (1978) 501-23.

___________. "Two Kinds of Ḥaṭṭa't." *VT* 26 (1976) 333-37.

___________. "Two Priestly Terms: šeqeṣ and ṭamē." *S. Gevirtz Memorial Volume*, forthcoming.

Milik, J. *Ten Years of Discovery in the Wilderness of Judea*. Tr. J. Strugnell. SBT 26. Naperville, Ill.: Allenson, 1959.

Morgenstern, J. "Amos Studies II: The Sin of Uzziah." *HUCA* 12-13 (1937-38) 1-20.

Murphy-O'Connor, J. "The Damscus Document Revisited." *RB* 92 (1985) 223-46.

Netzer, E. "Ancient Ritual Baths (Miqvaot) in Jericho." *Jerusalem Cathedra* 2 (1982) 106-19.

Neusner, J. "The Fellowship (חבורה) in the Second Jewish Commonwealth." *HTR* 53 (1960) 125-142.

__________. *From Politics to Piety: the Emergence of Pharisaic Judaism.* Ktav Publishing House, 1979.

__________. *A History of the Mishnaic Law of Purities: The Mishnaic System of Uncleanness*, XXII. Leiden: Brill, 1977.

__________. *A History of the Mishnaic Law of Purities: Parah*, X. Leiden: Brill, 1976.

__________. *A History of the Mishnaic Law of Purities*, XVIII. Leiden: Brill, 1977.

__________. *A History of the Mishnaic Law of Purities: Tebul Yom*, XIX. Leiden: Brill, 1977.

__________. *The Idea of Purity in Ancient Judaism.* Leiden: Brill, 1973.

__________. *Judaism: The Evidence of the Mishnah.* Chicago: University of Chicago Press, 1981.

__________. *Judaism in the Matrix of Christianity.* Philadelphia: Fortress Press, 1986.

__________. *The Mishnah.* New Haven: Yale University Press, 1989.

__________. *Rabbinic Traditions About the Pharisees Before 70 A.D.* Leiden: E. J. Brill, 1971.

__________. *Reading and Believing: Ancient Judaism and Contemporary Gullibility.* BJS 113. Atlanta: Scholars Press, 1986.

__________. *Sifra: An Analytical Translation*, 3 vols. BJS 138-40. Atlanta: Scholars Press, 1988.

__________. *Sifre to Numbers: an American Translation and Explanation.* 2 vols. BJS 118. Atlanta: Scholars Press, 1986.

__________. *The Talmud of the Land of Israel.* 35 vols. Chicago: The University of Chicago Press, 1989.

__________. *The Tosefta.* 6 vols. New York: Ktav, 1981.

The New Oxford Annotated Bible with the Apocrypha. Revised Standard Version. Oxford: Oxford University Press, Inc.

Newton, M. *The Concept of Purity at Qumran and in the Letters of Paul.* Cambridge: Cambridge University Press, 1985.

Neyrey, J. "The Idea of Purity in Mark's Gospel." *Semeia* 35 (1986) 91-128.

Nolland, J. "A Misleading Statement of the Essene Attitude to the Temple." *RQ* 9 (1978) 555-62.

Noth, M. *Leviticus.* Tr. J. E. Anderson from German. London: SCM Press, 1965.

Oppenheimer, A. *The ʿAm haʾAretz: a Study in the Social History of the Jewish People in the Hellenistic-Roman Period,* tr. I. H. Levine. Leiden: E. J. Brill, 1977.

Parker, R. *Miasma: Pollution and Purification in Early Greek Religion.* Oxford: Clarendon, 1983.

Plato. *The Republic.* Tr. D. Lee. Harmondsworth: Penguin, 1974.

Preuss, J. *Biblisch-talmudische Medizin.* [NY: Ktav, 1971.] Tr. F. Rosner. NY: Sanhedrin Press, 1978.

Pritchard, J. B. *Ancient Near Eastern Texts Relating to the Old Testament.* Princeton: Princeton University Press, 1969.

"Purity and Impurity, Ritual." *EJ* 13 (1972) 1405-14.

Qimron, E. "Notes on the 4Q Zadokite Fragments on Skin Disease." *JJS* 42/2 (1991) 256-59.

Qimron, E. and J. Strugnell. "An Unpublished Halakhic Letter from Qumran." In *Biblical Archaeology Today,* ed. J. Amitai, 400-407. Israel Exploration Society, 1985.

Rabin, C. *Qumran Studies.* Westport, CT: Greenwood Press, 1976.

von Rad, G. *Der Heilige Krieg im alten Israel.* Zurich: Zwingli-Verlag, 1951.

Rattray, S. "The Biblical Measures of Capacity" in J. Milgrom, *Leviticus,* I, AB, 890-901. Garden City, NY: Doubleday, 1991.

Rivkin, E. *A Hidden Revolution*. Nashville: Abingdon Press, 1978.

Rohde, E. *Psyche: The Cult of Souls and Belief in Immortality among the Greeks*, tr. W. B. Hillis. New York: Harcourt, Brace & Co., 1925.

Rothschild, J. "Tombs of the Sanhedrin." *PEQ* 84 (1952) 23-38.

Safrai, S. *The Jewish People in the First Century: Historical Geography, Political History, Social, Cultural and Religious Life. Compendium Rerum Iudaicarum ad Novum Testamentum*, I:2. Philadelphia: Fortress, 1974.

Saldarini, A. J. "'Form Criticism' of Rabbinic Literature." *JBL* 96 (1977) 257-74.

Sanders, E. P. *Jewish Law from Jesus to the Mishnah*. Philadelphia: Trinity Press International, 1990.

Sawyer, J. F. A. "A Note on the Etymology of Ṣāraʿat." *VT* 26 (1976) 241-245.

Schiffman, L. H. "Communal Meals at Qumran." *RQ* 10/37 (1979) 45-56.

____________. *The Eschatological Community of the Dead Sea Scrolls: a Study of the Rule of the Congregation*. Atlanta: Scholars Press, 1989.

____________. "Exclusions from the Sanctuary and the City of the Sanctuary in the Temple Scroll." *HAR* 9 (1985) 301-20.

____________. "Legislation Concerning Relations with Non-Jews in the Zadokite Fragments and in Tannaitic Literature." *RQ* 11/43 (1983) 385-87.

____________. "The Impurity of the Dead in the *Temple Scroll*." In *Archaeology and History in the Dead Sea Scrolls*, ed. L. H. Schiffman, 135-56. Sheffield: JSOT Press, 1990.

____________. "Purity and Perfection: Exclusion from the Council of the Community in the *Serekh ha-ʿEdah*." In *Biblical Archaeology Today*, ed. J. Amitai, 373-89. Israel Exploration Society, 1985.

____________. "The Temple Scroll and the Systems of Jewish Law of the Second Temple Period." In *Temple Scroll Studies*, ed. G. J. Brooke, 239-56. Sheffield: JSOT Press, 1989.

Schurer, E. *The History of the Jewish People in the Age of Jesus Christ (175 B.C.-A.D. 135)*, rev. by Geza Vermes, et al. Edinburgh: Clark, 1973-1987.

Sefer Eldad ha-Dani, Kitbe R. Abraham Epstein, I. Jerusalem: Mossad Harav Kuk, 1950.

Selvidge, M. *Woman, Cult, and Miracle Recital*. Lewisburg: Bucknell University Press, 1990.

Sifra debe Rab (Rome manuscript), ed. S. Y. Finkelstein. New York: Beit ha-Midrash l'Rabanim shebeAmerica, 1989.

Sifra: Sefer Torat Kohanim, ed. I. Meir. Jerusalem: 1890.

Sifre al Sefer Bamidbar v'Sifre Zutta, ed. H. S. Horovitz. Jerusalem: Wahrmann Books, 1966.

Smith, Robertson. *The Religion of the Semites*. London, 1927.

Snaith, N. H. *Leviticus*. Century Bible. London: Nelson, 1967.

Soler, J. "The Dietary Prohibitions of the Hebrews." *New York Review of Books,* June 14 (1979) 24-30.

Stegemann, H. "The Literary Composition of the Temple Scroll and Its Status at Qumran." In G. J. Brooke, *Temple Scroll Studies,* 123-48. Sheffield: JSOT Press, 1989.

__________. "The Origins of the Temple Scroll." *SVT* IOSOT Congress Vol., 235-56. Leiden: Brill, 1988

Sternberg, M. *The Poetics of Biblical Narrative: Ideological Literature and the Drama of Reading*. Bloomington: Indiana University, 1985.

Strack, H. L. and G. Stemberger. *Einleitung in Talmud und Midrasch*. Munich: C. H. Beck, 1982.

Talmud Bavli. Hebrew-English edition of the Babylonian Talmud, ed. I. Epstein. London: Defus Shontsin (Soncino), 1960.

"War, Ideas of." In *IDB,* IV, ed. E. S. Burke, 796-801. NY: Abingdon Press, 1962.

Webster's Third International Dictionary, ed. P. B. Gove, et al. Springfield, MA: G & C. Merriam Co., 1976.

Wegner, J. R. "Tragelaphos Revisited: the Anomaly of Woman in the Mishnah." *Jud* 37 (1988) 160-72.

"Weights and Measures." *EJ* 16 (1972) 80-88.

Weiss, I. H. *Dor, Dor v'Dor Shav*. Wilna, 1904.

Wenham, G. P. *The Book of Leviticus*. Grand Rapids, MI: Eerdmans, 1979.

Wertheimer, S. A. *Beʾur Šemot Hannirdapim ŠebbaTNK*. Jerusalem: Ketar Ve-sefer, 1984.

Wilkinson, J. "Leprosy and Leviticus: The Problem of Description and Identification. *Scot J Th* 30 (1977) 153-69.

__________. "Leprosy and Leviticus: A Problem of Semantics and Translation." Scot J Th 31 (1978) 153-66.

Winston, D. "Philo and the Contemplative Life." In *Jewish Spirituality from the Bible through the Middle Ages*, ed. A. Green, 198-231. NY: Crossroad, 1988.

Wise, M. O. *A Critical Study of the Temple Scroll from Qumran Cave 11*. Chicago: Oriental Institute of the University of Chicago, 1990.

Wold, D. J. "The Kareth Penalty in P: Rationale and Cases." *SBL Seminar Papers*, 1 (1979) 1-45.

The Works of Josephus. Tr. W. Whiston. Peabody, MA: Hendrickson Publishers, 1988.

Wright, D. P. *The Disposal of Impurity*. SBL Dissertation Series 101. Atlanta: Scholars Press, 1987.

__________. "Purification from Corpse Contamination in Numbers XXXI, 19-24." *VT* 35 (1985) 213-223.

Yadin, Y. *Megillat ha-Miqdaš*. (3 vols. 1977.) English tr., *The Temple Scroll*, 3 vols. Jerusalem: The Israel Exploration Society and the Shrine of the Book, 1983.

ABBREVIATION LIST

1QH	Hodayot, The Thanksgiving Scroll
1QM	Milḥemet Bnei ʾOr uVnei Ḥošekh, The War Scroll
1QS	Serekh ha-Yaḥad, The Manual of Discipline
4QFl	Florilegium
4QMMT	Miqṣat Maʿaseh ha-Torah
4QThrA1	Ṭaharot A1
4QOrdc	Ordonnances C
1QSa	Serekh haʿEdah, The Messianic Rule
11QT	Megillat ha-Miqdaš, The Temple Scroll
11QPs	The Psalms Scroll
AAR	American Academy of Religion
AB	The Anchor Bible
Ag. Ap.	Against Apion

Ant.	The Antiquities of the Jews
Arakh.	ʿArakhin
ARN	ʾAbot de-Rabbi Natan
AZ	ʿAbodah Zara
b.	The Babylonian Talmud
BASOR	*Bulletin of the American Schools of Oriental Research*
BB	Baba Batra
Bekh.	Bekhorot
Ber.	Berakhot
BJS	Brown Judaica Studies
BQ	Baba Qamma
CAD	*The Assyrian Dictionary of the Oriental Institute of the University of Chicago*
CBQ	*Catholic Biblical Quarterly*
Chap(s).	Chapter(s)
Chr.	Chronicles
Dem.	Demai
DJD	*Discoveries in the Judean Desert,* ed. J. Milik, et al. Oxford, 1955-62.
Dt.	Deuteronomy
Eduy.	ʿEduyot
EJ	*Encyclopedia Judaica*
Eng.	English
Erub.	ʿErubin
ET	*Enṣiqlopedyah Talmudit*

Ex.	Exodus
ExT	*The Expository Times*
Eze.	Ezekiel
Fig.	Figure
Gen.	Genesis
Git.	Gittin
HAR	*Hebrew Annual Review*
HAT	***Handbüch zum Alten Testament***
HTR	*Harvard Theological Review*
HUCA	*Hebrew Union College Annual*
Hul.	Ḥullin
IDB	*Interpreter's Dictionary of the Bible*
IOSOT	International Organization for the Study of the Old Testament
Isa.	Isaiah
Jb.	Job
JBL	*Journal of Biblical Literature*
JJS	*Journal of Jewish Studies*
Jl.	Joel
Jn.	John
Jos.	Joshua
JPS	Jewish Publication Society
JQR	*Jewish Quarterly Review*
JSOT	*Journal for the Study of the Old Testament*

Jud	*Judaism*
Kel.	Kelim
Ker.	Keritot
Ket.	Ketubot
Ki.	Kings
Lam.	Lamentations
LCL	Loeb Classical Library
Lev.	Leviticus
Lev. R.	Leviticus Rabbah
l(l).	line(s)
Lk.	Luke
m.	Mishna
Makh.	Makhshirin
Mekh.	Mekhilta
Men.	Menaḥot
Mes. Neg.	Meṣoraʿ Negaʿim
Mes. Zab.	Meṣoraʿ Zabim
Miq.	Miqvaʾot
Mk.	Mark
MQ	Moʿed Qaṭan
Mt.	Matthew
ms(s).	manuscript(s)
Naz.	Nazir

Ned.	Nedarim
Neg.	Negaʿim
Nid.	Nidda
Num.	Numbers
Num. R.	Numbers Rabba
Oh.	ʾOhalot
Pal. Tg.	Palestinian Targum
Par.	Para
par.	parasha
PEQ	*Palestine Exploration Quarterly*
Pes.	Pesaḥim
Ps.	Psalms
R.	Rabbi
RB	*Revue Biblique*
Ro.	Romans
RQ	*Revue de Qumran*
RSh	Rosh ha-Shana
RSV	Revised Standard Version
Sam.	Samuel
San.	Sanhedrin
SBL	Society of Biblical Literature
SBT	Studies in Biblical Theology
Scot J Th	*Scottish Journal of Theology*
Shab.	Shabbat

Shebu.	Shebuʿot
Shem. Sher.	Shemini Sheraṣim
Sif. Num.	Sifre Numbers
Sif. Zut.	Sifre Zuṭa
Sot.	Soṭa
SVT	*Supplements to Vetus Testamentum*
t.	Tosefta
Taan.	Taʿanit
Taz. Neg.	Tazriaʿ Negaʿim
Tg. Onq.	Targum Onqelos
Tg. Ps.-Jon.	Targum Pseudo-Jonathan
Toh.	Ṭohorot
tr.	translated by
TY	Ṭebul Yom
vol(s).	volume(s)
VT	*Vetus Testamentum*
Wars	The Wars of the Jews
y.	The Palestinian Talmud (Yerushalmi)
Yad.	Yadaim
Yeb.	Yebamot
Zab.	Zabim
Zeb.	Zebaḥim
Zech.	Zechariah

GLOSSARY

ʿAm haʾareṣ
: In Tannaitic literature: A Jew who is not trusted to properly tithe his produce or to maintain adequate purity standards with regard to food according to the standards of the ḥabēr. In later rabbinic literature: One who is ignorant of the Torah; an ignoramus.

Bertinoro
: Obadiah ben Abraham Yare di Bertinoro wrote the standard commentary on the Mishna. The commentary was written in Jerusalem and published in Venice (1548-49). Obadiah di Bertinoro draws liberally on Rashi and Maimonides.

Ephah
: 19.8 liters = 5 gallons (S. Rattray).

Genizah
: A storage area for worn out Torah scrolls, usually a room connected to a synagogue.

Gēr Tošab
: Lit. a resident alien = a gentile who identifies with Israel and resides in the Holy Land although he or she does not convert to Judaism.

Ḥabēr
: A Jew who has taken it upon himself to observe 1) tithing laws and 2) eating ordinary food in a state of purity.

Halakha — A majority ruling of the Sages; the traditional interpretation of Jewish law.

Ḥallâ — A contribution of dough to the priests to be separated from dough once it has been kneaded.

Ḥullin — Ordinary produce after the priestly contribution has been separated.

Log — A measure of volume equivalent to 1/72 of an ephah = .275 liters = 1 cup (S. Rattray).

Maddāp — 1) The degree of uncleanness conveyed by a zāb or zābâ to an object which is located above him or her; 2) the object, other than food or liquid, which is so affected, e.g., the bed cover.

Meṣōrāʿ — A person unclean with scale disease.

Midrāṣ — The degree of uncleanness conveyed by persons with impure flows to objects on which they exert pressure.

Miqveh — A ritual pool of water for immersion of the quantity of 40 seahs.

Miṭṭahēr — Lit., purifying one = a mĕṣōrāʿ who has been healed and is undergoing a 7-day purification as prescribed in Lev. 14.

Musgār — Lit., shut-up one. A person suspected of being affected with ṣāraʿat who is quarantined and inspected again after a 7-day confinement.

Negaʿ — An affection, sore, on the body which may indicate that the individual is unclean with scale disease.

Niddâ — A woman impure through menstruation.

Parashah — A section of the Torah according to the traditional weekly reading divisions. The Sifra also is divided according to parašot as well as according to its own chapter divisions.

Pharisee	A pre-70 C.E. predecessor of the Rabbis who maintained a high standard of purity with regard to food, even though not necessarily a priest, and emphasized an avid study of the Torah (Cf. Bibliography on S. Cohen, J. Neusner, and E. Rivkin).
Qab	A measure of volume equivalent to one-eighteenth of an ephah = 1.1 liters = 1 quart (S. Rattray).
Qōdôšim	Sancta: holy food (e.g., sacrifices) and objects (priestly garments, sanctuary furniture).
Rashi	R. Solomon b. Isaac, 1040-1105, of Troyes, France, medieval commentator of the Torah with a literalist-midrashic perspective.
Rashbam	R. Samuel b. Meir, ca. 1080-1174, the grandson of Rashi, medieval commentator of the Torah with the perspective of a literalist.
Seah	A measure of volume equivalent to one-third of an ephah = 6.6 liters = 6 quarts (S. Rattray).
Ṭebûl Yom	An unclean person who has immersed and is only waiting until the passage of time, e.g., until sunset, to be completely pure.
Tĕrûmâ	An agricultural contribution from the laity to the priests in addition to tithes.
Yaḥad	The community of Jewish sectarians, reponsible for the preservation of the Dead Sea Scrolls, who lived in the environs of the Dead Sea in the last few centuries B.C.E. until approximately 70 C.E.
Yôledet	A woman who has just given birth.
Zāb	A man with an abnormal urethral flow; gonorrheic.
Zābâ	A woman with a vaginal flow of blood outside the course of normal menstruation.